DUTY

THE LIFE OF A COP

DUTY

THE LIFE OF A COP

JULIAN FANTINO
WITH JERRY AMERNIC

KEY PORTER BOOKS

Library and Archives Canada Cataloguing in Publication

Fantino, Julian
   Duty : the life of a cop / Julian Fantino ; with Jerry Amernic.

ISBN 978-1-55263-874-3

   1. Fantino, Julian.   2. Toronto (Ont.). Police Service—Biography.   3. Police chiefs—Ontario—Toronto—Biography.   4. Police chiefs— Ontario—Biography.   5. Ontario Provincial Police—Biography.   I. Amernic, Jerry   II. Title.

HV7911.F35A3 2007   363.2092   C2007-901835-1

ONTARIO ARTS COUNCIL
CONSEIL DES ARTS DE L'ONTARIO

The publisher gratefully acknowledges the support of the Canada Council for the Arts and the Ontario Arts Council for its publishing program. We acknowledge the support of the Government of Ontario through the Ontario Media Development Corporation's Ontario Book Initiative.

We acknowledge the financial support of the Government of Canada through the Book Publishing Industry Development Program (BPIDP) for our publishing activities.

Key Porter Books Limited
Six Adelaide Street East, Tenth Floor
Toronto, Ontario
Canada M5C 1H6

www.keyporter.com

Text design: Jean Lightfoot Peters
Electronic formatting: Jean Lightfoot Peters

Printed and bound in Canada

07 08 09 10 11 5 4 3 2

Contents

· 1 ·

The Killing of
Michael Sweet

WE LOST HIM. WITH THOSE THREE WORDS MY WORLD just stopped. The doctor stepped out of the operating room at Toronto General Hospital and met us in the hallway. He had a sombre look on his face. He shook his head and said they did all they could. The brass of the city's police department was there. Waiting. Waiting for the news about Michael Sweet, the young police officer who had been shot during a holdup at a downtown tavern called George's.

Suddenly the noise that had been building over the last few hours was gone. It was like a switch had been turned off. The whole place went dead. Nothing but silence. Michael Sweet, thirty years old, the father of three little girls, had just died on the operating table with two bullets in him. It was shortly past six in the morning of March 14, 1980, and it had been a long night. A very long night.

Sweet had been shot just before 2:30 a.m. and lay bleeding to death on the kitchen floor of George's Bourbon Street for almost an hour and a half by the time they got him into an ambulance. The Munro brothers, a pair of small-time hoods who had bungled a robbery at the popular jazz club where gunplay was anything but common, had refused to let him go. They had refused despite his pleas and despite the attempts of two other police officers who had been negotiating with them for Sweet's release.

With the news, I felt like bursting into tears. The nurses were crying openly. All of them broke down right in front of us. It was a horrible scene. The doctor's head hung low. The nurses sobbing. And a lot of senior officers from the Toronto Police Department standing around in numb silence, feeling so powerless that it hurt.

I was there along with my fellow detective David Boothby. He had been planning to go away for the weekend with his wife, but at 4:30 that morning he got a call. Just like I did. We were both wanted at the hospital. Immediately. A police officer had been shot and Dave and I were the two investigators. I was thirty-eight years old and had been a cop for eleven years. My job that night was to interview everyone who was even remotely involved in what had happened. It meant trying to connect all the dots— all the confusion—that culminated in a policeman getting shot. I had my notebook out and was busy talking to people. Finding out who had arrived at George's and when. To the very minute. Car numbers. Police badges with the customary Date of Birth, as well as when each officer joined the force. In Michael Sweet's case, it was DOB 02-12-49 and 15-01-74. He was a six-year man. Thirty years of age. Three little girls at home.

I felt sick.

Police Chief Harold Adamson was there, too. He was a man who had a reputation for being tough but fair. Tall and always courteous, he wasn't one to be taken lightly. He had been chief for ten years and just the day before had announced that he'd be stepping down. The feeling at headquarters was that we would all go to hell and back for this man if we had to. He was that kind of leader but was on the way out now. It was time. But Chief Adamson was also deeply concerned about his son Eddy.

That night Sergeant Eddy Adamson had been in charge of the Emergency Task Force. The ETF. He had been overcome with tear gas when he and two other officers—Gary Leuin of the ETF and Barry Doyle of 52 Division—stormed the entrance of George's to take down the Munro brothers. And they did take them down. Eddy was being treated in this very same hospital, but unlike Michael Sweet he would be all right. Eddy was one tough guy.

Jack Ackroyd, the man who would be the next chief, was standing at Chief Adamson's side. Stout and bald-headed, he was called Kojak by everyone and did look like the TV character played by actor Telly Savalas. Also at the hospital were Michael Sweet's partner, Ron Crossley, and Doug Ramsey, the officer who was with Sweet when he was shot, and John Latto and Dave Moss, who were both involved in the events at George's. Dan Hayes, too. Dan Hayes wasn't part of what happened, but he was a close friend of Sweet's and had gone out in the middle of the miserable snowstorm that night to pick up Sweet's wife, Karen, and bring her to the hospital.

It was like a beehive in there with all those cops. A din that just seemed to keep escalating. People forever shuffling and milling about. Cigarettes. Coffee. And more than anything else—waiting. A lot of waiting.

It wasn't long after Karen Sweet was rushed into the operating room to be with her husband that the announcement nobody wanted to hear was made.

"We lost him."

I'll never forget those words.

So now we had a homicide on our hands. Strangely enough, farther down the hallway in another operating room were the Munros. Craig and Jamie. Both of them had been wounded in the hail of gunfire unleashed by Eddy Adamson, Gary Leuin, and Barry Doyle. Craig, the older brother, had a hole behind his right ear that could have been fatal but wasn't. He also had wounds to his nose and hand. Nothing life-threatening though. Jamie was another story. He had been hit by countless pieces of shrapnel. Enough to level a truck. The shrapnel had ricocheted off pots and pans and countertops in the kitchen at George's where the two had been holding Michael Sweet. Jamie had been hit in the middle of his back. In his kidney. In his diaphragm. In his stomach. That was the worst. His stomach. Three-quarters of it got blown away.

But somehow, both the Munros would survive. Why they would live and Michael Sweet would die, I will never know. It's a question I've asked myself a thousand times.

IT ALL BEGAN AN HOUR BEFORE midnight on March 13, 1980, when
Sweet and his partner, Crossley, climbed into cruiser 5209 and left 52
Division to begin their routine eight-hour shift. It was cold and a light
dusting of snow was whipping along the city streets courtesy of the
strong wind outside. A Thursday night. They had been assigned to
patrol the downtown area of Toronto, from Lake Ontario in the south
to King Street in the north, and from University Avenue in the east to
Spadina Avenue in the west. It wasn't a big area, but there were lots of
bars and taverns, so a few things were bound to be on the go. For no
particular reason, the two men strayed north beyond their zone of
patrol up to Queen Street.

They had been partners for two years and were known in police circles as the Pickering Express because Crossley lived in Pickering, a
satellite community immediately east of Toronto, while Sweet lived in
Ajax, the town next to Pickering. The whole region was solid city right
through those towns and farther east into Oshawa and all the way west
to Hamilton. You had millions of people packed into the biggest urban
centre in Canada—the Greater Toronto Area or GTA, as the traffic
reporters called it.

That night the usual number of drunks had to be driven to detoxifi-
cation centres and the regular parade of cars had to be stopped for
moving violations but, all things considered, it was shaping up like a slow
evening. The worst thing that had ever happened to Sweet as a police officer was getting jumped by a guy in the back of his cruiser. Crossley,
however, had seen much worse. In 1973, his partner Jimmy Lothian was
gunned down after chasing a car through city streets, and he died later in
hospital. Another partner of Crossley's had also been shot—in the
kneecap—but survived, and there was a joke among police that being
Crossley's partner was a bad omen.

On this night Crossley and Sweet wanted to get some coffee. The coffee would warm them up and help erase the smell of the last drunk who
had been in the back of their cruiser. Crossley opened the window and
let the air in.

It was approaching two o'clock in the morning.

Nearby on Queen Street was George's Bourbon Street. It was the city's top venue for jazz that often featured big-name artists. That night it had been singer Helen Humes. A jazz master from Louisville, Kentucky, she had been a regular with the Count Basie Orchestra and had sung with the likes of Nat King Cole. She and her band, all of them locals, had finished their last number on the ground-floor bar of George's and then left.

The club was on the north side of Queen, in the middle of the downtown core two blocks west of City Hall, an area known for bright red streetcars that passed in both directions, even into the wee hours. It was only a few steps from historic Campbell House, which back in the 1820s had been the home of Sir William Campbell, sixth Chief Justice of Upper Canada. The stately neoclassical building that boasted four white columns out front was the last remaining brick residence from the Town of York, the predecessor of Toronto, and had been moved to Queen Street and restored to its original elegance. A plaque on the lawn said this magnificent edifice was maintained by the Advocates' Society, a group of lawyers with an interest in history.

George's was at 180 Queen West and was the place to be if you liked jazz and good food. A number of restaurants, bars, and boutiques flourished on both sides of the street in this part of town. After the club had emptied for the night, three of the staff decided it was time to celebrate. Barman Bill Bambrough had just announced that he and his girlfriend were going to be married, so he and Tom Grindlay, manager of the Basin Street bar on the upper level of George's, and bartender Jim Kita opened a bottle of champagne. They were polishing it off just as a waiter was trying to usher two drunken customers out the front door. At the same time, assistant manager Erminio Guerieri was busy gathering the day's take—$25,000 in cash—into a brown paper bag.

The champagne done, Kita excused himself to go to the washroom while the soon-to-be-married Bambrough ventured off to the cloakroom for his backpack. The cloakroom was downstairs on the main level. The stairs were at the front of the club and another set of stairs was at the back.

At ten minutes past two that morning, Craig and Jamie Munro burst through the front door of George's with stocking masks on their faces. Craig, the bigger of the pair, went in first, flashing a .32 Colt semi-automatic. His younger brother, Jamie, followed right behind, brandishing a sawed-off shotgun.

"Through the glass of the cloakroom I saw the figures of two guys come in the front door and pull something over their heads," Bill Bambrough later told a *Toronto Star* reporter. "They pointed their guns at Cindy Shanks, the hat-check girl, and I heard one say, 'This is a stick-up. This is for real'."

Craig was the one in charge.

"The money, assholes," he said to the terrified staff. "Where's the fuckin' money?" He knocked Cindy Shanks to the floor and put the barrel of the Colt against her temple. "Tell us where the money is, little girl. This gun is big enough to blow your fuckin' head clean off."

Cindy, tears streaming down her face, pointed in the direction of the office where the safe was kept. The Munros herded everyone into the room, but one guy was moving too slowly so Craig hit him with the barrel of his Colt. The man screamed, and Craig hit him again. The brothers threatened to shoot the whole bunch unless somebody gave them the combination to the safe.

The Munros didn't know it, but the safe was empty. Assistant manager Guerieri had heard what was going on. Before the Munros spotted him, he had dropped the brown paper bag containing the $25,000 onto the floor and then kicked it under a table where nobody could see it. When the brothers finally did notice him, they said to come and join the others.

The manager of George's was on holiday at the time and Guerieri had been taking his place. Impatient, tempers flaring, the Munros ordered their hostages to lie on the floor. Using nylon cord, they tied their hostages' wrists behind their backs. One of the two drunken customers began pleading with them just then, saying he had nothing to do with this and had only come in for a couple drinks. They knocked him to the floor and kicked him in the ribs, before tying his hands. That was when busboy Bill Hoy appeared. He had just come down the stairs from the upper level, only to see two men with masks and guns. He laughed, thinking it was all a joke. Two men in masks with guns doing a hold-up at a jazz club like George's? He would later tell a reporter: "They grabbed my arm and told me to lie down and close my eyes and said, 'Listen, kid, you'd better co-operate. This is a powerful gun and we can blow your head off'."

It was no joke.

At that moment, Erminio Guerieri and Bill Bambrough thought about making a move for the two men. Said Bambrough: "Erminio and I looked at each other. I saw he was ready to go for one guy if I went for the other. I considered it, but I had that sixty-pound pack on my back. The one guy saw our eye signals and figured what we were up to. He knocked me down and gave me a couple of kicks. Then he tied my hands behind my back, but he wasn't much good at it. I kept my wrists stiffened and a bit apart, so all I had to do was put them together when he was finished and slip out of the cord."

Meanwhile, bartender Jim Kita was feeling a bit of a buzz from the champagne he had had with his friends. He was coming down the stairs from the washroom at the back of the club and wondered what all the commotion was about. He listened, then peeked around a corner to see one of the staff with his hands on the dial of the office safe, and another man he didn't know standing over him. It looked like the man had a gun. There was another man standing too. With a sawed-off shotgun pointed at the crowd of people. Kita knew the layout of George's like his own home. He slipped off his shoes, tiptoed back up the stairs, and went down the fire escape at the side of the building.

Outside in the parking lot he saw his boss, Tom Grindlay, sitting in his car warming up the engine. Kita told Grindlay what was going on and said to call the police. Grindlay didn't waste any time. He drove his car out of the lot and headed for 52 Division. On the way there, he saw a police cruiser, so he flashed his headlights and honked his horn.

Ron Crossley was behind the wheel and rolled down the window. A few seconds later the car was on its way to George's and Crossley's partner, Sweet, was on his police radio. "Dispatch, this is five-two-zero-nine. We have a possible armed robbery one-eight-zero Queen Street West. Request immediate backup. That's a possible armed robbery. One-eight-zero Queen Street West. Request immediate assistance. Confirm please."

Their cruiser, which was the second one to arrive on the scene, pulled up in front of George's. Sweet and Crossley got out and drew their service revolvers.

Jamie Munro saw them first. His hostages were lying on the floor and, when he saw the police, he jumped clear over the group of them. His brother realized right away something was up. One glance and Craig hit the floor. But that move gave his hostages the split second they needed. They got to their feet and rushed out the door. By now four police officers were inside—Sweet and Crossley, and the two from the first cruiser to arrive on the scene—Doug Ramsey and Dave Moss. There was a lot of screaming with tables and chairs going all over the place.

"Police officers!" Sweet said. "Drop the guns. Now!"

Three members of the staff were near the back door, unprotected. Craig shoved his Colt in their faces, then he and Jamie pushed them into the kitchen and shut the door behind them.

"Back off, you fuckers!" Craig shouted through the door to the police. "We've got people in here and we'll kill them all!"

Somehow in all the screaming and bustling the three workers from George's managed to open the back door and get out. So now it was just the two Munro brothers behind that door. There were no hostages. But then the police didn't know that.

"Jamie, watch those doors and kill anything that comes through them," ordered Craig. "Those bastards. They'll come up the back way. I'm gonna shut the basement door."

Craig ran from the kitchen and went down the stairs to the basement.

For some reason Tom Grindlay, the man who had first alerted the police about the robbery, decided to go back inside the club just then. Maybe he wanted to be sure in his own mind that Jim Kita's story, which Grindlay had thought incredible, was true. He headed down the back stairs to where all the trouble was now taking place only to have a police officer frantically wave him away.

"One of the robbers yelled, 'Someone is coming down the stairs, get him'," Grindlay said when he was interviewed later. "The cops heard the threat and had their pistols drawn, ready to fire. When I heard the robbers, I ran out of the door that was bolted and into the street. I thought I was going to get it in the back for sure."

By this time more police were on the scene. A few of them, all in uniform, took positions at the back of the building, while another group—Sweet and Ramsey were in this bunch—staked themselves at the front. Now the Munros were boxed in. Surrounded. All the entrances and exits to George's were secure. The ETF was on its way.

"Did anyone check the basement?" Ramsey asked.

As the events of that night would be related by scores of Toronto police for years to come, Ramsey had urged Sweet not to go into the basement. "I'm just going to do a quick sweep," he told Sweet, and said he'd go in alone. But Sweet insisted on coming, too. Just why, no one will ever know. Later it was said that Sweet may have been after the pinch and "a 159." A 159 was a commendation that would have gone on his record if he had been able to arrest the two suspects. It was helpful for a promotion.

"He was never worried about dying in the line of duty," Nick Tatone would tell a reporter. Tatone had been Sweet's next-door neighbour before the Sweet family had moved to Ajax. "He'd quote me all the statistics about what a safe job policing really was. He said the worst thing that ever happened to him was that he got jumped by a drunk in the back of his cruiser." Tatone said Sweet was a good neighbour and friend. "I have to travel a lot in my job and I remember how I always felt my wife and kids were safe because Mike was next door. When I was away, he'd always be around to check on them."

Said Constable Dan Hayes in a newspaper interview: "He was the kind of guy that was always in the background—a quiet guy and a steadying influence in the department. Not the kind of guy that would try to further his career with a one-fifty-nine. He did what he could to help anybody at any time and he went in there to help a fellow police officer because he felt it necessary."

According to Hayes, Sweet and a second officer went inside to check the basement to see if anyone else had to be rescued. They didn't know that no other civilians were down there. Sweet had entered George's at 2:18 a.m. and now it was 2:20. He had been in the place for two minutes, and the Munros had been inside for ten. With Ramsey guarding the door, Sweet edged to the top of the stairs leading to the basement. He said more people might be in the basement.

Ramsey started down the stairs with Sweet right behind him.

The basement of George's had a long narrow hallway with a single line of naked light bulbs hanging from the ceiling. The walls were whitewashed. A warren of rooms led off both sides from the hallway. It was a rat's nest if you didn't know the place. Sweet and Ramsey began checking the rooms, doing a quick sweep to see if any employees were there. Slowly. Carefully. They got to the end of the hallway and heard the Munros yelling and another officer, Nelson Lee Train, screaming at them through the back door from the laneway outside the building. Then a shot rang out. Craig had fired a blast clear through that closed door and Train let out a cry. He grabbed his arm. He knew right away how lucky he was; his watch had deflected the bullet and shattered.

The Munros had just upped the ante to attempted murder. But they weren't finished. After the shot, Jamie ran down the stairs to the basement to join Craig. Sweet and Ramsey heard the footsteps. Now the two officers knew no civilians were in the basement and the building was surrounded. A split-second decision had to be made. Either they move out to the hallway with the whitewashed walls and expose their backs to these men, who were obviously not afraid to shoot, or step into the dark room at the very end of the hallway. They chose the latter. They entered the room. It was the prep kitchen with a lot of tables piled one on top of the other. Nose-high, Ramsey would say. He was the first one in and could barely see Jamie crouching with his brother Craig half a dozen steps behind him.

"We've got six-shot, thirty-eight specials with very little firepower," Ramsey would say later. "They wouldn't even go through a windshield and this guy's got a sawed-off shotgun. A twelve-gauge. We didn't have vests either. There was no body armour. I realized I was outgunned."

Craig must have heard something, because he didn't waste a second. He fired his gun. Then he fired again. And again. And he kept right on firing that little Colt of his. Seven shots in all.

Bang! Bang! Bang! Bang! Bang! Bang! Bang!

One after the other. It was a semi-automatic. It didn't take long. Two bullets hit Sweet. The first got him in the chin and lodged in his right shoulder. It was a serious wound but not fatal. But the second bullet entered his chest under his left armpit and went through a lung. He fell. Ramsey saw him lying on the floor face down.

"Mike! Mike!" he cried.

Craig hollered back. "Get out of here! I've got your man! I've got a gun!"

Ramsey broke for the stairs and got himself out. Outside on the street the ETF was in full battle gear with Sergeant Eddy Adamson in charge. Ramsey, still out of breath from his narrow escape, described for Eddy the layout of the basement. Eddy wanted to go in right then and there, but an inspector showed up. He asked Ramsey if Sweet was alive or dead and Ramsey said he didn't know.

A decision was made to wait for the deputy chief.

Back inside, Craig had grabbed the fallen Sweet by his jacket and dragged him up the stairs to the kitchen at the back. One step at a time.

Thump. Thump. Thump.

Sweet was bleeding badly.

Plainclothes officer John Latto was a few blocks away on patrol when he heard the emergency call for help on his police radio. A thirteen-year veteran, he was working out of the detective office and would play a key role in the drama to unfold over the next hour and fifteen minutes as he would negotiate with the Munros for Sweet's release. Shots rang out from the basement immediately after he had arrived and there was no mistaking the screaming and yelling from down below.

"I was near the front and heard them coming through the kitchen door," Latto said later. "Then they stopped and stayed there."

As the downed Sweet lay bleeding on the floor, screaming and writhing in agony, Latto began a dialogue with the Munros through the two walls that separated them. His gun drawn, he told the brothers they should give themselves up, so Sweet could be taken to hospital.

"We've got one of your guys here and we're gonna kill him!" the Munros hollered back.

Another officer who was there that night said to a reporter: "They knew that Mike Sweet was hurt bad but they feared if they went in, the gunmen would go berserk, so it was a difficult decision." It was also felt that the Munros might kill themselves.

For the next hour and fifteen minutes, Sweet himself talked with the Munros. Pleading for his life. Telling them over and over about his three kids. He was talking about his kids when they dragged him into the kitchen. According to one eyewitness, Sweet said, "Please guys, I'm dying. Let me get to hospital. If I die then you know your lives aren't worth a nickel. Think of my wife and three young kids at home."

He was on his back on the kitchen floor, the blood seeping from his body. He knew he was dying.

There was a mess on the floor with his blood everywhere. For the second time, Craig picked up Sweet by the jacket and dragged him across the room. "I've been in Nam, pig," he told him, bending down low. "Put your hand over the holes and you won't bleed to death. Take it better, will you. You're getting on my nerves." Then he dropped Sweet on the floor like a bag of potatoes and looked into the eyes of his younger brother Jamie. Jamie was worried.

"We're gonna stand the fuckers off," Craig reassured him. "We're gonna get us a car and get the fuck out of here. Don't you sweat it, kid.

They'll never fuck with us! We've got one of them in here with us. You think they're gonna come in here blasting away if there's a chance the cop'll buy it?"

The Munro brothers were a brazen pair. When they had needs, those needs had to be met, no matter the consequences. Consequences never figured in their scheme of things. Once in the early stages of the drama Jamie had risked exposure by heading to the bar for some booze, but no one would take him down because Craig was still with Sweet.

Eddy Adamson, the son of Chief Harold Adamson, was getting antsy. He and the others who made up the ETF stalked around the front and back entrances of George's. Eddy had a shotgun and the others had semi-automatic AR15s fully loaded and ready to go if only the order would come. Eddy knew a cop had been shot and these two scumbags weren't releasing him and time was wasting. He was getting angrier by the minute. He paced. Negotiations were taking place and one member of the negotiating team was busy dialing the kitchen phone of the bar. The kitchen where Michael Sweet was being held by the Munros. Eddy wanted to go in. He wanted to go in now, and a senior officer kept telling him not yet. Not yet.

Eddy couldn't wait much longer.

At 3 a.m. Jamie Munro, of all people, showed his face outside the front door of George's. Right there on the street. He was walking out of the building with John Latto at his side and he didn't even have a gun on him.

Said Latto: "Jamie wanted to make a deal so he could go to his car. I walked him across the street. Craig had been yelling that if Jamie - doesn't come back he'd kill Sweet."

Neither Latto nor Jamie could see a single police officer, but cops were everywhere. They were hiding, kneeling by their cruisers, the cruisers with the red lights flashing, and there were press people all over the place, too. As Eddy got word that Jamie was making an appearance, he wondered if the Munros were finally giving themselves up. Did that mean they could go in and rescue Sweet? But no. Jamie, accompanied by Latto, headed for his car parked in a lot across the road. Dozens of guns were on him, but no one was going to shoot him. Much as they all wanted to. Were even itching to. Jamie yanked the car door and fumbled around before taking out a small bag. Then he returned to the club and went back inside. With his heroin.

The negotiations had been going on for more than half an hour and nobody on the street knew what kind of shape Sweet was in. But Latto kept hearing Sweet crying out, "Help me. Help me."

At 3:34 a.m. the still-pacing Eddy Adamson made his decision. For too long he had heard with his own ears what was going on, and he couldn't take it anymore. He could hear Craig hitting Sweet and mocking him, and he could hear Craig and his brother both taunting the young cop about his wounds and about his wife and kids and telling him he'd never see them again. Eddy had had enough. He told the negotiating team he was going in whether they liked it or not.

By this time Michael Sweet had been bleeding on the kitchen floor, dying a slow death, for an hour and fifteen minutes.

Eddy fired two rounds of tear gas through the closed kitchen doors. Then he and Gary Leuin—each of them wearing flak jackets with rifles in tow across their chests—burst through the kitchen entrance, along with police officer Barry Doyle. There was a lot of smoke but they could see the Munros. They followed up the tear gas with a barrage of gunfire. At the same time, their backup fired more shots through the steel-plated, rear doors—over a hundred shots in the diversion.

The Munro brothers fell.

·2·

Coming to America

I WAS BORN ON AUGUST 13, 1942, IN VENDOGLIO IN NORTHEAST Italy. It was during the war. Vendoglio (pronounced Ven-do-lio) was a village of fifteen hundred people in a region that is now called Friuli-Venezia Giulia. At one time this was part of the Roman Empire and was later taken over by the Huns and later still by the Hungarians and Austrian Hapsburgs. Historically, it has been a strategic area that has seen its share of conflict with the borders changing constantly. In 1866, the whole region was incorporated into the Kingdom of Italy.

Vendoglio is a small rural village and most of the families who lived there have left for Canada, the United States, Australia, and other countries where life is better. Not that it was so much better for us when we arrived, but it was still better than the old country. My earliest memory of Vendoglio is of having to do without. We didn't have much. There were no cars, no phones, and no heating in the home except for the kitchen stove. In the winter you would take a hot-water container to bed to warm up your feet.

I was the youngest of four children and our household included my parents, my grandfather, my uncle, and my aunt, making for nine people under one roof. But being the youngest didn't get me any special privileges. Back in Vendoglio it didn't matter if you were the youngest or the oldest. There was always work to do, even for me. There was work for everyone.

Of course, I wasn't known as Julian when I was born. I was christened Giuliano, Julian being an anglicized name, and that was because I got tired of having to spell Giuliano all the time. When I came to North America in the early '50s, people didn't understand an Italian name like that and no one could pronounce it, so changing my name to Julian made life easier. To this day my driver's license still says Giuliano.

The first time I went back to Vendoglio for a visit was in 1959, when I was seventeen. I met up with an old school chum who had some machine guns that had been abandoned after the war. We grabbed them and went hunting but never got anything. I don't think we even shot the guns, which is probably a good thing. But today the village isn't the same, because in 1976 an earthquake hit that part of Italy and our home—the home where my father and I were both born—was ruined and my old school was destroyed. Our house has since been rebuilt, but it no longer looks like the house where I grew up.

Vendoglio was a picturesque farming community with rolling hills. People worked in the fields with horses and cows, and if anyone acquired a tractor it was a real novelty, but even tractors were ancient, because they didn't have rubber tires, only steel wheels. Like other families in the village, we had farm animals—cows, pigs, and chickens—and lived in a house that was multi-purpose. It had a ground floor, an upper floor, and an attic, and was connected to a barn. There was a storage area for grain and a large workshop out back. We had a single light bulb in the kitchen and only one tap inside the house. We had no indoor facilities because there were no sewers, but the outhouse wasn't bad. In the winter, you went outside.

On that first visit back in 1959 my uncle and aunt were still living in the house, but they were older by that time and in the afternoon would take a nap. My uncle didn't have a car, but he did have a motorcycle and it was his pride and joy. He kept it pristine and parked it in the barn. While he napped, I took the motorcycle out, walked it down the hill and made sure not to start the motor until I was far away. Then I went for a ride. God help me if he had ever found out, because he didn't want anyone to touch it, never mind the price of gas he was always complaining about.

The first stop I make whenever I go back to Vendoglio is to the cemetery some distance from the church. The Church of St. Michael the Archangel. After putting my suitcases down at my brother Pietro's, we head off to the cemetery to visit the graves of our parents, our brother Luigi, and a lot of other people. It's very sobering to see the graves of old schoolmates who died so young—people who were born in 1942 and who died in 1992—especially when I hadn't known of their deaths until visiting the cemetery. I always make a point of wandering through that place.

When I was a boy, we walked everywhere. This might seem strange to people today, but visualize the place we are talking about and the times we lived in. It was just after the war, people didn't have any cars, and they didn't have any expectations either. Back then, you didn't grow up with expectations. If you bought food, you didn't buy it in bulk as we do now. You would buy a few grams of this and a few grams of that and make do. Selections were few and clothes were hand-me-downs and, as the youngest in my family, I certainly had my share of hand-me-downs. My shoes had wooden soles and in the winter I had to wear short pants. But we survived because the family unit was strong. We had a little farm with chickens and a couple of milk cows and I helped out. I would fetch water in buckets for the cows, clean up after them, and water the garden. Things like that. We all had chores to do. I'm glad I had this experience growing up because it helped me put my life in perspective. Even today I don't take anything for granted and don't like to waste.

In Vendoglio, the church was a lifeline for us. I was an altar boy, so I was always involved in funerals and things like that. Pretty well everyone in the village developed a social life within the church and our family was no different. I had an uncle who was a monsignor and an aunt who was a nun, so the church was a big part of our lives. Christmas was a festive season and, if you were lucky, you got a couple oranges and some nuts. That was it. There were no gifts, no Santa Claus, and no Christmas tree.

The parish priest was a man named Albino Fabbro. He was a tough old guy who was taken off to a concentration camp by the German ss during the war, but he survived. My memories of him are from after the war when he returned. He was balding, a little on the stocky side, and not too tall. One thing he hated was people being late for church, and he would even interrupt a sermon if anyone arrived late. I remember one guy who got under Father Fabbro's skin. This man never went to church and was a real rabble-rouser. When he died, I, as an altar boy, took part in his funeral. We picked him up in a casket at his home, then took his body to the church for a service. When his body was brought in, Father Fabbro muttered outside the door that finally this man had made it to church.

Father Fabbro was a disciplinarian who ruled the roost and was very demanding. I got into trouble with him a few times. He had a bunch of fruit trees in his yard and, one day when I was about eight, I helped myself to his fruit with a friend of mine. He caught the two of us red-handed. We had to face the music, go to confession, and get a lecture. He scared the hell out of me. But that was only one side of him. The other side of him was that every summer he would send us off to a camp at the beach. The camp was run by the church and he was the one who made it possible. So while Father Fabbro was tough, he also had a big heart. With Father Fabbro you knew there was a line you shouldn't cross. Unfortunately for me, the episode with the fruit wasn't the only time I crossed it.

When young boys misbehaved in church, they'd be in big trouble with him and that would sometimes mean a boot in the rear end. It was a reminder because he wasn't fancy with words. The most trouble I ever got into with him occurred when a friend and I went hunting for birds' nests and wound up destroying the roof of a building at the cemetery. Sparrows were nesting and our lifting the nests disturbed the tiles, causing the roof of the building to leak. Then came a meeting with Father Fabbro and more confession.

I got away with nothing as a kid. Either Father Fabbro or my mother were on my case. Things were such that, if you weren't behaving, people didn't hesitate to report to your parents or take you aside and straighten you out. Once, when I was carrying on in church, an older gentleman gave me a swat in the head and that was the end of it.

Probably the worst thing that ever happened to me was an incident that left a deep scar on my face. I got hold of a substance called carbide that, when mixed with water, would produce a gas. The idea was to put it under a can, make a little hole on top of the can, then plug the hole with your finger. After that you lit a match. As the gas built up inside, the whole can would explode. *Boom!* So that's what I did. But I forgot to turn my head away and the can hit me right between the eyes. I was nine or ten and there was a great uproar about it. People often comment about that scar and ask me if I got it on the job. I guess they figure thirty-six years and more as a cop and you're bound to show a few signs of it, but the truth is, it wasn't part of my badge of being a police officer. So I'd say no, this is not a battle scar, and then tell them about the can exploding. At the time, I was bleeding all over the place and they had to find my father, who took me on his bicycle to a doctor in the next town to get me stitched up. There were no painkillers or needles. Just raw sewing. I suppose that was an adventure, but I could have lost an eye. You have to understand; we didn't have any toys, so we had to make our own.

My father's name was Giovanni. During the war, the German ss came looking for him, but they never found him. The ss came looking for a lot of other people, too. They were after my father because he was a migrant worker in Germany when the war broke out, but then he took off like so many people did. Because I was born in 1942, my most vivid memories are of the postwar occupation and the American GIs who handed out chewing gum to the kids and who shared their food with us. I still remember their field kitchens. During the war, the Germans were much more feared than any Allied soldiers. The ss, in particular, had no patience with partisan saboteurs and it wasn't unusual for young Italian men to be executed or whisked away to concentration camps and never heard from again. One time after a German ammo dump was destroyed in the village of Nimis, which was twenty miles from Vendoglio, the German tanks moved in and destroyed the town. People were killed. Later, after the war, I remember my father telling me how everyone feared the ss.

What I learned above all in Vendoglio was the importance of family. I also learned about the importance of community. There was a deep sense of discipline and respect in Vendoglio and that included respect for your elders. Honesty and a work ethic were important, too. To tell you the truth, I don't think I ever saw a police officer in town even though there was a police detachment nearby. There just wasn't any crime. So while we may have been poor, there was a lot of love. And discipline and accountability. The reality was basically family, community, and church.

In our family, my mother, Maria, was the disciplinarian because my father was away six or seven months of the year. She was a short, chunky woman who spent the day working in the fields, tough, physical labour. All manual, no machines. She was strong, physically and mentally, and would be out there every morning at the crack of dawn, cutting grass or baling hay or plowing the fields and she wouldn't come home until night. My aunt had asthma and couldn't do that kind of work, so she looked after the house and my uncle, who was not a well man, and couldn't work the fields either. It all fell on my mother.

I think my mother was strict because she worked so hard and didn't have time for any nonsense. But she was also very generous. After the war, there wasn't much food, so she would carve up the eggs and give each one of us a piece. The only time we saw any meat around the house was when one of our chickens was put down.

My father, Giovanni, was a slender man, an inch or two under six feet, and he took on all kinds of jobs as a migrant worker. He would either send money back or bring it back himself. In the community, there were a lot of older people and they were all well looked after—there were no nursing homes or anything like that—and I remember that my father was always very respectful of his own father, my grandfather. He adored him. My father was a hard-working guy who made many sacrifices for his family. Because he was a conciliatory man who didn't like confrontation, there is no way he would have been a police officer. He might have been a missionary though, since he was very religious.

One sister and two brothers were ahead of me. My sister, Anna, has been a nun since 1951. When Anna said she was joining the church, my mother was devastated. Anna was the oldest of the four children and the only girl, and my mother had been counting on her to help out on the farm. Then, all of a sudden, she was gone. But later my mother accepted my sister's choice, and Anna has remained a nun to this day. After her was my brother Luigi. He became a priest in 1959 and remained a priest for ten years or so, but then left the church and wound up getting married and having a family. He died in 1996. Then came my brother Pietro. Pietro came to Canada with my mother and me in 1953, one year after my father's arrival.

My father came to Canada via New York in 1952, when he was forty-five. He had no trade and couldn't speak English. He arrived at Ellis Island after being sponsored by a neighbour who had come to Canada earlier. My father was in New York to visit his brother, who lived in Chicago and who was supposed to meet him. After a few days, my father planned to take the train to Toronto, but as soon as he got off the boat in New York, he got into trouble. The authorities noted that the surname on his documentation said "Fantino" while the surname of his brother was "Fantini." When they originally did the birth registry for my father in Italy, someone had made a mistake. In fact, the actual family name was "Fantini," but my father's birth registry said "Fantino." This kind of mistake was quite common in those days, but in the eyes of the authorities these two brothers had different surnames and that meant something was amiss. So my father was detained and placed in custody in a holding facility on Ellis Island. This was the introduction to America for a family that would one day spawn the chief of one of the biggest police forces on the continent!

My uncle had to borrow some money to post bond for my father. My father was given only a few hours to get out of the United States, and so he took a train to Toronto. He always said that whenever he looked at the Statue of Liberty, he cried, because he was so devastated by what had happened to him. Here was a man who had never been in trouble in his life, and the moment he sets foot in America he has his freedom taken away. He was emotionally wrecked over that. For the rest of his life, he would recount that story over and over. And the irony was that he could see the Statue of Liberty from the detention centre. After that experience, he was less than complimentary towards America and always figured the Statue of Liberty was a bit of a farce. Later, when we would drive to Chicago to visit my uncle, my father was always very apprehensive about crossing the U.S. border.

I didn't see my father for a year, until I came to Toronto with my mother and brother Pietro. We had gone to Naples to get our medical papers, and then we went to the Canadian embassy for the necessary documentation. On our way home, we stopped off in Rome and in Rome I thought I had died and gone to heaven. All those neon signs and buses were really something for a boy from a village in rural Italy. As for Canada, the only thing I knew about it was from my stamp collection. I was an avid stamp collector and Canadian stamps were highly sought because they were rare. So all this was a real adventure for me, but there was also a great deal of sadness because we were leaving my brother Luigi and sister, Anna, behind.

We left Genova, Italy, on a ship called *Conte Biancamano,* and what I remember most about that trip was the meals. Those meals were better than anything I had ever eaten. You got meat, a couple of courses and you were served, something I had never experienced before. I also remember people leaving families and friends behind. You had a thousand people and more going off on this great adventure. Some were going to the mines, some to lumber camps, some to build the railroad. Nobody was coming over to be an office executive.

I was eleven and thought that ship was just huge. I remember the rough seas. The ship bounced around and made a lot of people sick. In the dining room, as time went on and the weather got worse, fewer and fewer people showed up for dinner, but no matter how bad it was, I never missed a meal. Not once. Nowadays, whenever my wife and I take a cruise, my memory always takes me back to that first trip across the ocean. Cruises contain a real element of nostalgia for me, but then, that first one was no "cruise."

The day we left our home in Vendoglio, it rained cats and dogs. We had to catch the train to Genova and then go to Canada, but there was a problem with all this rain coming down. Somebody had a vehicle and they were going to give us a ride, but I held up the proceedings because the roof of our house was leaking. So there I was with these buckets and no one could find me and it was time to go. At the very hour we were leaving, I was still busy doing the things that would have been normal. Busy right to the end.

The whole journey—from the time we left our village and took the train to Genova and then the trip across the Atlantic Ocean to Halifax— took ten or eleven days. Pier 21 in Halifax is Canada's answer to Ellis Island, and like Ellis Island, the first thing you face is Customs and Immigration. Of course, we didn't speak any English, but people helped us out. It was like a production line where you got your eyes tested at one place and your documents processed at another. Then we were given ten dollars to buy a few provisions for the train ride to Toronto. My brother, who was about seventeen, did the shopping and came back with what I now realize was pineapple juice and white sliced bread. To Italians from Italy, white sliced bread is as foreign as can be and that began my journey into North American life.

Pier 21 in Halifax has always been special to me since it represented the first time I stepped on to North American soil. In 1992, I became involved in fundraising for Pier 21 and, in 2003, some members of the non-profit association Pier 21 launched a four-year plan to raise funds for a museum. I am happy to support such a cause. The idea behind the museum is to remember the stories of all those immigrants who arrived in Halifax, starting way back in 1867, the year Canada became a nation, and the purpose is to leave concrete testimonies for future generations. Another thing about Pier 2 1 is the Sobey Wall of Honour. It pays tribute to people and families who came from elsewhere and who helped build this country. You make a financial contribution and get your name carved on a brick at Pier 2 1 . I am proud to say that at Pier 2 1 , you'll see a brick with the names of my wife and me—Liviana De Bin and Giuliano Fantino.

The 1 9 5 3 train ride from Halifax to Toronto wasn't pleasant. While I was enthralled with the idea of being on a train, the cars on that one were hot and dirty with a lot of soot. My father met us in Toronto and it was a joyous reunion. Then we got a ride to what would be our home. We had two rooms—one room for my parents and another that doubled as a kitchen and a bedroom for my brother and me. Three families lived in the house, a total of ten people. It was a small, two-storey affair with one bathroom. We had no sink in the kitchen, so my mother washed the dishes in the bathroom. It was tight quarters and we lived with strangers who weren't Italian. Most people in the area were Polish or Ukrainian because their migration had taken place before the Italians.

Soon after our arrival, my father said we should eat and he wanted some bread. So I volunteered to buy it. There was a store around the corner and my father gave me a quarter and told me what to do. I marched over to the store and negotiated the sale and that was my initial foray into commerce on this continent. I said to the storekeeper "bread." It was my first word in English.

In Toronto, my father had been working in construction and I got myself enrolled in school. It was a challenge because I was the only kid in the class who didn't speak English, and the teacher, of course, spoke no Italian. The result was that a lot of kids didn't have any charity, as far as I was concerned. I was an outsider. I was eleven and was put back a couple of grades into Grade 3 . I sat at the back of the room and didn't have a clue what was going on. However, the teacher took an interest in me. She stayed with me after school and gave me kindergarten books about cats and dogs to help me with my English.

As time went on, my English improved, but I still felt out of place. I missed being back home in Italy and that was when reality set in. This was no longer an adventure. Now life was just plain difficult. I was from rural Italy and here I was in a big North American city. It was just overwhelming. I felt vulnerable and found it hard to adjust.

I also spent a lot of time by myself. My father was out working most of the time and my mother and brother worked as well; my brother was in construction and my mother operated a sewing machine in a factory. It was piecemeal work and the more you did, the more money you made. She often worked after hours on weekends and sometimes made more money than my father did. My parents were the kind of people who would go to work even when they were sick, so that first summer I was at home alone during the day. I had no friends, nowhere to go, and nothing to do. I would just look out the window and sometimes venture out, but I was always picked on and bullied.

Behind our house was a dairy and the workers were very kind. Across the road was an older gentleman with a garage. He had this old Ford truck and would take me with him when he went to pick up parts. I'd hang around his shop to kill time, but still I had nothing to do. There was a fire hall up the street and I was enamoured of fire trucks. The firemen would chat with me and give me the odd sandwich. So, during that summer, I had four points of reference in my life: the old gentleman with the garage, the folks with the dairy, our home, and the fire hall. My whole territory was a couple of blocks.

But the worst thing about that time was being rejected by other kids. My world shrunk with that. It's very difficult for a young person to leave familiar surroundings, leave members of your family and friends back home, leave a language you know, and leave your school. Then you come here and you're a fish out of water. You don't belong. You're not accepted. You have no way of assimilating. A year or so later we moved to another house and things were better because the family we roomed with was Italian and they had kids my age.

I look back on my first year in Canada as an apprenticeship. Do I regret it? No. It was a character builder and there is no denying the fact that such hardships make you stronger. They make you a survivor.

In 1957, we bought a house of our own. It cost $10,000. My father had found work with a company that raised houses so basements could be put in. It was a good company and he was treated well. He borrowed money from his employer for the down payment for the house, which was old and rundown and badly in need of repair, but we fixed it up and it was a really big thing for us. It was a sign that we had made it.

After a few years, I was speaking English just fine, but still I wasn't one of the crowd and that's because I was Fantino and not Smith or Jones or Brown. One day, I was walking down the road minding my own business, when I was approached by two boys. They had water pistols filled with dye and they sprayed me up, down, and sideways. Then they pushed me around and laid a beating on me with the usual choice words. I had to take it. Nobody came to help. So I got the beating and all my clothes were ruined and I went home and cried. There was never any talk about calling the police. That never even entered the picture. Who do you call? What do you do? What do you say? It never crossed anyone's mind. It was part of the apprenticeship.

So, there we were with a mortgage, and both my parents and my brother were working and I felt guilty about being in school. I was fifteen in Grade 8 and reached a decision. I was going to leave school and get myself a job. My parents didn't like the idea at all. They wanted me to stay in school, but I didn't feel right being there and watching how hard my family worked every day. Back in those days, you needed a permit to leave school before the age of sixteen.

Looking back, it was one of the biggest mistakes I ever made. I tell kids all the time to stay with it and not give up and I tell them what happened to me. I think I've influenced a lot of kids over the years about the importance of staying in school. In my travels as a police officer, a police chief, and a police commissioner I've come across a lot of kids, and I've always taken the time to give them some advice. Opportunities missed are opportunities that you rarely get back.

My first job was in a warehouse in Toronto's west end, and I was paid eighty cents an hour. I found out right away that a Grade 8 education didn't get you too far. The business was a housewares distribution centre and I was in shipping and receiving. It was physical work. I had that job for a few years, and then I got another job looking after the stock for a transport company. It was a filthy place to work. One of the things I did there was burn identification numbers onto truck tires. I did other jobs too, such as loading trucks and working on the production line for an electronics' manufacturer, and even driving cab part-time. The first day I drove a cab I must have worked twelve hours, but I made only seven dollars because I didn't know how the system worked. I didn't know that other drivers jumped the queue to get their fares. I was busy doing all these different jobs, but the big problem for me was that I had no trade.

In 1964, Yorkdale Shopping Centre opened in the north end of the city. Yorkdale had more than a hundred stores, wide air-conditioned halls, and high ceilings. With more than a million square feet of space to lease, it was the largest shopping centre in the whole country. So many people and cars descended on the place that more than a dozen police officers were needed just to direct traffic. Naturally, a lot of jobs became available, so I applied at Simpsons department store. Simpsons was one of the flagship stores in the new mall. I got a job in the stockroom, and after that I became a salesman in the hardware department. I really liked that, especially dealing with people. As it happened, this fellow who worked in security also happened to be a volunteer auxiliary policeman, and the guy who ran the store's security department was formerly with the Royal Canadian Mounted Police (RCMP). And that's how this whole police thing started for me.

·3·

Do You Speak Italian?

W HEN I WAS TWENTY-THREE, I HAD THREE JOBS. DURING
the day I was a security officer at Simpsons, at night I
loaded transport trucks, and on the weekend I drove a cab.
It was a full slate and having a full slate was something I got used to. It
was a good experience to have, especially later when I was rising through
the ranks of the police and eventually became a chief. Being able to handle many things at once and managing a busy schedule that never lets up
are prerequisites for such a position.

At Sions, I soon became involved in investigations, and around that
time I also joined the auxiliary police. It was a volunteer position, which
required taking auxiliary police training, and it got me a uniform. My
first. But my regular job working in security at Simpsons was plainclothes all the way. At the time, one case in particular stands out.

I was in the store watching a couple of teenagers and it was obvious
they were going to lift something. Teenage shoplifting was a big problem
then and many of the kids doing it were from well-to-do families. They
thought they had a God-given right to steal. By that time, I had learned
how to recognize their behaviour and was pretty good at it. I could tell
what these kids were up to by how they threw their eyes, how they
moved around, and sometimes by the shopping bags they carried. I

watched these two, went up to them, and told them to leave. They left, but when they got home they complained to their parents, then their parents complained to the store manager and I got taken to task. It was almost as if I had made a false arrest. I thought something was wrong here because, the way I figured it, my actions constituted an ounce of prevention and I should have been thanked for preventing a couple kids from getting into trouble. But the parents were long-time, affluent customers of Simpsons and that seemed to make all the difference. I didn't lose my job, but I did get reprimanded. I learned then that money talks.

I spent five years as an auxiliary police officer and then rose to the rank of sergeant. During that time I met Frank Barbetta. Our criminal cases were processed by 32 Division of the Metropolitan Toronto Police Department and Frank was a detective. Those cases required going to court, so he and I often went to court together. He coached me in how to present cases in court and showed me how to deliver my evidence.

Frank's reputation was larger than life, but then his whole life was his reputation. He was brave, committed, and dedicated, and would do anything to fulfill his oath of office. I thought he was the epitome of what a police officer should be. Frank and his partner, Jack Nicolucci, were doing the most dangerous work on the police department because back in those days there was no Emergency Task Force and none of the specialized equipment and training we have now. Those guys were kicking in doors and facing armed and dangerous people. Around the streets of Toronto, the Barbetta-Nicolucci team had a reputation and you didn't want to cross them. On the other hand, they were your best friends if you were a law-abiding person.

Frank died in 1998, when I was chief in London, Ontario, and I delivered the eulogy at his funeral. He spent thirty-two years as a police officer and became chief of detectives in Toronto, retiring in 1985 as staff superintendent. His nickname was "Supercop" and, believe me, he was that and his influence on me was huge.

One day when I was working in security at Simpsons, he asked me if I wanted to join the police force. I showed an interest and he continued to mentor me, but the first three times I applied I was turned down. That's right, I was rejected. You had to show academic qualifications and this was where I fell short. Later, I did a lot of correspondence courses and got my high-school equivalency, but I didn't have that when I first applied. Sure I was disappointed, but not crushed. I already had a good job. By that time, I had moved on from Simpsons and was managing security for the Ontario division of Steinberg's Miracle Mart department stores. I was earning considerably more money than an entry-level salary for a police officer. I was well treated, well paid, and had lots of freedom. I even had an expense account. Joining the police as a regular meant taking a big cut in pay, but I did it because of the opportunities, the variety of work involved, and the challenging nature of the work. In 1968, on my fourth try, I was finally accepted. By that time, I had obtained my Grade 10 equivalency through night courses.

Around that time, Italian organized crime was getting more established in Toronto. There were killings and bombings, but hardly any police officers who spoke Italian or who could interact with the Italian community. Not only that, but they didn't understand the culture. The Italian community had grown dramatically in the city, so my chances really improved because I spoke the language.

My starting salary as a police officer was $7,500 a year, which was a substantial cut from what I had made at Steinberg's. Some might say it was crazy to take such a pay cut, but I guess it was also crazy to come to Canada and go through the school of hard knocks. I look at these things as sacrifices made in order to get to a better place. When I was finally accepted by the Toronto police department, I was living in a basement apartment in a house owned by my cousins.

My wife, Liviana, came from an Italian background much like mine. She was born in Vittorio Venneto, which is near Venice. She was a young girl when her family came to Canada and, just like me, she came off the boat and couldn't speak English. We met in 1967, and by the time I joined the police and was going to police college, we were getting serious.

At police college I was twenty-seven and one of the older students. Most of the other guys were right out of university with good study habits, but I didn't have that and found it hard getting into the routine. There were thirty-five of us in the class. The first exam was on first aid and I didn't do very well. I knew right away that I was in big trouble. There was also a lot of discipline and regimentation. You were told what to do, when to do it, and how to do it. Many of the instructors were former military guys. You had to polish your shoes and parade in front of a sergeant to show him that you had shaved. I found it all very demeaning. I wondered then if I had done the right thing by quitting a good job in management, because here I was showing my superiors that I had shaved! But I was determined. So I told Livy we had to put our relationship on hold. We went out only one night a week and the rest of the time I poured my heart and soul into studying. It paid off because after three months of police college, I wound up at the top of the class and was also the best shot. I went from being a guy who could barely write an exam or pass a relatively simple test—first aid—to dealing with complex issues like the Criminal Code, Highway Traffic Act, Narcotics Control Act, and bylaws and procedures. There was a lot of learning to do, but I wasn't going to fail.

It didn't take me long to learn that being on the street was a lot different from being in police college. I remember my very first traffic ticket. It was a Sunday afternoon and I had been on the job for a week. I stopped a guy for going through an amber light and he kicked up a real fuss. He ranted and raved and called me everything in the book, then he took out a Kleenex box and a pen and wrote down my name and badge number. I figured I was in serious trouble. I phoned the desk sergeant and told him what had happened and he asked me what I did. I said I gave the guy a ticket and the sergeant said "good." Then he said I should've *arrested* him because he was causing a disturbance. Well, the guy never did make a complaint, but I felt so reinforced by the support I got from this old-timer. Many times since then I've had a similar response from people I've stopped, but I don't waste any time locking them up for causing a disturbance.

Never again did I put up with that nonsense.

I joined the police in 1969 and married Livy in 1970. By that time, we had a house and a mortgage. In those days, Toronto was much more peaceful and civilized than it is now. People didn't even lock their doors then. We also had the Vagrancy Act, which allowed us to deal with vagrants on the street. If they had no visible means of support, we would pick them up. Some people thought this pratice was inhumane, but it was the most humane thing to do because we took them to shelters or to special court where the judge would send them off to detox or to be fed or to get medical attention. The point is, it got vagrants off the street and directed them to the services they needed to survive. The Vagrancy Act was repealed long ago, but I think we need something to replace it, because today downtown Toronto is full of street people. We just let them die, and there is something seriously wrong with that.

However, even back in those days, the city wasn't very welcoming to newcomers. It was still very WASPY and stuffy. The hotels had separate entrances for women and men. There was no Sunday shopping. If you went to the liquor store, you had to fill in documents to buy a bottle. The crime was different too, with a lot of "booze cans." These were unlicensed liquor establishments where anyone could buy a bottle under the table on a Sunday. Drugs were just starting to come in.

On my first day as a police officer, I reported to 14 Division with the other recruits. The duty sergeant got us together and we were all spit and polish. He paraded us in front of his veteran officers and said this is how he expected them to look. Like us. Well, that didn't go over too well with the troops because later on we were all ribbed for it. There was a pecking order, and when you're new, you try to fit in. For example, when you went into the lunchroom you had to be careful where you sat. It was a reminder that you were new. On the other hand, those seasoned guys would come to your aid in a flash if you ever needed it.

What was it like being new? Well, you have experiences and you learn from them. When you start out, you don't get into a police car unless you are relieving one of the seasoned guys when he is on lunch.

One time I remember getting a car of my own and rushing out to a call. I didn't have much experience and was pushing the car too much. I hit a rise and the car went up in the air, right through a stop. It scared the daylights out of me. After that I always made sure to have full control of the car.

Another time, I stopped a man who was in his car with his wife. It was for a traffic violation and his wife slipped him ten dollars so he could hand it to me. He was an immigrant and I told him that in Canada we don't do that sort of thing, but he kept trying to stuff the ten dollars into my hand. He was very forceful about it and finally I had to arrest him for an attempted bribe.

In those days, Toronto police were mostly Scottish and English, and there was no such thing as community policing. Hardly any officers spoke Italian, which was my ace in the hole, but at the same time I found it almost surreal dealing with Italian mobsters. These people were pillars of the community. They were family men and business types who had all the outward appearance of being nice guys and yet, they were immersed in the underworld. When the movie *The Godfather* was released, it was a trip down fantasy lane. I thought it was pretty ridiculous, all drama, but with some elements of truth. For example, I remember a young fellow named Salvatore Palermiti, who was visiting Toronto from Italy. He was just eighteen. The Mob was after his father in Italy and they reached out across the ocean and killed the son over here. To this day that murder remains unsolved. Back when I joined the force, there was an upswing in organized crime, most of it involving drugs and extortion. Unfortunately, with *The Godfather* thing, whenever an Italian got into trouble everyone assumed it was Mob-related and most of the time it wasn't.

In those days, we did a lot of surveillance, when you'd be out alone all hours of the day and night. It was dangerous because some of these guys played for keeps. But that was why I got onto the force in the first place. I spoke Italian and understood the culture. It was a good fit. And back then, of course, we had far more latitude than we do now. By that I mean tools were more readily available to us, laws were more permissive as far as being a police officer was concerned, and the restrictions on police were not nearly as severe as they are today. So, all in all, we were doing very effective police work in the underworld. That meant surveillance, following people around, and doing electronic investigations. All this gave you a pretty good picture of who was doing what. But the problem, which still exists today, was not having enough resources dedicated to doing long-term investigations.

Of course, being able to speak Italian was a big help. One time we had information that a certain individual was in possession of a large amount of jewellery that had been stolen in a robbery. I went along with the investigators as part of the raid team, and we had a search warrant at the home of an Italian guy. We searched his house and couldn't find anything. Then he and his mother started up a conversation in Italian, not knowing that I spoke the language. It turned out that the jewellery was in the mother's possession and she was telling her son that everything was okay because she had it on her. I grabbed onto those clues and we had her searched by a policewoman. Sure enough, she had the stuff and they were both arrested.

Another time, I was brought out of uniform to work in plainclothes. A prostitute was working out of a restaurant, and the owner was keeping a bawdy house. The woman was Italian and her clientele were Italian, so I was told to make contact with her and set up a date. According to the plan, the place would be raided by plainclothes officers while I was there. I was given instructions about what to do, what not to do, and what to say. The one thing I was strongly cautioned about was not to engage in any kind of sexual activity. But I still had to get in. I made the appointment and showed up, and was I ever nervous because never before had I been in a situation like that. They had told me they'd give me a few minutes and would arrive on time, but one thing I knew even then was that nothing ever works on time. And there was no way I was going to allow myself to get compromised. So I tied my shoelaces into knots, thinking that would buy me time if I had to undo those knots to get my shoes off. Sure enough, those guys were late, and thank God I had those knots, because this woman was all ready to go. She was in business and had other appointments to keep. I was hurried up and there I was trying to get my shoes off! I delayed and delayed and was damn nervous about it, but in the end we locked her up and we locked up the owner, too. The knots in the shoes saved the day and whenever I get knots in my shoes now I think about that time.

There are all kinds of little tricks a cop can use on the job. Take domestic situations, which are always trouble because you never know what to expect. Many times I was called to a house because the husband was abusing and threatening his wife, and my concern was always that the violence would start up again as soon as I left. So I'd encourage the husband to speak to me on the sidewalk. If he was still ranting and raving and being violent out there I could deal with him because now he was in a public place and I could lock him up. Of course, sometimes the wife would turn on you as well.

You had to be careful in those situations because they could easily turn violent. And sometimes soccer games were violent, too. If there was ever trouble with a soccer game it was definitely the matches between the Serbians and the Croatians. They were men's teams and these people had very bitter feelings towards each other. The soccer matches became a battleground and sometimes we had to respond with paddy wagons and horses. I remember once when somebody in the stands threw stones, and before you knew it, stones were flying everywhere. A sergeant spotted a few guys throwing them, so he vaulted over a fence, went into the crowd, and grabbed the men. He handed them over to us and we locked them up. You could be sure that there would be fights when the Serbians were playing the Croatians.

Generally, most immigrants were just good, decent people trying to build a life. However, one experience from those early days really disturbed me. I was in uniform on a Sunday morning. The patrol sergeant told me to patrol an area that comprised a lot of immigrants and I'll never forget what he said: "Get those WOPS off the sidewalk." I found that very hurtful. Here the local Italians would come meet their friends after church. They'd have their espresso, Italian newspapers and magazines, and some of them would have shortwave radios so they could listen to the soccer games from back home in Italy. They would gather on the sidewalk and chat and were as harmless as can be. Obstructing nothing. Bothering no one. Just socializing. But some people complained and saw this as threatening in some way, so I bit my tongue and figured that was part of the apprenticeship, but I sure didn't throw anyone off the street. There was no need. I'd drop by and chat with them and I thought that was the greatest form of community policing you could do.

Like most immigrants, Italians brought a great work ethic to this country. They came here with no expectation other than to work and contribute and raise a family. They'd buy a house, fix it up, and pay off the mortgage. Just look at how all those communities with Italians, Greeks, Portuguese, and other immigrants changed over the years. All those old houses got fixed up and the neighbourhoods really improved. As they tried to get ahead, many immigrants also kept boarders. In fact, my father was a boarder during his first year in Canada.

But still there were distinct differences between their cultures and what you had over here. In those days, Italians were very hesitant about calling the police. When my brother was nineteen or twenty he was working as a labourer at the Royal York Hotel in downtown Toronto and his wallet was stolen. He was told to report the theft at the local police station. He couldn't speak English very well and got into a disagreement with the police. He ended up being thrown out of the police station, which was a very bitter experience for him. He went for help, but got the boot and after that he'd always say to me, "Why do you want to be one of them?"

This reluctance to get the police involved is no longer the case with the Italian community, but it does happen with other groups who are relatively new. In the '80s, a number of extortions were taking place in Toronto's Chinatown and it was very difficult for the police to investigate because so few people would come forward. They mistrusted the police, which goes back to the culture the Chinese came from. More recently, the same problem has existed in certain elements of the Sri Lankan community and also the black community. It's difficult doing your job when no one wants to talk to you, is intimidated by you or, worst of all, has no respect for you. They also think that if you're a police officer, you must be on the take. The longer people are in Canada, however, the more they learn that we treat policing as a profession.

By the time the '90s rolled around, Toronto was being called the most multicultural city in the world. Even *National Geographic* said so. And it *is* an incredible city where people from many different ethnic groups live side by side, for the most part in peace and harmony. But like everything else there are always bad apples and that's why we have police.

It's important for any police force to recognize the demographic makeup of its community, and when I joined that was a big drawback. There were virtually no inroads into the Italian community and just being able to talk the language wasn't enough. You also had to know the culture. Here's what I mean. As an Italian immigrant, one thing I always understood about immigrants, especially those from Europe, was the importance of wine. One Saturday afternoon I got a radio call in a Portuguese community. There was smoke coming from this house and the owner wouldn't let the fire department in. I chit-chatted with the guy, who spoke broken English at best, but he was reluctant to let the fire department into his basement because, as it turned out, he was cooking grape *mash*. As any European immigrant can tell you, *mash* is the remnant you express from grapes during wine-making. This guy was making moonshine and a lot of Italians used to do this as well. The word Italians use is "grappa" for grapes. But he wasn't just making it. He was also running a business. An illegal business. So I called the RCMP, and two of their plainclothes officers took a sample to be analyzed at the lab. The guy had a garage at the back and it was full of barrels of wine. The Mounties broke them open with axes and let all that wine run down the drive into a drain on the street. That didn't seem to bother them at all, but it sure bothered me. It was a real disappointment to see all that stuff going down the drain. A waste of good wine. As an Italian, I could readily appreciate that.

When *The Godfather* came out in 1972, the city's Italian community felt that the Mafia legend was overblown, and it was. Antonio Nicaso, a journalist and an expert on the Mob, has been a friend of mine for many years. According to his book, *Deadly Silence*, cowritten with *Toronto Star* writer Peter Edwards, less than 0.02 per cent of Toronto's Italian community had ties to organized crime, which meant that 99.98 per cent of the Italian community did not. But whenever anyone whose last name ended in "i" or "o" got picked up, it was always assumed they were Mafia. It's true that back in the early '70s the Mob was flexing its muscles and executing people. We had bakery explosions and killings, and for many years the government was terribly naive about the level of organized crime operating in Canada, as was the public in general. But the reality was still nothing like *The Godfather*.

By saying this I don't mean to make light of the very serious problem of organized crime. Believe me, I'm the last person who would make light of that. In 1952, the Bonnano family appointed Vic Cotroni as their representative in Montreal and he worked the Buffalo connection and it spread to Ontario with extortion, narcotics, loansharking, illegal gaming, and sometimes bombings and murders. I was exposed to this soon after I joined the police department, and while Toronto had this image of being "Toronto the innocent," in fact, there was nothing innocent about it at all. There was a problem and no one—not the politicians, not the local Italian community, and not even the police—would acknowledge it.

In the summer of 1972, Ontario Secretary for Justice Allan Lawrence said there was no problem with the Mafia and denied that such a criminal organization even operated here! Well, he was wrong. But the real problem was not having a strategy in place to deal with organized crime and, as far as the Italian community was concerned, not having a connection between the police and that community. I guess that's where I came in.

While other G7 countries were trying to deal with the same thing, Canada had no currency laws, no anti-gang legislation, and no recognition that there was a problem. I'll get into this in more detail later, but suffice to say that the Mob was very well established in the '70s and also that alleged connections to organized crime for anyone with an Italian name had reached the point of absurdity.

I did an interview with the *Toronto Star* in 1972. The title of the article was "Toronto's Italians say Mafia legend is over-exploited." I mentioned how I used the Italian language every day on the job patrolling the streets of Little Italy. I explained how in Italy a driver might lean on his car horn to make a statement, while that sort of thing didn't wash here, or how in Rome a large gathering on the sidewalk would be considered an "obstruction" on this side of the ocean. I related the story of Nino Daversa, whose bakery in Toronto's Italian area was bombed by extortionists. An Italian mobster had approached him with an offer—pay $5,000 or expect another bombing. But to his credit Daversa came to the police and we made an arrest.

A few years later, when I was in homicide, three small-time hoods paid with their lives after they broke the so-called code of honour among criminals. The three men were fences—they would buy stolen goods from break-and-enter artists and sell the hot items on the black market for whatever they could get. The triple slaying happened in an apartment when one of the guys—Bill the Greek—agreed to meet the men he had swindled. The guns came out and you had a triple murder. One of the killers was convicted of first-degree murder and is still in jail today, while the other one got second-degree murder.

So, sometimes things did get ugly, and in later years the problem with organized crime got much worse, and still the government had blinkers on. It's funny when I think about this now, but I can probably thank Italian organized crime for giving me the opportunity to become a law enforcement officer. And while I had a lot of trouble trying to understand those mobsters—after all, I shared their heritage—what was more traumatic for me in the early '70s was the killing of a police officer. In a little over a year, four Toronto police officers were gunned down on the job and it was a real rough time for the city's police department. Let me explain.

On October 6, 1969—that was the year I joined—David Goldsworthy was patrolling the factory areas in the northwest end of the city. It was a remote and lonely area with a lot of farmland, and some break-ins had occurred in the vicinity. Goldsworthy didn't report off duty that morning and had been marked off by the desk sergeant because it was just assumed he had gone home. But then a coffee-truck guy found his body in a field. He had been shot through the chest. One of the bullets went through his memo book in his breast pocket, and we later learned that in his dying moments, he had scribbled the name of the man who shot him. That man, Vincenzo Fazzari, was later convicted of what was then non-capital murder and sentenced to life imprisonment. He initially had been charged with capital murder, which at the time called for the death penalty in the killing of police or prison guards, but the charge was later reduced to non-capital murder. Fazzari, an Italian national, was later deported to Italy.

Before he died, Goldsworthy also jotted down the names of his wife and son. Those were the very last things he wrote. He was a 31 Division officer and I knew him through my dealings with that division when I had worked with Steinbergs. With his death coming so soon after I became an officer, the dangers of the job quickly sank in for me. But then, you never think it will happen to you.

By and large, being a police officer is underappreciated by the public. Most of us who do this for a living could be making a lot more money doing something else. People don't understand the enormous sacrifices that are made, and not only by police officers, but by their families as well. It's a job where you're always under the microscope. The media is constantly in your face and there are a lot of day-to-day demands. This creates a lot of added stress on your life and on your family. So does shift-work. You might finish at midnight and then be back at work at seven in the morning, so you go from night to day shift over a space of five or six hours. You don't have time to unwind and then you're right back at it again. This was the "short changeover" and sometimes between shifts you also had to go to court, so there were times when you could go *three or four weeks* without getting a single day off. The thing people don't realize is that, like everyone else, police are human beings who are subject to pressures and family issues, and sometimes they get unfairly pilloried in the media. People really have no idea about the kind of trauma that goes on in a police officer's family.

The police constitute a family, too. It's known as the Blue Line and it exists. It has to. You learn to rely on other officers. It's like a soldier who must count on his buddies for survival. And the family goes beyond that. In my time, when you walked the beat, your best friends were the cab drivers because they would always radio for help if you needed it. There are also people on the beat like shopkeepers whom you can count on. One fellow who owned a pool hall in a tough neighbourhood—he was a rough-and-tough kind of guy—was always ready to jump in if I ever had a problem with somebody. By the same token, there would be rounders—criminals and low life—who would jump you if they got an opportunity. When that happened, you gave as much as you got, only you tried to give a little more. First you try to talk your way out, but if you can't, then it's time to dance, and if you should ever face imminent danger, you sure can't wait for people to take you down. The police have a saying: *It's always better to be tried by twelve than to be carried by six.*

Over the years, I've had my share of scrapes and bruises, however, I always felt good about it at the end of the day because the bad guys usually went to jail. But this is why it's such a terrible thing when a police officer is killed in the line of duty. We all feel it. And as bad as the death of David Goldsworthy was, it really hit me when two good friends of mine were killed on the same night.

Mike Irwin was my instructor at police college. He was a decent guy who took great interest in the recruits. He was always open, welcoming and encouraging, and a real model and mentor to the young guys. There was a humanity about this man I deeply respected. Police college can be very intimidating to newcomers, but Mike understood that we were new and he used his experience to mold and shape us. I met Doug Sinclair when I was seconded to the Intelligence Unit, and we became good friends. He was happy-go-lucky, good humoured, and enjoyed the job. He had a positive energy that was great to be around. We went hunting together and I got to know his family. Doug was a detective and I was only a new officer, but he treated me like his own. These were two guys who went the extra mile and were decent to the core.

On Sunday morning, February 27, 1972, I was in 14 Division and had just come in for duty when I was told what had happened. Mike and Doug, both detectives, had answered a call about a man who was seen firing a gun off his balcony in an apartment building. The man's name was Lewis Fines. When Mike, Doug, and a third officer, Samuel Fox, arrived, they found Fines standing in the middle of the corridor with an automatic rifle in his hands. Before they could do anything, Fines shot Doug twice through the chest. He died instantly. Fines was told to drop the gun, but he fired again and shot Mike in the head. Mike died later in hospital. The other officer, Fox, later said Fines had fired seven shots in that hallway. Fines took off and went to the basement garage of the building. Fox chased him, then turned around and went back to give mouth-to-mouth resuscitation to Mike, and while he was doing that, he heard footsteps coming up the stairs. Fines had returned and now he was pointing his rifle at Fox, so Fox fired his .38 revolver three times. Fines was hit in the head, chest, and arm, and died on the spot.

I'll never forget that day. My heart sank. These two men weren't only police officers, they were also mentors and personal friends of mine. The tradegy hit home big-time. I formed part of the honour guard at Doug's funeral and there was a huge turnout. For me, it was just like losing family. The night Mike died at the hospital, his wife, Barbara, signed consent forms to allow his corneas to be used for two blind people. She is a wonderful woman who never remarried, but when Mike died she was left almost destitute with four children to raise. Her pension was negligible. So she made a point of addressing these things, and because of her courage and determination and what she did, a lot of changes were made to improve the lot of police widows. Today, two of her children and a granddaughter are Toronto police officers, and her son-in-law is with the RCMP.

On January 11, 1973, less than a year later, another officer, James Lothian, was killed by a couple of speed freaks after he stopped their car. One of them was out on bail at the time. Lothian and his wife, who had an infant son, had just bought a house. Then, a mere three weeks after that, we had yet another shooting. Leslie Maitland was chasing a suspect after a bank robbery and wound up taking four bullets. He had two little kids and his wife was pregnant with their third child. After that there was a big debate about getting two-man patrols in cars during the 7 p.m. to 2 a.m. shift because the dangers of the job were becoming increasingly obvious. Back then Toronto was one of the few cities in North America that still allowed one-man units.

So, in less than a year, four Toronto police officers were killed on the job. This was a horrible time for Toronto cops, and during it all Chief Harold Adamson was a tower of strength who provided tremendous leadership when we were all really traumatized. Let's face it, these were not traffic accidents. There was a lot of talk in the guard room and angst about the job. Many guys were getting heat at home from their families who wanted them to quit. My own mother was always fearful about the job and she also urged me to quit. We felt very vulnerable and that we were being used as target practice by these idiots. We thought society was letting us down, because there was a lack of appreciation for the safety issues of police officers in the line of duty. Both by the public and especially by politicians.

There weren't enough officers out there and, to make matters worse, we had inadequate equipment. Take our holsters. They had a simple flap and could be opened easily. You know what we called them? *Widow-makers.* But that's all we had. When you went into a brawl, you had to worry about protecting your gun because it was easily accessible. It wasn't until the 1980s that we got safer holsters and not until the '90s did we get semi-automatics. That was a real battle for us because you had some voices saying the police would now be going around shooting people. But then, these characters weren't walking the streets at night, were they? Another safety problem was the leather cross-straps that went across the chest. They could be grabbed with no difficulty at all. And the knotted ties. It wouldn't have been too hard for someone to strangle you with your tie. Today there are no cross-straps, we have clip-on ties, and it's a lot harder for someone to try to pull your gun out.

But my point is, any time an effort was made to provide the police with basic tools to help us do our job and just be safe, there was always a pushback that we would be abusing that authority. Abusing the public. And that's what frustrates the police to no end. It's not the danger of the criminal element out there. We know we have to deal with that, know it's part of the job, and accept it. What frustrates the hell out of police officers and their families are those who are always critical and who always feel that we are dishonest.

All these deaths were a powerful lesson and made us realize how vulnerable we were and that we should never take officer safety for granted. At the same time, it enhanced my own pride in being a cop, and made me think that when I picked up my badge, I didn't surrender my rights as a citizen. And I didn't.

·4·

The Munro Brothers

E DDY ADAMSON SPENT THE LAST TWENTY-FIVE YEARS OF HIS LIFE CONSUMED BY guilt over the death of Michael Sweet, and when Eddy himself died in November 2005, he took that guilt to his grave. On that ominous night in March 1980, Eddy was the sergeant in command of the Toronto Police Department's Emergency Task Force. The Munro brothers were in the midst of botching a robbery at George's Bourbon Street, and Sweet just happened to be in the wrong place at the wrong time. He got himself shot, not once, but twice, and the two gunmen wouldn't let him go. Sweet was dying slowly, and the Munros refused to release him even as he pleaded with them about his wife and family. On and on it went and all Eddy kept hearing was that he couldn't go in yet for the rescue. A police team was negotiating with the Munros, trying to engineer Sweet's release, and Eddy had to wait.

Finally, when he couldn't wait any longer, he, Gary Leuin, and Barry Doyle gave the signal to storm the place. They let loose with tear gas and gunfire. The Munro brothers went down and then they and Sweet were rushed to hospital, as was Eddy. It was the effect of the tear gas and he had to be treated. But Eddy would be all right and even the two thugs who started the whole thing would be all right. But not Sweet. A few hours later, the thirty-year-old father of three little girls died on the operating table.

Every day for twenty-five years Eddy thought about that. He thought about it a lot. He talked about it all the time, and whenever his mind returned to that hor-

rible night, he told himself that he shouldn't have listened to his orders and waited as long as he did. He should have gone in right away and taken those two guys down. And they could have gotten Sweet out of there and he would have lived and those little girls of his wouldn't have lost their father. It had been tearing Eddy up ever since.

BACK IN 1865, IN UPPER AND Lower Canada any crime involving murder, rape or treason called for the death penalty. The method was hanging. Prior to that time, death was the sentence meted out for as many as 120 different crimes. People convicted of crimes that did not warrant death could be whipped, branded, or placed on public display in pillories or stocks, and sometimes they got banished to other countries.

During the nineteenth century, however, a new philosophy of corrections was beginning to take hold in England and was gathering steam in Canada and the United States. The idea was to incarcerate offenders in penitentiaries where they would be kept from society and have time to consider what they had done and, hopefully, to repent. In fact, Canada's first such institution opened its doors as early as 1835, when the Provincial Penitentiary of Upper Canada in Kingston, Ontario, admitted six inmates.

It wasn't until 1976 that the death penalty was formally abolished in Canada. The last executions had taken place fifteen years before then. In 1961, Arthur Lucas and Robert Turpin—the latter had murdered a police officer—were both hanged at Toronto's Don Jail. At the time, the crime of murder was either capital murder or non-capital murder. Capital murder was for premeditated murder and the murder of a police officer, prison guard, or warden. It carried the death penalty, while non-capital murder did not. Interestingly enough, the Canadian military retained the death penalty, at least, on its books, until 1998 when the Canadian National Defence Act removed the death penalty and replaced it with life imprisonment with no eligibility for parole for twenty-five years. This put the military in line with Canadian civil law.

The military has long had its own brand of justice and corrections, separate from the country's civil system. While the underlying philosophy of Canadian penal institutions over the past thirty years can be explained in one word, rehabilitation, the military approach isn't quite the same. Today, Canada maintains one military prison, the Canadian Forces Service Prison and Detention Barracks at Canadian Forces Base, Edmonton. Here there is no such thing as parole or temporary passes, but inmates can reduce their sentences by earning privileges through an award system. When an offender arrives, there are no rights at all; they must be earned. Each morning everyone is up at 6 a.m. with reveille. Cells must be kept spotless. Girlie posters are not permitted. Dress codes are rigidly adhered to. Elbows are not permitted on tables in the cafeteria. And as recently as 2002, inmates who caused trouble could be placed on a restricted diet, bread and water, for up to three days.

For what it's worth, in the military prison the rate of recidivism, which is the percentage of inmates who serve their time and are released only to be returned to the institution for new offences, is about 2 per cent. The rate of recidivism in Canada's civil system is much higher. How much higher? That depends on whom you talk to.

The Correctional Service Canada has a booklet called *Myths and Realities—How Federal Corrections Contributes to Public Safety*. It was published in 2000. One of the so-called myths is that "most offenders commit new crimes while on parole." The "reality," says the booklet, is that most offenders do not commit new crimes while on parole. It then cites a review of 1,796 cases in which full parole ended in the 2000-01 time frame and says, that in 1,333 of those cases or 74.2 per cent of them, the terms of release were "successfully completed." This means a success rate of 74.2 per cent or about three out of four, meaning a recidivism rate of about 25 per cent. Anyone can make whatever they want out of figures, but the jails are full of recidivists. If the system is supposed to rehabilitate people, it's certainly not doing a very good job of it.

Prisons and statistics aside, human history is rife with the most diabolical punishments imaginable, and the idea or philosophy behind such punishments has been to deter future acts of criminality. Indeed, deterrence has long been part and parcel of the whole concept of punishment. In ancient Rome, a person convicted of murdering their mother or father was submersed in water in a sack that contained a dog, a rooster, a viper, and an ape; guilty parties would fend for themselves and "justice" was seen to be done. In the Middle Ages, a person condemned to death might undergo a public display of debasement and humiliation by being tarred and feathered before the *coup de grâce* was delivered by quartering, which was anything but a tidy form of execution.

Today, in Canada, things are much different, and thankfully so. But has the system gone too far the other way? Has it gone too far when a convicted police killer can raise a family while incarcerated and spend his time in an institution that is anything but hard time? Has it gone too far when a convicted police killer can marry a foreigner, legally change his name, and get paroled to another country where he can live in absolute freedom without being watched or supervised at all? This is exactly what happened to Craig and Jamie Munro.

In 1981, the two brothers were convicted in the killing of Michael Sweet. Craig Munro, as the shooter, was convicted of first-degree murder and sentenced to life with no eligibility for parole for twenty-five years. Jamie Munro was convicted of second-degree murder and sentenced to life with no eligibility for parole for twelve years.

The murder of Michael Sweet was far from the first time these two men had broken the law. In fact, at the time of Michael Sweet's killing, the Munro brothers were already long-time career criminals who, like many other offenders in Canada, had been making a mockery of the country's justice system for years. They made a mockery of it because of light sentences handed out for serious crimes, some sentences so light as to stretch one's belief, and because of repeated early releases granted to them even despite their continued propensity for reoffending while free. Time and again, over a period of many years and after a litany of offences that eventually resulted in the cold-blooded murder of a police officer, the Munros would serve minimal time, if any time at all, for their convictions. And during those times when they were incarcerated, they would invariably receive parole, which must be applied for, or the automatic mandatory release which comes to virtually all offenders after two-thirds of their sentence has been served. Which begs this question: Are such forms of early release designed to keep the number of inmates inside Canadian institutions as low as possible?

Correctional Service Canada's *Myths and Realities* that quotes the 74.2 per cent "success rate" says the answer to this question is an unequivocal no. It says the size of the federal prison population is not a factor considered by the National Parole Board when it reviews an inmate's application for parole. However, a 1981 federal government study that looked at crimes committed by offenders out on early release over a four-year period from 1977-80, which was the same period of time when the Munros were most active in their criminal careers, begged to differ. The study was the Solicitor General's Study of Conditional Release and the report of the working group came out in March 1981. The report was not meant for public consumption, but was an internal government document. On page 43 it stated: *Penitentiaries have a strong interest in seeing as many full releases as possible occur in order to save costs.*

The reason behind that philosophy was simple; then as now, it was much cheaper to supervise an offender in the community on parole or mandatory release than to keep the offender behind bars. According to Correctional Service Canada, in 2003-04, the average annual cost of incarcerating male offenders in federal institutions in maximum security was $110,000, in medium security $72,000, and in minimum security $74,000. But the average annual cost of supervising an offender on parole or statutory release was under $20,000. Does it all boil down to money then?

It might. One look at the record of offenders like the Munros and it's painfully clear that the system doesn't place a very high regard on the safety and protection of the public. What is blatantly obvious from scrutinizing the criminal records of the Munro brothers and their lifetime of crime is this: The system is far more interested in having such offenders outside in the community where they can wreak havoc on society than it is in having them inside a penal institution.

But for two murderers like the Munros it doesn't end there. Even after their murder convictions for the killing of Michael Sweet, they have continued to wage war on Canadian society, with the support of the government of Canada. Craig Munro remains incarcerated largely due to my own efforts to keep him behind bars. During his years of incarceration, he has been in trouble with authorities many times, often receiving no punishment for his behaviour. On the inside, he is regarded as one with a "personality disorder, passive-aggressive type," according to his Parole Eligibility Report from October 9, 1996. Still, he has managed to produce a family, courtesy of conjugal visits with his wife. He is currently incarcerated at Fenbrook Institution, which is located in the midst of Ontario cottage country.

Meanwhile, Jamie Munro, who was convicted of the lesser charge of second-degree murder, has managed to forge a much better deal with authorities than his brother Craig. He was able to work out a special arrangement. By marrying an Italian national and legally changing his name to Massimo Marra, he was allowed to leave Canada, obtain a Canadian passport, and take up residence in Calabria, Italy, where for many years he has operated a gym. During all the years he has lived in Italy, he has never once reported to a parole officer or been monitored in any way whatsoever.

If we take another look at Correctional Service Canada's *Myths and Realities*, on page 13, it says:

> A life sentence means life. Never again will an offender serving a life sentence enjoy total freedom. Although "lifers" may not spend the rest of their lives within an institution (i.e. they may eventually be paroled) they will always remain subject to conditions and supervision.

Apparently, they forgot about Jamie Munro. And maybe some other offenders as well.

THE MUNROS' STORY BEGINS WITH their father, Lawrence Munro. He was a heavy drinker and a gambling man who was often away from his family because he worked as a truck driver. At different times in his life he ran a small-engine business and an asphalt company. He and his wife, Frances, had a big family, eight sons and three daughters, and the children came along at regular intervals, about every year and a half. Their first child was born in 1947 and the last in 1964. Craig Alfred Munro, their fourth son, was born on December 3, 1951, and Jamie, their sixth son, was born seven years later on October 30, 1958. Lawrence Munro died from leukemia in 1977, when Craig was twenty-six and Jamie was nineteen. By that time, Craig already had a lengthy criminal record and Jamie had started to build his resume.

It all started for Craig in February 1968, when he was just sixteen. After stealing a car and smashing up a kitchen, he found himself charged with Malicious Damage and Possession of a Stolen Vehicle. When youngsters stole cars in those days, it was known as "joy riding." Craig was young and a first-time offender and, as is the case with first-time offenders, the authorities decided to go easy on him. He was convicted of both charges, but received only a suspended sentence and two years' probation. That meant he had a record but wouldn't do any jail time and would be under the supervision of his probation officer. However, going soft on the young Craig did not have the desired effect because three months later, when he was still on probation for that first offence, he faced three new charges: two counts of Take Auto Without Owner's Consent, which is essentially auto theft; and one count of Common Assault. He had been in a fight and had given the other guy a black eye. Craig, still sixteen years of age, was convicted on all counts and sentenced to fifteen days in jail with a $72 fine thrown in.

In June 1969, seventeen-year-old Craig struck a bus driver and was found guilty of Assault Causing Bodily Harm. For that he received a sentence of three months. In the Canadian scheme of things, three months means you may apply for parole after one-third of your sentence which, in this case, was a month. If you don't apply for parole or are turned down, the law is such that you will be released into the community on "mandatory release," which used to be called mandatory supervision, after doing two-thirds of the sentence.

In October 1971, Craig, now nineteen, was convicted of Possessing Stolen Property Over $50 and handed a six-month sentence. His case file said he had been in possession of an air conditioner and a cassette deck. Only one month later, in November 1971, he was convicted of Dangerous Driving and for that was fined $100.

On February 10, 1972, he was paroled after serving four of the six months for his earlier Possession-Over-$50 offence. He was able to stay out of trouble for seven months. In September of that year, he and a friend beat up two other men. For his trouble, Craig was convicted of Causing a Disturbance in a Public Place and Dangerous Driving.

He was now twenty years old and a long way from being a first-time offender. The sentence for causing a disturbance? A $25 fine. That was it. Three weeks later, he was tried and convicted of the Dangerous Driving charge and fined $150.

In April 1973, he was convicted of Robbery, which was more serious than anything else on his record until then, and Possession Over $200. He said he was the driver in a $5,640 robbery from the R. G. Foreign Exchange Service in Toronto. Finally, Craig was handed his first stiff sentence. He got three years for Robbery and another year for Possession Over $200, for a total of four years. For the first time in his life, he now found himself in a federal institution, namely Collins Bay Penitentiary in Kingston, Ontario, 200 kilometres east of Toronto on the north shore of Lake Ontario.

Collins Bay was built in 1929 and opened a year after that. The second-oldest federal institution for men in the province of Ontario, it is a medium-security facility and over the years has housed many of Canada's most notorious criminals. Although it once held over five hundred inmates, it would eventually hold less than half that number. It was at Collins Bay in 1975 where Craig obtained his Grade 10 education; he had quit formal school in Grade 9 at the age of fifteen.

Four years of prison time meant his sentence was due to expire in April 1977. But one year before, in April 1976, he was out on mandatory supervision, the same automatic release that offenders get after two-thirds of their sentence, even if they were previously denied parole. So, technically speaking, Craig was still "serving" time, but in the jargon of correctional services he was serving his time in the community. However, Craig violated the conditions of that early release by reoffending and was sent back to Collins Bay. Still, that didn't mean he would be denied his next mandatory release. And he wasn't.

Four months later, on September 2, 1976, he was found in possession of stolen identification, which meant he had *once again* violated the terms of his mandatory release. So, he had that release revoked and was convicted of Possessing Stolen Property Under $200. By this time, Craig was a multiple offender with a long string of convictions over a period of several years and had been convicted of such serious crimes as Assault, Theft, Robbery, and Possession. He had done federal time. He had violated his day parole. He had violated the terms of his mandatory release. So what did this long-time, repeat offender, who on more than one occasion had violated the conditions of his early release, get for his latest conviction of Possessing Stolen Property Under $200? Thirty days. Less than four months later, he obtained his next mandatory release, which meant Craig Munro was back on the street again.

In 1977, he had still more run-ins with the law. In April, he was acquitted of the charge of Assault Causing Bodily Harm and a charge of Mischief was withdrawn. In September, he was acquitted of another charge of Assault Causing Bodily Harm, but was convicted of three brand-new offences: Unlawfully in a Dwelling, which got him fifteen months; Assault Causing Bodily Harm, which got him six months; and, for the first time in his life, Possession of a Prohibited Weapon, for which he received six months. These new charges stemmed from an incident in which Craig and another man had forced their way into an apartment looking for drugs and then held the occupants at bay while they searched the place. Craig had assaulted a man and had threatened him with a switchblade. The man wound up getting cut.

In spite of all that, Craig was still given the benefit of the doubt. The total time he would have to serve for these three new convictions was only six months. And that was the case because the sentences would not run consecutively but concurrently, or at the same time. As with any offender, he was eligible for parole after one-third of his sentence, which in this case was two months, and he would get his mandatory release come hell or high water after two-thirds, which was four months.

Craig was granted his parole after two months and, true to form, he got into trouble almost immediately. On November 18, 1977, he was convicted of Possessing Stolen Property Over $200. He got six months for that. While doing his time at the Guelph Correctional Centre in Guelph, Ontario, he got into a fight with a recreation officer and was convicted of Assault Causing Bodily Harm, which earned him another six months.

He served the six months for his latest assault conviction, and while out on his latest mandatory release, was convicted of Conspiring to Possess Stolen Property. For this he got another nine months, and three months later he was out again only to be convicted of Dangerous Driving. The sentence this time? Seven days. Seven days even though he had yet again violated the terms of his release. What's more, that seven-day sentence was to be concurrent with his other previous offence, which meant it would not be an additional seven days but instead would be served at the same time as his other conviction. In the mathematics of criminal justice, that means it doesn't count.

In March 1979, Craig was charged with Obstructing a Peace Officer, but the charge was dismissed. In April, he faced two charges of Assault Causing Bodily Harm and Possession of a Weapon, and both these charges were withdrawn.

In late September of 1979, he was released once more on mandatory supervision, despite his Parole Eligibility Report, which stated that his behaviour had "deteriorated" and that he was involved in many institutional charges, including an assault on a prison doctor. A security report, dated September 19, 1979, said he should not return to Joyceville Institution, a multi-security penitentiary northeast of Kingston, "in the event that he re-offend in the community." That same security report described him as being "very aggressive and threatening." Craig was considered a risk. A risk to the public.

He was out on mandatory release when, in November 1979, he was charged with Mischief. The charge was dismissed. Two months later, however, in February 1980, which was only one month before the shooting of Michael Sweet, he was convicted of Possessing a Weapon Dangerous to the Public Peace and fined $1,000. It was for this $1,000 fine that he and his brother Jamie decided to rob George's Bourbon Street on the night of March 13, 1980.

What is truly remarkable about Craig Munro's treatment by federal authorities is this: The automatic mandatory release date for his latest conviction, a conviction that merited jail time, would have occurred in October 1979. That mandatory release was suspended. But a few months later, on February 18, 1980, a mere five days after his latest conviction for possessing a dangerous weapon and only twenty-three days before the killing of Michael Sweet, the National Parole Board cancelled that suspension and let him out yet again on mandatory supervision.

While offenders on mandatory supervision are supposed to maintain regular contact with their parole officer, Craig's own Parole Eligibility Report states that during this time "supervision contact was sporadic." But still he was let out.

On June 17, 1980, three months after the bungled robbery at George's and the shooting death of Michael Sweet, Craig's next mandatory supervision release stemming from a prior conviction was revoked because he was now charged with first-degree murder.

What about Jamie Munro? Craig's younger brother was seventeen the first time he got charged with a crime. That occurred in 1975, for Possession of a Restricted Weapon, and he received only a conditional discharge and three months' probation. And why not?

Jamie was a first-time offender.

In January 1976, Jamie was convicted of Possession of Property Obtained by Crime Under $200 and he received another conditional discharge and was put on probation for one year.

In April 1977, he was convicted of Causing a Disturbance and fined $100. Five months later, it was three counts of Common Assault and fines of $50, $50, and $150, respectively.

In November 1978, he got thirty days for impaired driving. This was now his *seventh* conviction and for that he would do his first jail time, which was essentially a slap on the wrist.

In March 1979, he was fined $100 for Common Assault. In April, he got nine months for Criminal Negligence in the Operation of a Motor Vehicle and another three months for Possession of a Weapon. On July 17, he was *paroled*. So this means that, on the night of Michael Sweet's death, Jamie Munro was roaming the streets of Toronto because he was free on parole.

His older brother, Craig, was a ticking time bomb. He was a career criminal with a hankering for guns. He was especially fond of shotguns and rifles. He had a taste for heroin and had taken up boxing, karate, and weightlifting. But on the night of March 13, 1980, Craig Munro, a man deemed too dangerous by officials to reside in a minimum-security penitentiary, was walking the streets of Toronto because he was out on mandatory release. The Correctional Service Canada, on its website, www.csc-scc.gc.ca, explains the reasoning behind it under the category of Supervision:

> The purpose of conditional release supervision is to protect society by helping offenders become law-abiding citizens by ensuring control and by providing them with assistance and programs in order to minimize the risk of their committing new offences.

It's the law. As for the National Parole Board, on its website, www.npb-cnlc.gc.ca, under the section Myths and Realities, this is what it says about releasing criminals:

> The protection of society is the overriding consideration in any release decision.

Read it and weep.

·5·

The Speed Capital of
North America

I N THE 1970S, I WAS PART OF A FIVE-MAN SQUAD WITH THE
Toronto police. In layperson's terms, it was the street-level "drug
squad," even though at the time there was no such formal unit. In
fact, we were just street cops working in "old clothes," or plainclothes
if you will. But the big difference between us and the other police officers on the force was that while we worked out of 14 Division—we
were simply called No. 14 Division Old Clothes Unit—we had the
autonomy to work in whatever area of criminality we wanted. It was
high-end stuff and we concentrated on the drug scene because it fuelled
so much crime.

Our leader was an officer named Mike Burke, who was a constable
then, but later was promoted to sergeant. Mike was one of the most
intelligent people I've ever met in police work. He had a fantastic memory, a very strategic mind, and lots of valuable contacts and informants.
I don't think I've ever known another police officer with his qualities. He
was an icon in the police department and was even profiled in *Reader's
Digest*. Mike was a personality who was well known in the courts and
well known to the media. It always seemed that somebody was doing a
story on him. One day Mike went to the unit commander and asked if I
could join his crew, and that's how I got involved.

We were a tight unit and were given much more latitude than regular, uniformed police officers. We were free to roam the criminal haunts of Toronto and had the whole city at our disposal. We reported directly to the unit commander, which meant we didn't have to report through intermediate levels, and sometimes we received assignments right from the chief himself. We were free to work the hours we wanted and to tackle the criminal element on its own turf. There was no formal structure as to our hours, but we usually worked the night shift from 7 p.m. to 3 a.m. and, believe me, we were busy. The city was in the grips of a dramatic upsurge in violent crime and criminal activity, most of it due to drugs. In those days, Toronto was known as the "speed capital of North America" because of the proliferation of methamphetamines, speed houses, and all the speed freaks in town. This reputation was deserved.

On the street, speed is called meth or crystal. Speed is basically a chemical containing amphetamines and phenyl-2-propanone. Through a process of mixing and cooking and filtering, you get crystal, which is as pure a substance as you can get. Eighty per cent of purity would be considered extremely high quality. The crystal is then diluted with dextrose or sugar powder and, depending on how good the chemist is, some of it might look like dirty powder or even sugar itself. It is usually diluted and then injected. What it does is stimulate the central nervous system and lead to heightened paranoia. Users can go days and days without sleep. The doses came in about a third of a gram, with twenty-eight grams to an ounce. In the 1970s, speed quickly became a huge criminal underworld enterprise because a whole marketplace of speed dealers was concentrated in Toronto.

It was dangerous work for us because of the kinds of people we dealt with, people who would arm themselves with sawed-off shotguns and rifles. There were many times when we faced sawed-off shotguns. Once, after we kicked in the door of a drug den, we found a guy in a sofa chair. He reached under the cushions of the chair and pulled out a sawed-off rifle. We managed to overpower him, but I don't think there was any doubt about him using that gun of his. Of course, a warrant was needed to search a place that we suspected might house a dealer, but we also needed something else. The element of surprise. At the first hint of a raid, these characters would try to drop their drugs down the toilet. They had lookouts and their own brand of countersurveillance because they knew we were looking for them, which is why we did undercover buys, and that was dangerous work, too.

Anything could happen in a raid. One time we were going into a fortified crack house, and I was the lead guy who was supposed to kick in the door. It was snowing and I was wearing rubber boots. I kicked the door with the heel of my boot and it gave way, but my heel got stuck between the door and the frame. I was hanging upside down and couldn't get out. Considering the potential for what might have happened, and the kind of people we were going after, that could have been really bad. Fortunately, we forced our way in and made the arrest, but not until my colleagues had a good laugh at my expense.

Another time we had a warrant to search the penthouse suite of a major drug dealer. We were worried that he'd get rid of the drugs before we busted in, so we climbed onto the flat roof—it was a three-storey building—which gave us access to an external door leading down to his apartment. We knew this guy had a cat and that sooner or later he'd have to open that door to let the cat out. So the plan was to nab him when he opened the door, go in, and find the drugs. But getting to that door meant we had to jump over the roofs of buildings nearby. They were all three-storey buildings with a gap of maybe four feet between each of them, and you had to jump clear over those gaps or it was a long way down. What's more, it was cold and dark with a steady drizzle of rain. The problem for us was Mike Burke. He was a very intelligent guy, but not too agile, and a little overweight. The rest of us had to keep pushing him and pulling him, so he could get from one roof to the next. It's funny when I think about it now, but it sure wasn't funny at the time. Anyway, we got to the door and waited several hours out there in the cold and rain. Finally the door opened, out came the cat, and we got our man.

That's how it was, sometimes very tedious and not too pleasant, and other times so many things were happening at once that you needed your wits about you. Many times, of course, we would execute a search warrant and find nothing. These people may have been dangerous, but they were also very enterprising. They stashed their drugs behind bricks in a wall, behind a furnace, up in the ceiling, around vents, or inside mattresses. Usually we went in with a plan. For example, there were up to five of us in the group and the idea was to create confusion with our guys coming and going and then, amidst all this confusion, one of our group would stay behind inside the apartment. He'd stay in a closet or hide behind a couch and, when the rest of us left, these characters would invariably start talking about how smart they were and how they had the drugs stashed away in such-and-such. Fifteen minutes later we would all come back, and the guy who was concealed inside would tell us where to find the drugs.

In those days, we had no bulletproof vests and there was no Emergency Task Force for backup. At the same time, we had to assume that these people were armed. Many times when we broke through a door someone would reach for a gun, like the guy I mentioned on the sofa chair, but luckily none of us ever got hurt. That was because we relied on our intelligence and on stealth and because we always did our homework and worked as a team.

Dealing with this kind of person was not only a criminal issue, but also an economic and health issue. Speed freaks never looked healthy. They had skin diseases, rashes and sores, and their behaviour could often be irrational. They resorted to crime to buy drugs. As I say, it was a prolific time for drug dealers and a lot of money was made. Big money. A hit of speed cost five dollars and that was for a third of a gram, but our quest wasn't to go after the speed freaks. It was to find the illegal labs.

The drug scene involved a lot of middlemen, and on one particular investigation, we were able to work the distribution chain or ladder through twelve different stages from the street to the lab. That meant twelve different stages of dealers. The way it works is like this: As you move up through the chain, you keep getting a higher quantity and quality of product. The lab may put out pure crystal, but after that it starts getting diluted and broken down until you wind up with the street product. The more additives you add, the bigger the profit. As mentioned earlier, crystal meth was usually diluted with a powdery substance called dextrose.

The crack houses were all over the city, not just downtown, and desperate addicts would trade stolen goods for drugs, so it fuelled a great deal of crime. The biggest centre of this drug scene was Rochdale College, which back then was supposed to be a futuristic learning centre but, in fact, was a known haven for bikers and criminals. It was a place where drug dealers would come from just about everywhere to make their purchase.

Rochdale College was a co-op residence connected to the University of Toronto. It was billed as Canada's first "free" university and got its name from Rochdale, England, which was where the world's first co-operative housing development was created in the mid-1800s. Rochdale College opened in 1968, and became not only the largest co-op residence on the continent but also, according to the CBC, "North America's largest drug distribution warehouse."

Rochdale was an eighteen-storey high-rise on the south side of Bloor Street on the fringes of the University of Toronto campus and not far from Yorkville, which in the '60s and early '70s was Toronto's and Canada's focal point for hippies. Was Rochdale really an educational institution? Well, that's a matter of opinion. It had no structured courses, no structured curriculum, and no exams. The so-called students were the ones who set the curriculum, whatever curriculum there was. What Rochdale did have, however, was a lot of hallucinogenic drugs such as MDA (methylenedioxyamphetamine) and LSD, as well as speed, hashish, and marijuana. It was still the early days for heroin and cocaine, but some of that existed, too. Of course, everything, no matter what drug you were talking about, involved money. Lots of money.

Marijuana was smoked in cigarettes and sold in "nickel" or "dime" bags. The street cost for a single cigarette was $2 and it went up from there. A half ounce was $15, an ounce $25, a quarter-pound $75, a half-pound $125, and a pound $225. A person who was found in possession of one pound of marijuana could divide it into 906 cigarettes, which had a total cash value of

$1,812. They could also divide it into 128 nickel bags with a total cash value of $640, or into eighty dime bags with a total cash value of $800.

Hashish was even more expensive. The street price for a gram of hash was $10. An ounce was $80, a quarter-pound $275, a half-pound $500, and a pound $800. A person in possession of one pound could divide it into 454 dimes with a total cash value of $4,500, or into 1,000 nickels with a total cash value of $5,000.

And those were just the "cheap" drugs. The street price for one pound of LSD was $5,000 and for one pound of cocaine $10,000. Heroin fetched even more. A pound of that could have been $15,000. Drugs like cocaine and heroin became more popular later, but when I was working in the No. 14 Division Old Clothes Unit in the early '70s, by far the biggest problem was speed.

A hit of speed, a third of a gram, cost $5 on the street. A quarter-ounce was $40 and a half-ounce could fetch $80. An ounce could go for $150, a quarter-pound $500, a half-pound $1,000, and a pound up to $1,600. Do the math and it's easy to see how much money could be made. A person with one pound of speed could divide it into 1,364 nickel hits, which would bring a return of $6,820. Or they could divide it into what was called sixty-four "weight quarters," which brought $2,560 or, failing that, 112 "street quarters," which brought $3,920.

The quality of speed sold on the street was 20 per cent, and a heavy speed user would take up to five hits a day. The total quantity required for that amount was about two and a half grams. Every single day. Once we made an arrest, the charges usually involved possession for the purpose of trafficking, or trafficking, or a combination of both. There has never been any charge only for possession. These then were all offences that contravened the Food and Drug Act.

Rochdale was also a haven for American draft dodgers—this was the era of the Vietnam War—and for squatters and bikers who dealt in drugs. In fact, the building's own security force included members of a biker gang. The place eventually closed in 1975, and the day it closed, the police had to forcibly carry out residents who refused to leave. But for several years Rochdale was definitely the hub of the drug scene, and not just in Toronto, but for the whole country and even the whole continent.

Orders would come in to Rochdale from all over. It had an international reputation and it helped make Toronto well known to the U.S. law enforcement community as the "speed capital of North America." In fact, American law enforcement agencies recognized the problem and set up special task force units that sought the experience of local drug enforcement officers within the Toronto police. A constant liaison was maintained between American officers working with the Drug Enforcement Agency and my own unit. I think it's fair to say that by 1972 and 1973, the illicit use of speed had reached epidemic proportions in the city.

In 1971, our unit made 571 arrests representing 1,051 criminal charges. In 1972, it went up to 779 arrests representing 1,549 charges and, in 1973, it was up another 50 per cent over that. In early 1973, we made a concerted effort to trace the flow of speed from the street level up to the manufacturer. At the end of March that year, we were able to arrest nine people who were running a multi-million-dollar, speed-trafficking operation that reached deep into the United States. The top honcho in this organization was a businessman named Benno Sternig who lived in Mississauga, immediately west of Toronto.

Sternig owned an aircraft-leasing company called Stern Aircraft and a chemical company called Alpha Chemicals. It was suspected that Stern Aircraft would fly raw, speed-making ingredients into Canada and later fly the finished product out to points throughout Canada and the United States. Alpha Chemicals was the front set-up for the illicit drug laboratory and it made possible the easy purchase of controlled chemicals and the importing of these chemicals from Europe. It was a well-organized operation with so-called respectable people at the top while those below were the more typical criminal types. There were also "musclemen," legal advisers, and others who all played a role in the distribution of speed as if it was a legal business.

When we finally took down the enterprise, some eighty-one charges were laid against sixteen people. The charges included Conspiracy to

Traffic, Possession for the Purpose of Trafficking, Possession of Stolen Property, and Possession of Restricted and Unregistered Firearms. On a single day—March 29, 1973—nine raids were carried out simultaneously by joint forces of the Toronto police and the Royal Canadian Mounted Police, and the whole operation was coordinated by Mike Burke and my Old Clothes Unit. We seized more than $200,000 worth of speed along with other drugs, a quantity of stolen property, about $40,000 in cash of which over $20,000 was hidden in a freezer, of all places, and a lot of guns. For sure, the potential was there for this operation to generate millions of dollars. Sternig would become the first person in Canada to receive the maximum sentence for making speed, which at the time was ten years.

When I think back to those days I find it hard to believe how many arrests we made. It felt like we were on a production line. For example, in January 1972, we arrested seventy-five people and laid 122 charges on them. In that month alone, we seized various quantities of speed, marijuana, hashish, heroin, and cocaine with a total street value of over $150,000. Keep in mind that this was 1972.

But making a bust was never easy and it was always dangerous, especially in a place like Rochdale College where they had a warning system to tip people off. If we had a search warrant for a particular apartment, we would sometimes find that the number had been switched with that of another apartment, effectively screwing up our search warrant. Because it had such a concentration of drug dealers, Rochdale was a very dangerous place to raid. It was always a game of wits to try to get in there and do a bust and then get out safely.

What typically happened was that we would get to an apartment, someone would pull the fire alarm, and then everyone on the floor and throughout the building—and I mean *everyone*—would gang up on us. Many times we were involved in punch-ups. But there would be such a crowd that it was hard to pin drugs on any one person. So we used to keep observations on Rochdale—all the comings and goings—and do our homework and figure out who was there to buy drugs. We would do street stops and most of the time we were right.

One Sunday morning in my very early days in uniform, before I was working with Mike Burke and his group, I was on routine patrol in a cruiser by myself, following a car driven by three men. The car was registered out of town and I was suspicious. I flipped on the lights and siren, but for the longest time the driver refused to pull over. It wasn't a high-speed chase or anything like that, but I kept on him and halfway across the city he finally pulled over to the side of the road. I got out of my car and approached their car. I told the people inside to get out, and when I began to do a physical search, there was some pushing and shoving and then they ganged up on me. Fortunately, the backup I had called for arrived, and we arrested them. Naturally, these three men had been to Rochdale to buy drugs. A glance at one of the characters and it was obvious his crotch was bulging; it turned out to be a block of hashish.

Everyone knew what was going on at Rochdale. You had to be comatose not to know, but there were other notorious crack hangouts in the city, too. Norm's Grill was on the north side of the corner of Dundas and Pembroke Streets in downtown Toronto, and the New Service Tea Room was on the south side. People who were either involved in criminal activity or on the run from the law would converge on such places to buy or sell or to make contact or to recruit others for criminal purposes. A great many times these spots were the scenes of violence where people got stabbed, and we made a lot of arrests right on the premises or nearby. And as much as these types may have despised the police, what they despised even more were other drug dealers who were trying to rip them off or screw them out of money. It's no surprise so many violent incidents occurred there.

Now, while I admit many of the characters we encountered were pretty smart about their operations, there were also some who weren't very bright at all. One day, after we had been out all night and were tired and just wanted to go home, we came across this guy at Norm's Grill. He said he was from out of town and was eager to make some fast money, so we told him we knew about a place we could break into but that we needed someone to be our lookout. It didn't take much for him to volunteer. We took him in our old car down a side street and pointed to a building that just happened to be 14 Division which, of course, was one of the biggest police divisions in the city. But he didn't know that. We told him to scout it for us, so he did, and when he came back he was in a real huff and said the alarm must have gone off because the parking lot was full of cop cars! We sent that guy on his way and had a laugh. Unfortunately, we were never short of warrants to execute or people to arrest. In those days, it was hard for us just to keep up with the street drug scene.

We were out there mixing with the low-life and dressed the part. For example, we drove an old beat-up car. It was a real mess, full of empty takeout food boxes and coffee cups, and it had only one headlight working. Some of the guys in our unit grew long hair and wore scruffy old clothes and no way would you ever think they were police officers. If I didn't know better, I would have been afraid and intimidated about meeting them in a dark alley myself. They looked the part, they acted the part, and they were very convincing. One of them was short and skinny with a strong Scottish accent and with a real gift of the gab and he could talk his way into anything. He was very adept at undercover work. Another one was more rough and tough and looked like a biker. He talked like a biker, dressed like a biker, and put on the biker routine.

Mike Burke, our leader, was roly-poly and walked with a bit of a waddle. He was six feet tall, weighed 240 pounds, and could put on any accent and get away with it. He was one of those guys with a photographic memory and he used it to good advantage, like tracking stolen cars. He was very good at that. He had long, curly black hair, and a moustache, and he'd wear a headband or a Stetson or a wig, and never in a million years would you figure him for a cop. But then, you'd never figure any of us for a cop. Well, except maybe for me.

My end of things was more in line with intelligence, paperwork, and preparing warrants and cases for court, so I never grew my hair long or looked like a biker. I preferred to stay neat and tidy, but for a while I did allow myself a moustache, even though I wasn't too crazy about it. My family didn't like it at all. I still have a photograph of me in a suit at church the day we baptized our son, and in this picture I have that moustache.

One of the big problems with policing drugs at the time was the lack of laws involving drugs. In the case of speed, there were no laws prohibiting or criminalizing the importing of precursor chemicals. As mentioned earlier, the main ingredient of methamphetamine is phenyl-2-propanone or P2P, the precursor compound necessary for making methamphetamine or speed. Back then, Canada had no legislation or regulation or any controls whatsoever for the importation of this chemical. A lot of it came from countries like Germany, and because there were no controls, there was no registry for it either.

And the labs were everywhere. They could be in somebody's home or apartment and there would be pots and pans and pumps and beacons and chemicals, some of which were very volatile, all over the place. It just looked like a messy, dirty laboratory. Some of the speed was good quality, but some of it was bad, with impurities that ended up in people's veins. The trouble was, many of the labs were hard to find because they were so well insulated. Some of them were set up behind legitimate businesses, and quite often the people running them had no criminal record. But the labs and chemicals presented a dangerous situation for us because, in those days, we had no real training and wore no protective equipment. By training I mean that in those days we just saw these people as criminals. We didn't see them as people who needed help. Today police, and society in general, are much more in tune with trying to get help for such individuals. We have come a long way.

One of the places I remember well was the Caledonia Pharmacy. It was a legitimate business whose principals just happened to be dealing crystal speed at a very high level and, in addition to that, they dealt in methaqualone, a drug that came in tablets. We tracked down labs like this and it usually meant a long, protracted, labour-intensive investigation. But I'll never forget the Caledonia Pharmacy because it was special.

We knew this lab existed but didn't know where. We needed $500 to make an undercover purchase of crystal, which would allow us to move up the chain and get closer to the lab. So we went to the morality unit of the Toronto police and made our case, but they turned us down. They were suspicious of a bunch of street guys like us, maybe because of how we were dressed, while they considered themselves to be the elite. We were frustrated by that, but we had a backup plan. By that time our unit had built up a good relationship with the RCMP drug squad in the city, so we went to their office and made our pitch. It was the exact same case we had put to the morality unit. And with no questions asked, their unit commander handed us five brand-new hundred-dollar bills and all he wanted in return was a photocopy of the money.

With that money we bought a quantity of crystal speed from a shady character named Bruno Orticello who, as it turned out, had been making trips to Colombia. He led us to another guy, Giuseppe Roccari. Roccari was found to be in possession of a quantity of speed, not to mention restricted weapons, and was later charged with armed robbery. He, in turn, had direct contact with a speed chemist, a businessman who owned a medical building. A joint investigation involving our unit, the Niagara Regional Police Force, the Guelph Police, and the Niagara Falls RCMP Intelligence Unit, was carried out over several months with a lot of surveillance work. We found that the speed was coming from two brothers, Morton and Mel Canton, whose business was called the Canton Group and who also owned the Caledonia Pharmacy. We traced the flow of speed from Morton Canton to Roccari and the quantities were twenty pounds per week. That was an awful lot of speed. Roccari would make contact with Samuel Backus, a buyer from St. Catharines, and then he would distribute the speed to motorcycle clubs in the Niagara region where it would be distributed across the whole country. We kept up twenty-four-hour-a-day surveillance of Roccari and the Cantons and overheard conversations involving drug deals at their meetings in secluded restaurants and shopping plazas. We discovered that Morton Canton was also dealing in thousands of methaqualone pills. These would be purchased by two characters who would sell them at a large profit to drug dealers in the United States. This got the United States Bureau of Dangerous Drugs involved in the case and that was when we started making arrests; in one car alone we found 75,000 methaqualone pills! The street value for all that would have been more than a million dollars, which was an incredible amount of money in those days.

Finally, we identified the illicit speed lab we'd been looking for, namely, the Caledonia Pharmacy. But things were happening at other locations, too. For example, in the basement of one building we found seven pounds of crystal speed, an assortment of raw chemicals used to manufacture the drug, and a psychedelic hallucinogenic called MDA or methylenedioxyamphetamine. We also found 28,000 Valium pills in a closet, of all places. At the Caledonia Pharmacy itself we found eleven large cartons of pills, each of which contained 25,000 methaqualone tablets. That meant we were talking 275,000 tablets. More than a quarter-million of them.

Bruno Orticello was found to be in possession of six ounces of speed and he had also stashed methaqualone in a locker at the Guelph Bus Terminal. When we got him, he had just returned from Colombia. Giuseppe Roccari had 7,000 methaqualone pills at his business address. Mel Canton was arrested and found in possession of hashish, not to mention an automatic pistol with ammunition. But Morton Canton's story is the most interesting of all. A movie could be made about this guy. He absconded bail, went to Italy under an alias, and became a licensed medical doctor who eventually wound up in a Florida hospital specializing in geriatric care!

The Caledonia Pharmacy was probably the single-biggest operation our unit ever uncovered and when it all went down it was very satisfying for us. It was a major trafficking operation that was making crystal speed and methaqualone. And I can't say enough about the RCMP who gave us all kinds of support with surveillance and vehicles, and the whole thing started with that initial $500 buy; those crisp C-notes made everything possible.

All these criminals were convicted but, as for the actual time they served, well, that's another story. In those days, the maximum sentence for manufacturing this stuff was ten years. But because there was so much money to be made and because parole might be granted after just three years, that sentence didn't deter people in the least. The fact remains that a lot of people made huge amounts of money and never got caught, so it's fair to say we had an epidemic on our hands. The police were always lobbying for precursor chemicals to be put on a controls list and eventually they were, but as always, it was too little too late. At the time, there was a real need to look at sentencing, the importation of chemicals into the country, and the money-laundering-and-seizure laws that were totally inadequate. In fact, when a forfeiture was made, meaning we actually seized money, Health Canada, which meant the federal government, would get involved. Looking back, I think the public didn't realize how bad things were and, for sure, the policy-makers were naive about it. We often dealt with the same people over and over again. They went in and out of jail. It was a revolving door. A production line. Amongst ourselves we would often talk about the obvious inadequacies in the system. Senior Toronto officers like Deputy Chief Jim Noble were very outspoken about things like the deportation of illegals, but that wasn't our end of things. We were just the guys in the trenches. One thing was for sure though; we knew we were in a growth industry.

In those days the police were dealing with a very serious problem and doing it with minimal tools. And it was dangerous. We didn't have the laws and, as I said earlier, we didn't have the right equipment either. But what we did have was experience, resourcefulness, and an in-depth understanding of what the threat levels were and, of course, whom we were dealing with. We relied on ourselves to look after one another. We did everything as a team and never took unnecessary chances, although there was always an element of risk. And we didn't take shortcuts because we knew the consequences would be severe. It could literally mean life or death.

Naturally, we encountered some interesting people along the way. Doc was a guy who dispensed drugs that would normally be purchased with a prescription. Gimpy Morgan was called Gimpy because of his bad leg. And Ian Francis Tonner was an Englishman, a chemist who had been trained at

Oxford, of all places; we nailed him for operating a speed lab in a house in the east end. Because of their drug dependency, many addicts were incapable of holding down a job, so they turned to crime to facilitate their drug habit. To be honest, some of them looked like death warmed over. They were undernourished and had all kinds of diseases. And because the lifestyle they were leading perpetuated violence, their lives were often short. Overall, it wouldn't have been so bad if we'd had more enforcement, better laws, and better prevention systems. By prevention systems, I mean more places where people could go and detox. Mind you, the speed freaks were never our primary target anyway. They were just the bottom-feeders in the chain, but we had to deal with them to work our way up so we could find the traffickers, the suppliers, and the chemists.

My own life was a real contrast at this time. I would come home to family and friends and socialize with normal, hard-working people. Then I'd be out at night around these types who, at least, on the surface looked quite legitimate and who wanted to be thought of as decent, upstanding pillars of society while, at the same time, they were immersed in the kind of activity that only brought down society. They exploited people and they destroyed people. Mike Burke called them "merchants of misery and death" and that's exactly what they were. The way I looked at it, behind every hit of speed going into the veins of some young person, there was a criminal making a ton of money. He lived a lavish lifestyle and liked to project himself as a respectable businessman, but it was all at the expense of others. And, of course, you also had lots of young people in the prime of their life overdosing on these drugs. It happened all the time.

A prime example of the violence and paranoia associated with this subculture was the murder of Toronto police constable Jimmy Lothian. He was shot and killed when he was making a street stop of two known drug dealers. They shot him for no reason at all and this was the kind of environment our own unit operated in. When these guys got paranoid and high, they would arm themselves and use their weapons, sometimes even on themselves. These two characters in particular were well known to the police and I helped track them down. After they shot and killed Lothian, they took off and went on the run, and that night we chased after them from speed house to speed house to speed house. Eventually we caught up with them, but by the time the holdup squad arrived, both had already committed suicide.

One thing we never forgot about were all the victims. I'm not talking about the users who overdosed, but the people who were victimized by the crimes committed by those users. You can't lose sight of all the cars that people broke into in order to steal eight-track tape decks or stereo units just so these things could be converted into hits of speed at some speed house. It was incredible how much stolen stuff we found back then. Indeed, some of those addicts were doing very serious robberies and break and enters. It was a vicious cycle of drugs, crime, and violence. Lots of violence.

Still, I loved the work, but at the same time it took a toll on my family. My two children were born in 1972 and 1975, and that was a time when I was totally immersed in this professional lifestyle. I worked mostly at night and spent the day in court. I hoped to get a day off on Saturday or Sunday if I didn't have umpteen things on the go, like paperwork for court or another warrant to execute. I just wanted to crash at home and recharge my batteries. It meant I wasn't much of a father or much of a husband, but at least I was a good breadwinner. Mind you, I didn't have much time to enjoy my own life, and I certainly wasn't the only one like that. Mike Burke was the same. Fortunately for us, we had families who were very understanding and supportive.

Mike Burke died of skin cancer at thirty-five years of age and he had five children. He would come to work with blood on his shirt and would always slough it off as nothing serious. He was too busy to go to the doctor. The man was dedicated to his job and his family and was such a hard-working guy. I remember when we'd come out of court and change from a shirt and tie into old clothes and I'd see this circle of blood on his shirt get bigger and bigger. So finally I went to our unit commander and said he had to order Mike off so he could see his doctor. That was when they detected his skin cancer. But the man never gave up, right to the very end. Police work and his family were his passions.

Steve Sherriff was a Crown attorney who prosecuted many of our cases. We even thought of him as a member of our unit because he did great work and got some very good sentences for our convictions. When Mike died, a group of us, including Steve, got together and held a fundraiser for Mike's family. It was a dinner and hundreds of people showed up, not only police officers and judges and attorneys, but also people whom Mike helped convict and who did their time and then went straight. There were quite a few of those. I gave the eulogy at his funeral and remember seeing police officers and criminals alike weeping in the pews. Mike was buried in his police uniform. He was a very respected police officer. In fact, he was so respected that the RCMP and the U.S. Drug Enforcement Agency (DEA) used to ask him for advice all the time. Steve, who was the executor of Mike's estate, became the trustee of that fund and, in the end, that fund put Mike's children, all five of them, through school. Today two of Mike's children are police officers and one of them even has his father's badge. Number 26.

So, for sure, it wasn't an easy life and all our families sacrificed a great deal. That's why, now that I have grandchildren, I'm committed to spending quality time with them. If I don't see them for a day or two, I go into withdrawal. When my own kids were young, I was away all the time and missed out on an important part of my life. Do I regret it? Sure. But do I feel guilty? No, it was my job. The long and short of it is that my wife, Liviana, basically raised our children on her own and she did a wonderful job. She and the family had to deal with extraordinary hours. Broken engagements. Missed Christmases. Cancelled vacations. The job really did run the family. To be honest, my wife should be the one wearing all the medals I have received over the years. She earned them more than I did. She and my family have always been very supportive of the work that I do. But that's how it has to be when you're a cop.

·6·

Fighting the Mob

WHEN I WAS CHIEF OF POLICE IN LONDON, YORK REGION, and Toronto, and later when I became commissioner of the Ontario Provincial Police (OPP), New Year's Eve would always find me on patrol. During all those years, I didn't spend New Year's with my wife, much as she wanted me to, because I figured this was part of the sacrifice of being a police officer and especially of being a chief. The reason I did this was to make sure I never lost that sense of appreciation about who was doing the work, and the one doing the work was most definitely the officer on patrol in the middle of the night. So every New Year's Eve I would be out there doing spot checks. If you want to get an idea of what it's like being a cop, this is a great learning experience. When I was chief of the York Regional Police, immediately north of Toronto, I once brought along a good friend to join me on patrol on New Year's Eve. Senator Consiglio Di Nino. I was in uniform, but that didn't exempt us from being stopped by the Reduce Impaired Driving Everywhere (RIDE) program. An OPP cruiser pulled us over to check us out and Senator Di Nino was very impressed. A few weeks later, on February 17, 1999, he rose in the Senate in Ottawa and made this passionate speech about the police:

This past new year's eve I spent the evening and early morning hours patrolling York Region, a part of the Greater Toronto Area, with its Chief of Police, Julian Fantino. We drove the streets and visited police stations, communications rooms and command centres. We even spent two extremely cold hours with a RIDE team. Everywhere we went I was struck by the courtesy, the decency and the professionalism of the officers.

As Chief Fantino and I drove about, the police radio was our constant companion. I was shocked at how many domestic disputes police officers are called upon to deal with. Usually alone, and often confronted with violent situations, these brave officers do their best job to solve the often unsolvable, using whatever common sense God has given them and whatever street sense the job has taught them.

Backing them up are surely the unsung heroes of police work. The public knows very little about the critical role played by the communications staff, in particular, the dispatchers. Usually civilian, mainly female, dispatchers are a police officer's lifeline in times of trouble and need.

All in all, my night with the York Region Police was both an eye-opener and an education. In the space of a few short hours I had the privilege of seeing a number of exceptional and dedicated Canadians at work and meeting some courageous men and women who daily put their lives on the line, and willingly so, to keep our communities safe.

I am happy to salute them, and all police personnel in Canada. They are truly one of the reasons why this country has been judged the best place in the world in which to live.

Obviously, that night on patrol had a great impact on Senator Di Nino, as did a similar experience with Ontario premier Dalton McGuinty on the last day of 2006. After leaving the Toronto Police Service as chief in 2005 and becoming commissioner of Emergency Management for the government of

Ontario, I got to know Premier McGuinty pretty well. I knew he was concerned about the carnage on our highways and the issue of impaired driving, so on December 31, 2006, I asked him if he'd like to come along on a RIDE spot-check program that afternoon. He accepted. A RIDE program was already set up on Highway 417 in Kanata, just outside Ottawa, and he was able to see first-hand how it operated. He joined me and some OPP officers on one of the ramps to the highway, and we had him outfitted with a proper safety vest. He spoke to the media and was definitely on top of the issues. As commissioner of the OPP, and also in my previous job with the government of Ontario, I have always found McGuinty to be in tune with matters of public safety, policing, national border issues, and security. I think it would be good if more politicians spent time with the police on spot checks or out for a night in a cruiser. It might open up their eyes a bit. The fact is, many of them are hopelessly out of touch with reality and, unfortunately, this can go right to the top.

On July 30, 2003, the Rolling Stones headlined a huge rock concert in Toronto to help the city recover from the SARS outbreak that took place earlier in the year. Almost half a million people showed up to hear the likes of the Stones, AC/DC, Justin Timberlake, the Guess Who, and others. The idea was to help the city get back on its feet, and the concert was a big success. The federal government, the government of Ontario, Canadian brewery Molson's, which was the chief sponsor of the event, and the Rolling Stones themselves donated money to help fight SARS.

I've never been much of a fan of the Rolling Stones, but I must give credit to Mick Jagger for what he did, especially when he took to the stage and said Toronto was back and booming. The police were responsible for security for that event, and when it was all over, Molson's presented me with an electric guitar. I still have it in my office along with other keepsakes collected over the years, such as the photograph of me meeting Pope John Paul II when he came to Canada in 2002. That was a real highlight and the picture is still on my office wall.

The reason I mention this is that I met with Paul Martin at the time. He was running to become the next prime minister of Canada, and told

me to contact him when I was next in Ottawa. He became prime minister the following December and two months later, in February 2004, I
followed up on his offer. I was in Ottawa and we had a meeting. I spent a
full hour with him, one-on-one. My intention was to provide the new
prime minister and his staff with some insight into important public-
safety issues in the country. It was a great meeting and I was impressed
by the prime minister because of the time he spent with me—he even
went over the allotted time, and was very engaging.

To prepare for that meeting, I put together a report with background
material on key issues of the day. It was extensive and required a lot of
work. I knew the prime minister was a busy guy, but I thought his staff
could review it and recommend policy both to him and his government.
When I was leaving, I told him I was available to discuss any of these
issues with his staff or to elaborate further. He said that his office would
be in touch.

My report comprised eight sections. The first section was a review of
the criminal justice system and explained why trials that used to take
days and weeks to complete were now taking months and, in some cases,
even years. I got into such issues as disclosure obligations that had
become so onerous that the police and Crown attorneys didn't have the
time or resources necessary to make timely disclosure. I explained how
all of this was contributing to the delay of trials. I explained how the
whole justice system was bogged down and that we desperately needed
more judges, more prosecutors, and more courtrooms. Crown attorneys, who were being driven ragged trying to keep up, had an enormous
workload and were trying to do their job but were short-staffed. This was
and still is a very serious problem.

Section two of the report was about gun violence. I proposed a mandatory, ten-year minimum sentence for anyone convicted of gun crimes. The
best we had was a mandatory, four-year minimum sentence for certain gun
crimes, but this wasn't deterring criminals because they could be paroled
in sixteen months. This section also contained material about the relationship between guns, gangs, and drugs, and the trends in gun crimes over the

previous five years, and the Canadian Firearms Registry, which I have always opposed. I have opposed it because, while it has some good things going for it, like background checks and safe storage requirements, the fact remains that while I was chief in Toronto, I didn't know of a single case where a firearms offence was solved by any data or information received from the firearms registry. Who is going to register a sawed-off shotgun?

Section three was about child protection. It got into criminal voyeurism—such issues as the covert photography of children—and the very serious problem of child pornography. I suggested that Parliament consider imposing mandatory minimum sentences on crimes that involved the harm and sexual exploitation of children. I also outlined a National Operational Strategy for better ways to investigate the proliferation of child pornography on the Internet.

Section four contained recommendations about DNA legislation. In 2000, the Canadian government finally passed legislation related to the gathering of DNA evidence and established a National DNA Data Bank. It was long overdue. But there was still a big problem with offenders who were convicted of violent crimes before that time because their DNA was not in the data bank. I also recommended expanded criteria for the collection of DNA from suspects accused of a crime at the time of their arrest.

Section five focused on marijuana, the ever-increasing problem with commercial grow ops, and how all this was tied in to organized crime.

Section six was about high-risk offenders and included a series of recommendations I had given to Anne McLellan when she was federal minister of justice and attorney general of Canada. The recommendations included things like how to improve the management of high-risk offenders.

Section seven discussed immigration and why we shouldn't allow a person like the rapper 50-Cent into Canada because of his criminal background and because of the violence that always occured at his concerts.

Section eight was about terrorism and included a presentation I had given to the Senate Committee on National Security and Defence in 2002. I suggested an audit by the federal government on what safety measures had been implemented across the country since 9/11. Nothing like that had ever been done before.

So this was the report I prepared for Prime Minister Martin for our meeting in Ottawa in February 2004. That meeting lasted over an hour and, as I said, it was just him and me. I came out of that meeting really buoyed and felt much had been accomplished. It was an encouraging meeting and the prime minister told me I'd hear back from him on these issues. But I never heard from him again. Or from anyone on his staff. I was so disappointed. It was a major letdown. As police chief of the biggest city in the country, I figured the least I deserved was a follow-up.

That wasn't the only time something like this had happened to me. In May 2000, shortly after I became chief in Toronto, I wrote to then Prime Minister Jean Chrétien about the increasing problem we were having with raves. Raves were large social gatherings of young people, most of them under the age of sixteen. The problem with raves emerged in the early '90s and peaked around 1997. They were usually held in abandoned buildings, warehouses, parking garages, and even open fields, and they involved dancing, loud music and, of course, drugs. The most popular drug at raves was E, which is also known as ecstasy or MDMA, but there was also marijuana, ketamine, and cocaine. I explained in my letter to Prime Minister Chrétien how organized crime was involved with raves and that there was profound national ignorance about what was going on at these events.

One Friday, I met with the press and was asked if I would invite the prime minister to join me at a rave, so I did. I wrote Prime Minister Chrétien and extended an invitation for him to come to Toronto, with me as his personal escort, so he could see for himself exactly what was going on at raves. This wasn't just a Toronto problem. It was a national problem. So what happened? I never even got an acknowledgment from his office that he had received my letter. What really irked me about that is that a few years earlier, when I was chief in London and we were investigating a child sexual-exploitation ring, a pedophile whom we had arrested and who was later convicted had written to Chrétien accusing me of all kinds of things, and he got a response from the prime minister. But I didn't.

Being ignored is one thing, but being courted and, by all indications, supported by, someone who is in a powerful office, only to be dropped like a lead balloon after an election takes place is another. But that is exactly what happened to me with Allan Rock, when he was the federal minister of justice and attorney general of Canada.

I met with him when I was chief in London. At the time, we were having a serious problem with outlaw motorcycle gangs. Rock said he wanted to meet with the Canadian chiefs of police and I happened to be chairman of the Criminal Intelligence Service Canada (CISC), National Strategy on Outlaw Bikers, an organization that encompassed Canadian police chiefs. On April 11, 1997, Rock came to a CISC meeting in Ottawa that had thirty-seven Canadian police leaders in attendance. At that meeting, he very much wanted to get onside with us. After the meeting, he tabled anti-gang legislation, which is something police all over the country had desperately wanted for a long time, so we could better deal with organized crime. That anti-gang legislation was Bill C-95.

After the meeting with Rock, and after he had tabled his anti-gang legislation, at his request I sent him a proposal about how to fight outlaw motorcycle gangs. In my letter, I explained that the Canadian Association of Chiefs of Police (CACP) had first discussed a national strategy to combat outlaw motorcycle gangs at its conference in Regina, Saskatchewan, two years earlier, in 1995. That was when outlaw biker gangs in Quebec were escalating their murderous war that resulted in the death of an eleven-year-old boy during one of many biker bombings. I told Rock about a meeting of fifty-four police leaders that had been held in Ottawa in February 1996. That meeting identified common issues and concerns, and the result of it was *unanimous* approval amongst all the police chiefs about developing a formalized national strategy to fight outlaw motorcycle gangs. The letter concluded with a funding proposal calling for provincial coordinators and regional sub-committees with personnel dedicated to the task at hand. The total funding request was for

$1,140,000, which wasn't much of an outlay for the federal government but would have gone a long way to getting this strategy off the ground.

Attached to the letter were three things: the Joint CACP/CISC Communications Strategy, the administrative/operational plan called A Canadian Strategy for Combating Outlaw Motorcycle Gangs, and an organizational graph of the CISC sub-committee. Copies of my letter were sent to Phil Murray, who was commissioner of the Royal Canadian Mounted Police, and to Richard Phillippe, who was director of the CISC. Why did I go to all this trouble? Because during that entire period, Rock had given me and Canada's police community every indication that he was standing with us on this important issue and was anxious to help us.

Well, never before in my life have I been so blindsided. Before the federal election in June 1997, Rock had promised us the moon. After the election, however, he did absolutely nothing. We never heard from him again and we—the entire law enforcement community—felt betrayed. We felt betrayed because organized crime was a growing problem in Canada and he had just washed his hands of it, as well as of the police leaders of the country.

ORGANIZED CRIME WAS NOT new to Canada. In fact, it had been around this country for a long time. The Mafia has been in Canada since before World War I, but it wasn't until 1982 that a judge ruled that the organization even existed in this country. In the Ontario judicial district of Hamilton-Wentworth, Judge David McWilliam ruled in the landmark *Regina versus Fumo, Luppino and Luppino* case that the so-called Honoured Society, or Mafia, was a fact and was here. The Mafia is one of four Italian-based criminal organizations. The others are 'Ndrangheta, Camorra, and Sacra Corona Unita. But the Mafia is the oldest.

Canada's traditional Mafia centres are Hamilton, Toronto, and Montreal, but the Mob—which is police vernacular for organized crime—has also been well entrenched in many other places, too. This includes such Ontario cities as London and Guelph and other cities like

Winnipeg and Vancouver. But Hamilton, Toronto, and Montreal are the keys because of their close proximity to the U.S. border. The reason these three cities are so attractive to the Mob is simple. You have a long, undefended border, though that is starting to change because of 9/11, and a country that is wealthy and stable and with a long tradition of being soft on organized crime, dare I say crime in general. On top of that, Canada has long lacked legislation, which has existed in other countries, to fight organized crime. Put all this together and you have a veritable gold mine for organized crime groups.

Not only has Canada lacked effective legislation that makes it illegal to be part of organized crime, but for a long time it has also lacked money-laundering legislation, even though other countries had this. This then is what makes Canada so appealing to organized crime and to terrorist organizations as well.

For a long time Canada has been an easy mark for organized crime. Ottawa's usual reaction to fighting it is to make lots of promises about how to make our streets safer from organized crime and then to not adequately fund law enforcement focused on this very issue. Look at the United States. In 1970, the U.S. Congress passed the Racketeer-Influenced and Corrupt Organizations Act, more commonly known as RICO. RICO, which targeted the Mafia and especially La Cosa Nostra, identified the nature of a criminal organization as a criminal enterprise and allowed authorities not only to go after them, but also to go after their criminal assets. The Federal Bureau of Investigation (FBI) then put together units to target specific crime families such as the Bonnano family in New York City. RICO enabled people like Rudolph Giuliani, when he was a prosecutor for the state of New York, to convict and lock up such Mafia kingpins as John Gotti.

What about other countries? Italy has had generic, anti-gang legislation since the late nineteenth century. In the early 1980s, it passed legislation that targeted members of the Mafia and allowed the police to seize their assets. In the mid-1990s, Japan passed its anti-gang legislation, which was much like RICO, to target the Yakuza or Japanese Mafia. These

countries also had tough legislation against money laundering that
allowed them to deal with their own homegrown, organized crime problems. Legislation in the United Kingdom came even after Canada's, but
they have always had Scotland Yard (the headquarters of the Metropolitan
Police in London) to look after this problem, and Scotland Yard traditionally wields a lot more authority in the U.K. than the RCMP does in
Canada. The whole hierarchy of policing in the U.K. is under the Home
Office, which is a national ministry, and they also have more DNA laws
than we do. They can do DNA harvesting on impaired driving. They can do
DNA harvesting on shoplifters. They can do it on break and enters. We
have a long way to go on this in Canada.

As usual, Canada was late off the mark. In 1989, the Canadian government passed the Proceeds of Crime legislation, but it wasn't very
good and had to be amended ten years later to give it real teeth. We really
got our first taste of anti-gang legislation with Bill C-95 in 1997, but it
was never used. Why not? The government was afraid to use it, figuring
it wouldn't stand up to challenges to the Charter of Rights and
Freedoms. It wasn't until 2001 that Bill C-95 was amended, and another
bill gave the country a real currency law. Until then, Canada was the only
member of the G7 without a currency law and, believe me, other countries in the G7 had been lobbying Canada to get its act together. What
does it mean not to have a currency law? It means that anyone can bring
into the country any amount of cash they want. There are no limits. And
what was the result? Criminals, organized crime, and terrorists took
advantage of the loopholes, but they weren't even loopholes. They were
more like gaping canyons laying out a welcome mat for organized crime.
And that's exactly what happened. The first time this anti-gang legislation
passed the Charter test wasn't until 2005, when a judge in Barrie,
Ontario, declared the Hells Angels motorcycle gang to be a criminal
organization. So in 2005, Canadian authorities finally discovered organized crime—which was only about a hundred years after the fact.

Adrian Humphreys, who is now with the *National Post*, is a veteran
crime reporter who has written two bestsellers on organized crime—*The*

Enforcer and *The Sixth Family*. He neatly summed up the situation in an article that ran in the *Ottawa Citizen* on June 8, 1998. It was called "Canada makes it easy for the Mob: Lax bank rules make it a prime money-laundering location."

> Why does the Mob love Canada? Let us count the ways: weakened banking regulations, close proximity to the United States, a generous parole system, the presence of large casinos, a diverse ethnic population, stable economy, absence of laws banning organized crime association, and lack of reporting rules for money crossing our borders.
>
> It's a potent mix that makes the Great White North a pretty good place for laundering massive profits from the drug trade and other dubious deals around the world.
>
> Selling tonnes of dope through connections in Venezuela? Launder that dirty money in Montreal.
>
> Smuggling booze and cigarettes across the U.S. border? Recirculate the cash in Toronto.
>
> Part of a large cocaine cartel? Wash out your profits in Vancouver.
>
> And why not? Canada has what it takes.

In that same article Humphreys quoted me. I was chief in London at the time and also head of the organized crime committee of the Canadian Association of Chiefs of Police. I was quoted as saying: "This is a very soft country with respect to immigration laws, with respect to our money transfer laws. Money laundering is an easy feat here."

The long and short of it is that Canada has been important in the organized crime scheme of things because of its proximity to the United States and because of its long-time lack of meaningful legislation. In Canada, it has always been much easier to collect, receive, and transfer money than it has been in the U.S. Make no mistake, Canada is a wonderful country—I have already explained how much love I have for this country as an immigrant who came here with very little—but at the same time, it's a naive country that takes things for granted and acts only after the fact. Only after something really horrible happens. I have stated many times that the system of justice in Canada is broken and is in need of a complete overhaul.

The simple truth is, Canada has never had a proactive strategy to fight organized crime.

At one time, the Mafia was the most visible element of organized crime, with its influence in the construction industry, especially in Toronto, Hamilton, and Montreal. The Mob managed to infiltrate trade unions and get involved in extortion, narcotics, loan sharking, gambling, illegal gaming houses, prostitution. You name it, they did it. In the '70s, Mob hits and bombings of bakeries and other storefront operations were typical. Around that time, the trafficking of heroin took off and with that, really big money was being made. And when you were making big money in heroin you needed help. You needed an accountant. You needed a lawyer. You needed a banker and a stock market broker. These mobsters had them.

Still, at the time, the Italian community said there was no such problem as the Mafia and politicians said the same thing. The trend was to deny. Traditionally, in Canada, politicians never like to focus on a particular ethnic group, even if that group has a known, albeit small, criminal element in its midst. The Mafia originated in Italy, but in Canada it wasn't until the 1990s that you could publicly say the words "Mafia" and "Italian" in the same sentence. To cite a more recent example, the Toronto area has had a problem with the Tamil Tigers, a dangerous violent group that wreaks havoc on the local Sri Lankan community, with extortion and fundraising for terrorist activity. But it wasn't until 2006 that the federal government labelled this outfit a terrorist organization.

So this explains why I feel how I do about Allan Rock, and I'm not alone. Fortunately, not all politicians and not all governments are of the same ilk. In August 2000, the government of Ontario hosted a conference called Taking the Profit Out of Crime: The Ontario Government's

Summit on New Approaches to Fighting Organized Crime. It was an international summit that attracted experts from the United States, England, Ireland, Wales, and South Africa. Attendees included police officers, prosecutors, and people from the private sector and the financial sector. On the first day, the keynote speaker was Gerald McDowell. He was chief of the Asset Forfeiture and Money Laundering Unit in the U.S. Department of Justice, and he spoke about his department's success in following the trail of illegal money, seizing the assets of organized crime, and shutting down money-laundering schemes. I was impressed with what he was able to do, and also envious, because we didn't have the tools to do that sort of thing in Canada.

I spoke at the conference as well and the themes I touched on were, first, how the public must understand that organized crime affects us all, and second, that we need tougher laws. And I added my bit on "life must mean life" and compared how the U.S. and Canada have treated two major organized crime figures.

John Gotti, who was known as the Dapper Don and the Teflon Don, was head of the notorious Gambino Mafia crime family in New York City. In 1992, he was convicted of RICO charges and sentenced to life with no possibility of parole. He was put in a maximum-security institution that was locked down for twenty-three hours a day. Ten years later in 2002, he died from cancer while in jail. I know there are voices in Canada who would call this cruel and unusual treatment—even for a Mafia don—but I'm not one of them.

Now compare that to Canada's treatment of Alfonso Caruana, who was head of the equally notorious Cuntrera-Caruana crime family. I'm sure most Canadians have no idea who he is even though they most certainly have heard of John Gotti. Caruana led what was alleged to be the biggest drug-trafficking, money-laundering organization *in the world*. It had been operating for thirty years in North America, South America, Europe, Thailand, and India. For many years, it was believed that Caruana had been living in Venezuela, but it turned out he was living in Canada, in Woodbridge, just north of Toronto, and no one even knew. Of course,

Caruana was no dummy; he had his Canadian citizenship. Great work by the RCMP and OPP, as well as the Toronto police and local regional police, cracked the code for telephone numbers used by this crime family.

In January 1998, hundreds of kilos of cocaine were being shipped from Colombia through Venezuela to Canada and that was when the police made their move. They closed in on Caruana just as he was making plans to flee the country. As it turned out, only 200 of the estimated 14,000 kilos of cocaine from that shipment were ever seized. Caruana was convicted of conspiracy to import and traffic in a controlled substance and sentenced to eighteen years, which meant, at the time of sentencing, he was eligible for day parole in 2003 and full parole in 2005. And while John Gotti was kept in maximum security during his entire period of incarceration until his death in the U.S., Alfonso Caruana did but one year in a Canadian penitentiary before being moved to Fenbrook Institution in Southern Ontario, which is basically an open concept with all kinds of liberties. In short, it is soft time. This is the same place where Craig Munro, the killer of Toronto police officer Michael Sweet, has been staying as a guest of the Crown.

Alfonso Caruana, no ordinary criminal, is prima facie evidence of what a joke Canada is in terms of sentencing and also what a joke it is in terms of the ease with which world-class criminals obtain parole. Consider this: Canada's National Parole Board actually *approved* Caruana for day parole after he served one-sixth of his sentence and approved him again for *full parole* after one-third of his sentence! But the only reason he wasn't released is that three days before his eligibility date for day parole—April 14, 2003—he was slapped with an extradition request from Italy where he is wanted for conspiracy, conspiracy centred on drug trafficking, and the continued aggravated importing, possession, and sale of large quantities of drugs.

The language used in the National Parole Board's decisions on Caruana illustrates how out of touch the system is with such criminals. Day parole for Caruana was granted because, in the words of the NPB Accelerated Parole Review Decision Sheet:

You have been convicted of extremely serious drug offences and are said to be a member of an organization known to use violence to achieve criminal objectives. There is, however, no information available in your case linking you personally to any possession or use of weapons or to any acts of violence. You have no known criminal history for any assaultive or weapons-related behaviour. There are, moreover, no noted concerns in the areas of family violence, substance abuse, or mental instability. Under all the circumstances, therefore, the Board is satisfied there are no reasonable grounds to believe you are likely, if released, to commit an offence involving violence before the expiration of your sentence.

The report goes on to say that, while Caruana is considered a flight risk since he has been sentenced, in absentia, to a "very lengthy prison term in Italy," the Correctional Service of Canada "recommends that full parole be directed."

The only thing we can conclude, then, is that the Canadian justice system regards drug trafficking as a non-violent crime, even for a man like Alfonso Caruana, and this is why most offenders sentenced for drug trafficking in Canada get day parole after serving one-sixth of their time. It truly boggles the mind and brings into question the credibility of the system.

Canada's incredibly lax justice system is well recognized around the world. In 1999, this is what the U.S. Department of State said about Canada's efforts in fighting international drug cartels and organized crime. It also explains the mindset behind the treatment of men like Caruana. This information was retrieved on April 22, 2006, from the U.S. government website www.state.gov/p/inl/rls/nrcrpt/1999/920.htm:

While the RCMP has mounted effective operations against narcotics and other criminal organizations, the impact of these efforts has been undermined in numerous cases by court decisions. Canadian courts have been reluctant to impose tough prison sentences, often opting for fines, reflecting a widespread view that drugs are a "victimless" crime or simply a health issue, not a criminal or public safety concern. For example, one court dismissed charges against an individual arrested for snorting crack in a public restroom, calling it an invasion of his privacy. The Supreme Court has questioned the legality of police involvement in "sting"-type operations, undercover "buys" and other techniques now commonly used around the world in drug investigations, largely on privacy grounds, as a potential violation of the 1982 Canadian Charter of Rights and Freedoms. Canadian press reports indicate that only 20% of those convicted of growing marijuana in Vancouver receive jail terms, and that British Columbia has the highest rate of acquittal rates in the nation. In January, a judge ruled that a convicted criminal, who had already been deported by the GOC [Government of Canada], must be returned to Canada at GOC expense to pursue his request for refugee status, despite having aided two Colombian drug traffickers to escape from jail.

Criminals feel safe in Canada. According to sources, Caruana believes that Canada, for wanted criminals, is the safest place to live, with a much lower risk of detention and prosecution than in the United States or Europe. No wonder that a mastermind like Caruana lived in Canada for so long. In what other country could he get such treatment? The fact remains that many violent and dangerous criminals serve less time in Canada than they would in other countries, so why wouldn't they want to operate here?

If you want to know about the frustration of being a police officer in Canada, think of those who were involved in the Combined Forces Special Enforcement Unit, which was the integrated joint forces operation responsible for apprehending Caruana. That unit comprised various police forces, Citizenship and Immigration Canada, and the Criminal Intelligence Service Ontario. The cost of the operation was more than $8 million, which isn't much when you consider that the Cuntrera-Caruana organization controlled much of the billion-dollar cocaine trade that came out of South America.

Is it any wonder then that journalist Antonio Nicaso, an expert on organized crime who has written fourteen books on the subject, created the biggest waves at the Ontario conference on organized crime (Taking the Profit Out of Crime: The Ontario Government's Summit on New Approaches to Fighting Organized Crime, in August 2000) when he said Canada had become a haven for every major organized criminal group in the world? I'll never forget what he said: "It's tougher to import a case of cheese into Canada than a suitcase of dirty money."

The Canadian Charter of Rights and Freedoms embodies sound principles, but the problem is how these principles are interpreted. In some cases those interpretations have turned the justice system upside down to the benefit of the criminal element. I even have a personal example from my own family. In 1990, the Ontario Supreme Court's Askov decision ordered that charges must be dropped in any case that takes more than eight to ten months to go to trial. I have already explained how the system was bogged down and the Crown attorneys were overworked. This court decision was all about "justice delayed, justice denied" and, because of it, more than 40,000 criminal cases in Ontario alone were thrown out. Well, one of those cases involved my son. When he was seventeen he was out driving and got hit by an impaired driver. He was injured and the car was a writeoff. This was the second impaired-driving offence for that particular individual. So I went with my son to court, the Charter arguments about unreasonable delay were brought forward, and the case was thrown out. I'll never forget when we left the courthouse that day. My son couldn't believe this was how things were done.

WHO HAS REAPED THE GREATEST benefits from the Charter of Rights and Freedoms? I would argue that if it isn't common criminals, then it must be the Hells Angels. Canada, and especially its politicians, have spent thirty years underestimating the problem of biker gangs. Never has there been a proactive strategy on the part of the government to fight bikers. Biker gangs grew and eventually became bigger than the Mafia. Today, out-

Six-year-old Julian's first communion in 1949 in Vendoglio, Italy. (First row, fourth from right.) Standing at the back on the right is Father Albino Fabbro.

The Fantino family house in Vendoglio where Julian, his siblings, and his father were born. Three families lived in the house and shared a kitchen.

Passport photo of Julian, age 10, with his mother Maria in 1953, the year they came to Canada.

Julian's Picture Card and License to drive a cab in Toronto in 1965.

Officer Fantino in front of his cruiser at the Canadian National Exhibition in 1970. One year on the job.

Officer Fantino as a member of the drug squad in 1973.

Sergeant Mike Burke, leader of the No. 14 Division Old Clothes Unit.

Sporting a moustache while working with the 14 Division Old Clothes Unit.

Police Constable Michael Sweet, killed at George's in 1980, was a 30-year-old father of three. Julian was a homicide investigator on the case. [*Photo credit: Toronto Police Service*]

Posing with another cache of drugs seized in a raid.

Two future chiefs of police: Julian and David Boothby working in homicide.

Patrol Sergeant Fantino at work in Toronto's No. 32 Division in 1981.

Julian escorts murderer Craig Munro from courthouse following guilty verdict in the trial for the death of Officer Michael Sweet. [Jim Wilkes, *Toronto Star*]

Principals involved with the Michael Sweet murder trial, left to right: (front row) Staff Sergeant David Boothby, His Lordship the Honourable Mr. Justice Frank Callaghan, Sergeant Julian Fantino; (back row) Defence Counsel John Rosen, Defence Council Harry Frymer, Defence Counsel Earl Levy Q.C., Deputy Crown Attorney Robert McGee Q.C., Assistant Crown Attorney Michael McGrann, Defence Counsel Rebecca Shamai, Law Clerk Frederick Maefs.

Being sworn in as chief of the London Police Service, October 1991. With him are daughter Andrea, son Gregrory and wife Liviana. [*London Free Press*]

Being interviewed by reporter in London, Ontario, outside clubhouse of notorious Outlaws motorcycle gang in May 1998.

Formal portrait as chief of York Regional Police Service, August 1998.

Former chiefs assemble for luncheon following swearing in as chief of the Toronto Police Service in 2000. Left to right: Harold Adamson, Jack Marks, Bill McCormack, Julian, Dave Tsubouchi (then Ontario minister of community safety and correctional services), and David Boothby.

Chief Fantino receiving a rosary from Pope John Paul II at World Youth Day at the Vatican in Rome in 2000. With him are wife Liviana and Toronto Cardinal Aloysius Ambrozic.

Chief Fantino visits Toronto police officers stationed in Kosovo in June 2000.

Alone at Ground Zero in
New York City shortly
after 9/11.

With fellow police officers at Ground Zero.

law motorcycle gangs are by far our biggest problem, with organized crime, but it took the death of a young innocent boy on the streets of Montreal to wake the country up. Daniel Desrochers was an eleven-year-old boy who was killed in 1995 by flying debris when a booby-trapped Jeep blew up. At the time, two rival biker gangs, the Hells Angels and the Rock Machine, were engaged in a bloody war in Quebec. In that province alone, some 160 people were murdered, most of them bikers, and many others were almost murdered over the course of a few years.

There was enormous outrage after the boy's death, and with a federal election in the offing, the government wasted no time in passing Bill C-95. Bill C-95 defined organized crime as any group, association or other body *comprising five or more persons* whose primary activity was to commit indictable offences. So now the police, after years of trying, were finally given new tools to investigate outlaw biker gangs. We were given things like expanded access to wiretaps and access to income tax returns. The bill provided penalties of up to fourteen years for being associated with a criminal organization; however, Bill C-95 was anything but all-encompassing. It stipulated that the targets must have a record of criminal activities committed only *within the previous five years* and, as I pointed out, it was restricted to organizations with five or more persons. So, after the bill passed, what did the Hells Angels do? They opened a new chapter in Ontario and filled it with members who had no criminal record over the previous five years. And they could have opened up new chapters all over the country with four people in each chapter and be in the clear. According to Bill C-95, the Hells Angels would not have constituted a criminal organization.

This is typical of how Canada does things. Piecemeal and in dribs and drabs. Police descend on Ottawa and put forth reasons why new legislation is warranted and are treated like any other special-interest group. I've been to Ottawa many times myself, and this is the kind of reception we get. There always seems to be a lot of trepidation on the part of politicians to put through any meaningful legislation that would really make the country safer. And why? Because they're afraid of their political rear ends. While the federal government was totally absorbed in whether to make marijuana legal, the bikers were busy doing their thing uninterrupted right across the country. The Hells Angels even set up its own public relations machine and put in place a defence fund, which allowed them to hire high-priced criminal lawyers to defend them. Unfortunately, it took the tragedy of that young boy in Montreal to turn political attention around.

Bill C-95 remains the only anti-gang legislation we have, so it's better than nothing. Fortunately, in 2001, it was amended and improved considerably, and not by Allan Rock, who, as I have said, will forever be known to the police community as the justice minister who betrayed us, but by his successor, Andy Scott. Among the amendments to the Criminal Code were these:

- All provisions related to organized crime activities were brought together in a specific part to be entitled Enterprise Crime, Designated Drug Offences, Criminal Organizations, and Money Laundering;
- The number of participants constituting a criminal organization was reduced from five to three;
- The requirement that some or all members of the criminal organization have committed indictable offences within the preceding five years was removed;
- Sentencing judges were allowed to order that the offender serve the full sentence of incarceration without any form of conditional release.

To his credit, Andy Scott delivered on his word and I respect him for that. I still remember the day he reported to the House of Commons on the state of organized crime. That was a real learning experience for me in terms of how Ottawa operates. The chiefs of some of the biggest police departments in the country were in the gallery to watch Scott get up and speak, but to my surprise hardly anyone was sitting in the House. It was almost empty. I was amazed. One of my colleagues, a fellow chief who was far more familiar with Ottawa than I was, pointed out how the TV cameras were set up and a few MPs strategically positioned to avoid showing the empty seats. "It's all show business," he said. And that's exactly what it is.

In January 2007, a trial in Montreal effectively lowered the bar as to what defines a criminal organization. Quebec Court judge Jean-Pierre Bonin won plaudits from police everywhere when he said that the local Pelletier Street Gang was a criminal organization. He found all of the accused guilty of trafficking in crack cocaine and five of them guilty of gangsterism.

Why do we need anti-gang legislation? Because without it any crime the police deal with has to be treated as an *individual* crime. Crime that results from a *conspiracy* of people in a well-oiled organization—such as the Mafia, Asian Triads, Colombian drug cartels, biker gangs, Russian Mafia, or terrorist groups, and they're all here—love Canada because of the lack of legislation to fight them. You have to understand the criminal mind. Most criminals don't mind doing time; they even regard it as part of the cost of doing business. But go after their assets and that's another story. And that's why we needed money-laundering legislation. Other countries have long had money-laundering legislation, but Canada didn't pass any until 1989 and even that was lousy legislation.

The fact of the matter is, every major criminal organization operates in Canada, and for too long we have made it far too easy for them to be here and remain here due to weak immigration laws and processes.

Earlier I mentioned the Law Enforcement Summit that was held February 17-18, 1996, at the Canadian Police College in Ottawa. There were fifty-four leaders of the police community in attendance at that meeting and the purpose was twofold: 1) identify on a national scale those issues and concerns dealing with organized crime and, in particular, outlaw motorcycle gangs; 2) develop a national strategy that would disrupt and dismantle outlaw motorcycle gangs operating in Canada. Canada's police community did both these things but, as always, the problem was getting the federal government to come on board.

The Hells Angels were formed in 1948 in California and, over the years, have grown into an organization with chapters all over the world. A CISC report on the Hells Angels, in 1997, included a two-page spread of its international organization. The headquarters or Mother Chapter was in Oakland, California, with fourteen other chapters throughout the state of California. There were also twenty-nine chapters in sixteen other states. In Canada, sixteen chapters were established in five provinces: five in British Columbia, three in Alberta, one in Saskatchewan, six in Quebec, and one in Nova Scotia. There were also chapters throughout England and Scandinavia, in every corner of western Europe, and in such countries as Australia, New Zealand, Brazil, and South Africa. Affiliations (called hangaround status) existed in Argentina and even in Russia. That was the structure back in 1997.

The Hells Angels first came to Canada in 1977, and over the next twenty years established chapters coast to coast. In the beginning, they had trouble penetrating into Ontario, which was the domain of another gang, the Outlaws. In Quebec, the Hells Angels were at war for many years with the Rock Machine. But today the Hells Angels are entrenched all over Canada and are easily the biggest and most dangerous biker gang in the country. They are also the biggest and most dangerous organized crime entity in the country.

By 2006, it was estimated that the Hells Angels had about 500 full-fledged members in thirty-two chapters across Canada. The Greater Toronto Area, which over the years had absorbed members from other gangs, such as the Para Dice Riders, Satan's Choice, and Last Chance, was said to have about 100 full-patch members. This means the Greater Toronto Area now has *the highest concentration of Hells Angels in the entire world*. How's that for a mention in the *Guinness Book of World Records*?

When I was chief in London, we had a growing problem with motor-cycle gangs. In 1997, a group called Los Bravos held a big celebration for their thirtieth anniversary. Bikers from all over the country, including the Hells Angels, came to town for the celebrations. At the centre of it all was the Los Bravos clubhouse. You had bikers—notorious criminals—

doling out hot dogs for kids and even signing autographs. These guys were very good at public relations and, unfortunately, some people fell for this.

One year later, London was the scene of killings attributed to the biker wars. The slain bikers were Jeffrey Labrash and Jody Hart, who were both members of the London Outlaws, a large chapter that had been around since the 1960s. At the time, the Outlaws were all over southwestern Ontario with chapters in London, Windsor, St. Catharines, Toronto, Ottawa, and Sault Ste. Marie. As is the case with most bikers, Labrash and Hart were no strangers to police. Five years earlier both of them had been front and centre in a seven-month police probe called Project Bandido. After raiding the homes of some known bikers and their clubhouses, we seized $52,000 in cash along with almost $200,000 worth of cocaine and marijuana, not to mention sawed-off shotguns and tear gas. The kind of thing law-abiding citizens keep in their homes, right? At the funeral for Labrash and Hart, hundreds of bikers showed up from Ontario, Quebec, and the U.S. And three years before that, in 1989, which was just before I became chief in London, a million-dollar cocaine cartel had been smashed by police. There were raids on biker homes and clubhouses in Montreal and in eight Ontario cities, London being one of them.

More recently, in April 2006, the biggest mass murder in Ontario history took place when eight bikers from the Bandidos were shot to death. They had been slaughtered in a farmer's field in southwestern Ontario. The Bandidos had moved into Canada in 2000, when they took over the Rock Machine. In fact, what many people don't realize is that the Rock Machine was actually created by the Mafia so it could compete with the Hells Angels. Well, the Hells Angels won that war and then tried to crush the Bandidos in Ontario. This led to a civil war among the Bandidos, after the Hells Angels recruited a prominent Rock Machine leader to join them.

But anyone who thinks biker activity is confined only to bikers is seriously mistaken. This is big-time, organized crime and, just like with the

Mafia in an earlier era, it affects us all. When you talk organized crime, you are talking about threats to our citizens and to our communities. You are talking about threats to our businesses and to our financial institutions. You are talking about threats to both national and global security. But until recently, the police in Canada were engaged in a fragmented fight against organized crime. We were under-resourced, had outdated laws, and were largely discounted by those very people who were responsible for developing public policy. Over the years, Canadian police leaders have been frustrated by inadequate criminal and civil laws, and by the erosion of other tools and resources available to law enforcement. The result? All this undermined our ability to keep pace with the extraordinary advances made by very sophisticated, transnational, organized crime enterprises.

Criminal Intelligence Service Canada is a model organization well suited to serve as an ideal host to coordinate the fight against organized crime on both a national and international level. But a big impediment has been a lack of willingness and ability on the part of the police themselves to share intelligence information. In fact, in this regard, efforts by the law enforcement community as a whole have been less than stellar, somewhat uncoordinated, and often lacking in a strategic focus that would allow us to tackle and dismantle these criminal organizations. Fortunately, over the last few years, this situation has been changing for the better and that is a good thing. Not only does organized crime take advantage of committing criminal acts across jurisdictions, but so do individual criminals. Look at a killer like Paul Bernardo. He was a transient criminal who operated in different jurisdictions, so when the investigations began, different police departments were involved. And what happened? Police were not able to connect the dots. That led to an inquiry by Justice Archie Campbell and things have since improved. The result has been better case management, more centralization of information, and improved coordination of the records management systems of police forces. Today a police officer on the streets of Vancouver, for instance, can check a data bank from London, Ontario.

With new legislation, and greater powers of search and seizure of property, the police have been better able to get convictions of the Hells Angels and other members of organized crime organizations. But arriving at that point has been a long and hard battle for us, and it's not over.

On January 12, 2001, when I was chief in Toronto and chairman of the National Strategy on Outlaw Motorcycle Gangs, I made a presentation in Ottawa to the Solicitor General Canada's National Committee on Organized Crime. In my presentation, I said that the system of sentencing, parole, and probation for members of organized crime wasn't working and further, that outlaw motorcycle gangs were using their extensive networks, as well as legal defence funds, numerous legal challenges, and dream teams of defence lawyers, to make it increasingly difficult for them to get convicted. I proposed that members of criminal organizations receive mandatory minimum sentences with no chance of early parole. It's a fact that no member of the Hells Angels or Rock Machine has ever quit a gang while in prison. Every single one of them, 100 per cent, have returned to gang and criminal activity after their release. I also proposed that gang members, while incarcerated, be segregated from fellow gang members or moved to other locations in the country.

Two examples I cited in that presentation illustrate how ineffective parole and probation have been in preventing criminal activity by members of criminal organizations, and also how ineffectual light sentences are.

Example 1: This individual became a full member of the Quebec City Hells Angels in 1999. In 1991, which was eight years before that time, he already had a lengthy criminal record that included breaking and entering, assaulting a police officer, fraud, and destruction of property. In 1991, he was charged with causing a disturbance and fined $75. In 1992, while he was on probation, he was charged with discharging a firearm and assault, and fined $300 and given one year probation. In 1992, he violated the probation conditions and nothing happened to him. In 1997, he was charged with illegal possession of a firearm. Now this was his *twenty-second* offence and what did he get? Two years's probation. In 1998, again while on probation, he was charged with assaulting a police officer and fined $1,500, and given another two years' probation. Up until then, he had never served a single day in jail! In 1999, he was charged with drug trafficking and illegal storage of a firearm, for which he was sentenced to five and a half years. He wound up serving two. It was this record that allowed him to become a full member of the Hells Angels in 1999.

Example 2: From 1987 to 1997 another member of the Quebec City Hells Angels was charged with seventy-three crimes. During this ten-year period he was either on parole or probation, but the consequences were negligible.

This is not how you fight organized crime.

The fact remains that, just as it has long been relatively easy for the Mafia to operate in Canada, so too has it been easy for biker gangs. Michel Auger, a crime reporter with the tabloid *Le Journal de Montréal*, was shot five times in September 1999 after reporting extensively on biker gangs. But he survived. Auger once addressed the annual confer-ence of the Canadian Police Association and this is what he said: "There are some politicians who say [Canada] is the best country in the world. Criminals seem to think the same thing."

Consider a little item that I gleaned from the *Globe and Mail* of April 24, 1997. According to this article, on the very same day that Ottawa announced its albeit flawed anti-gang legislation that was chiefly designed to fight Quebec-based bikers, the province of Quebec gave $71,000 in government money to two members of the Hells Angels. Why? So they could renovate a building that the police had raided two years earlier!

This is not how you fight organized crime either.

On June 22, 1999, Phil Murray, when he was commissioner of the RCMP, delivered a speech called Organized Crime and You to the Canadian Club of Ottawa. This is part of what he said:

The tentacles of organized crime reach far and wide; its effects are not only pervasive and deadly, but are economically devastat-ing. Legitimate business suffers because organized crime creates competing businesses using laundered money, money that was illegally obtained from drugs, prostitution and violence. Society suffers through a loss of tax dollars. Health-care costs escalate. Drug use among our children grows. Telemarketing fraud steals life savings and ruins futures. Property and violent crimes escalate which reduces the feeling of security in our own homes. Humans are smuggled into the country illegally which fuels the underground economy. And the cycle continues.

Organized crime is not something that occurs on the television and in the movie theatres. It is real and it is about undermining the social fabric of Canada. It is about your elderly parent who is conned into investing in something that isn't real. It's about insurance fraud that makes your rates go up. It's about your stolen car from your street. It's about the fourteen-year-old girl, someone you could know, who is forced into prostitution. And it's about our children developing an addiction to drugs.

All this business about gangs and guns and drugs is driven by organized crime. According to Commissioner Murray, and remember this was 1999 when he said this, money-laundering activities in Canada accounted for *$20 billion to $30 billion a year*, which was obviously taking a sizable bite out of the country's economy.

So far I have largely restricted my thoughts on organized crime to the Mafia and outlaw motorcycle gangs. But organized crime also includes many other groups and for virtually all of them guns are involved. Street gangs are notorious for carrying and using firearms. In recent years, the problem with street gangs has been huge, especially in Toronto. But right across Canada, we also have Asian gangs, the Russian Mafia, and many other groups. They are all here and over the years they have shown us that they like how Canada treats them: for the most part, with kid gloves.

In February 2001, the Ontario government's Standing Committee on Justice and Social Policy was examining Bill 155, which was an act to provide civil remedies for organized crime and other unlawful activities.

At this gathering, the Toronto police were given twenty minutes to make a presentation. I delivered that presentation along with Staff Superintendent Rocky Cleveland and Counsel Jerry Wiley. Many other groups were also there—the Ontario Ministry of the Attorney General, the Canadian Civil Liberties Association, the Office for Victims of Crime, the Canadian Bankers Association, the Canadian Bar Association, and the Criminal Lawyers Association.

Finally, here was a law in Canada that would take the profit out of organized crime. Bill 155 meant that the profits gained from unlawful activity could be seized through the use of the civil process rather than through the criminal process. This bill would provide a mechanism for compensating persons who suffered monetary loss or other damages as a result of unlawful activity. What's more, it recognized the need to compensate municipalities for losses and expenses incurred in the investigation and enforcement of this law, so presumably, some of this money could be directed to defraying the expenses of the police.

As Phil Murray made so clear in his 1999 speech to the Canadian Club of Ottawa, it is foolhardy to think that something like drug trafficking is a victimless crime. Consider the terribly tragic case of Louise Russo. When I was still chief in Toronto, in 2004, this forty-five-year-old Toronto mother was shot in a bungled underworld hit. She was standing in a restaurant buying her youngest child a sandwich when the place was suddenly sprayed with bullets. One bullet shattered her spine, paralyzing her and confining her to a wheelchair for the rest of her life. It also meant she could no longer care for one of her other children who was severely disabled and not able to feed herself. As the mother, this woman had been that child's primary caregiver. Later, six men—five of them known, organized crime figures and the other a member of the Hells Angels— were convicted on a variety of charges, including attempted murder and conspiracy. Louise Russo was awarded $2 million, which included $670,000 seized from the homes of the accused when they were arrested by police. It was a lump-sum payment. Without such compensation, this woman would have had to sue the guilty parties for damages in civil court and those damages wouldn't have been much. Ontario's Criminal Injuries Compensation Board allowed a maximum lump-sum payment of only $25,000 and a maximum monthly payment of only $1,000. Indeed, innocent victims of crime have long been the ones who get shafted in the justice system. While nothing can bring back this woman's former life, at least that money will help.

But those criminals shouldn't have been out on the street in the first place.

Canada still desperately needs a strategy to deal with organized crime. It needs tougher sentencing and truth in sentencing with mandatory minimum sentences for certain types of crime. It needs to completely overhaul its system of parole and early release. And more than anything, it needs to take a long look at exactly what organized crime is and how it affects everyone. The goal of any organized crime strategy should be to make Canada the absolute worst place in the world for organized crime to operate and to profit.

Not the best.

·7·

The Sweet Investigation

THE DAY AFTER THE MURDER OF MICHAEL SWEET, DAVID Boothby and I stopped off at the city morgue where Sweet's body lay on a table. The first thing we noted was the morgue tag on the big toe of the left foot. It was standard procedure. Big toe, left foot. Dave and I were both seasoned homicide investigators and Michael Sweet was far from our first case, but there was something very poignant about that solitary white tag on the foot. It was a symbol of the stark finality of life. Here was a young man in the prime of his days. He was the father of three little girls, a cop who was just doing his job. He and his wife had just bought a house a few weeks earlier. What a waste. Such a needless, senseless waste. And it was a waste because he could have been saved. Even despite being shot, he most definitely could have been saved.

Michael Sweet was a thirty-year-old man with a long forehead and slim face. He had brown hair with tinges of grey and liked to wear a moustache. He kept his hair short in a clean-cut style that seemed a throwback to the '50s. In uniform he looked tall and handsome and he projected everything that a police officer was supposed to project. Neat. Professional. Approachable. But still the figure of authority. Dave had known him from 52 Division and remembered him as a young officer, a gentleman at all times, who always did his job and looked good doing it.

But today Michael Sweet was not in uniform. His battered body had only a morgue tag and a white sheet draped overtop. There were abrasions and bruises to one of his thumbs, an entrance hole from a bullet at the upper right side of his chest, another bullet hole in his chin just to the right of centre—the exit of that bullet hole was in his right cheek—and yet another entrance hole on top of his right shoulder.

Dave Boothby and I were the two homicide investigators on the case. I was a sergeant and he was a staff sergeant. Later, in 1995, when I was chief in London, Dave became chief of the Toronto Police Service, and after he retired I succeeded him as Toronto's chief. On first impression, he cut an imposing figure as a cop. He was a towering six feet five inches, and a solid six feet five inches at that, so his sheer physical stature was more than enough, and then there was the uniform and cap topping it off. Dave always exemplified what a police officer should be. But despite his size, those who worked with him knew he wasn't intimidating. He was soft-spoken and calm, with a quiet, soothing demeanor. Like me, Dave was very passionate about this case, but he had closer ties with it than I did because he knew all the officers who were involved; Dave himself had worked in 52 Division and he had known Michael Sweet.

Joining us in the examination of the body were two other men who would play important roles in the investigation. Sam Barbetta, a firearms expert with the Ontario Centre of Forensic Sciences, was the younger brother of my old mentor, Frank Barbetta. Sam was an accommodating man who was always dressed in a lab coat and, because of that, looked just like a doctor. He was very knowledgeable about firearms and trajectories and was an excellent witness in court. Sam studied Sweet's body up close and scrutinized the entrance and exit wounds for every one of those bullet holes. No one was better than Sam in performing an analysis of all the shooting that had taken place at George's the previous night. The other man present was Dr. John Hillsdon-Smith, a respected pathologist. He was an Englishman who was meticulous in his work and who used to lecture about homicide investigations at the

Ontario Police College. What I liked about him was that he would walk
you through everything, and I learned a lot about human anatomy from
this man. At Michael Sweet's autopsy, he had recovered two bullets, one
from the back of the body and the other from the shoulder. In his mind,
the cause of death was perfectly clear. Internal hemorrhage due to a
gunshot wound to the lung. There was no question that was the fatal
shot. Once the bullets were extracted, we conducted a careful washing
of Sweet's hands to see if there was any sign of gunshot residue. This was
routine forensic procedure in those days.

After leaving the morgue, Dave and I went straight to the crime
scene—the basement at George's—to begin a very careful examination
and take samples. The biggest problem for us was the powdery residue
that still remained from all the tear gas that had been released by Eddy
Adamson, Gary Leuin, and Barry Doyle immediately before they had
stormed the place to take down the Munro brothers. The residue of that
tear gas was in the air, on the floor, on the doors, on the walls. It was
everywhere, and whenever Dave or I made even the slightest motion,
that residue got stirred and went into our faces. It is a white powder that
gets into the air when initially fired. It settles down but gets airborne
again with any movement, and so it wound up in our eyes. It stung to no
end and we were constantly wiping our eyes. The tear gas aside, we went
over every inch of the floor where Sweet had been shot and over every
inch of George's where Sweet and Constable Doug Ramsey had been the
night before. That meant the upstairs as well as the downstairs. We
wanted to retrace every step they took. So Dave and I started seizing
exhibits, and gradually we began to reconstruct all the events that had
taken place to result in the death of a young cop.

We both knew there was something different about this case. It was
a homicide and we were professionals who knew what had to be done,
but the victim was a fellow officer who had been shot. Now he was dead.
What had happened to Michael Sweet could just as easily have happened
to me or Dave or any other officer with the Toronto police department.
What's more, here we were in the very same place where Sweet had been

murdered. Every item that Dave and I collected was yet another marker, another piece of evidence.

We sifted through the evidence, piece by painstaking piece. Swabs of blood. Shell casings. Lead fragments. Indeed, the carnage from the night before was shocking. Dozens of bullet holes were plain to see, as were even more holes from all the pieces of shrapnel that had struck various things. But it was those little remnants of Michael Sweet that really hit home for us.

On the ground-floor landing, we found a set of handcuffs and the key that went with them. His cuffs. We also found two keys with the familiar Chrysler logo embossed on them. They were to his cruiser. No. 5209. A wood baton. A pair of brown gloves. An officer's tunic. Some torn buttons. A police-issued black tie. A black flashlight. A holster. And an officer's hat with the badge and number 4794 on it. All this was found at the scene and all of it belonged to Sweet.

The hat would have to be retrieved for the funeral, which was to be held in a few days. Then it would be given to Sweet's wife, Karen, now a widow with three little girls to raise. Also on the floor amidst all the other debris was a sawed-off shotgun that was still loaded with one live shell. Number 6 shot. The serial number on the gun had been chiseled off. Some rope, shotgun shells, and a purple sports bag were also on the floor. From the debriefing we had done earlier with the officers who had been on the scene, we knew these things belonged to the Munros. And, of course, there were those tear gas canisters. The air was a potent reminder of that.

Around police headquarters, I had a reputation as a stickler for detail, and when doing a homicide investigation I had my own system of identifying pieces of evidence. For every item I retrieved, I would make an entry in my notebook and number it with a capital "S" for Scene. So, the first item in my notebook was S1, the second was S2, and so on. Some ten hours later Dave and I were done, at least with the initial examination, and I had no less than eighty-three items dutifully recorded in my notes. Every one of those items was placed in a plastic bag or a glass container or some kind of receptacle to carry it away in and, of course, labelled accordingly. We were careful to make sure nothing was damaged or altered, which would have rendered the evidence inadmissible. While still at the scene, I also made notes about the two penetrating bullet holes to the southeast corner of the fridge in a south-to-north direction, the six bullet-impact marks at knee level on the bottom sub-door of the front of the fridge, and anything else that would help build the case against the Munros.

Joining Dave and me was firearms specialist Sam Barbetta, who was able to offer keen insight into what had transpired the night before. He examined each and every shell—what size it was, where it was found—and observed the many bullet holes so he could re-create the scenario. Also involved in these early stages of the investigation was a police photographer, who took hundreds of shots of the crime scene, and a crime artist, who made sketches to help illustrate measurements and depth to scale.

Dave and I had arrived at George's at 6:15 p.m. on March 14, and remained there doing an exhaustive examination and collecting every bit of evidence we could find until 3:55 a.m. the next morning. When we finally left the crime scene, which was guarded by police officers, it was almost exactly twenty-four hours after Sweet and the two Munro brothers had been carted off to the hospital.

After our ten-hour examination of the scene, we went to Toronto General Hospital. Wing 3 West. It was still the middle of the night. We got there at 4:10 a.m. and headed to the room where the Munros were recovering from their wounds. Both of them were heavily bandaged and under police guard. Neither Dave nor I were in uniform. We were wearing suits. We read the Munros their rights and formally charged both of them with first-degree murder in the death of Michael Sweet. That done, Dave asked Craig how he was feeling and Craig said he was in bad pain.

"Do you know who we are?" Dave asked him.

Craig said he knew we were police. Then he said he had nothing more to say and that he was in enough trouble already.

"We had to do it," he suddenly blurted out. "I can't bring your buddy back. It was either him or us."

He told us he had to talk to his lawyer.

Jamie was the more seriously hurt of the two and couldn't make any conversation. No fewer than twenty-seven holes were found in the grey coat he had been wearing the night before, all of them due to pieces of flying shrapnel. He had at least fourteen entry wounds in his body and had to undergo a three-hour operation for damage to his spleen, diaphragm, lung, stomach, one of his kidneys, and his liver.

After seeing the Munros, Dave and I left the hospital at 4:30 a.m. and returned to the office to prepare reports and begin processing exhibits. There were lots of exhibits. It was noon before I finally reported off duty and went home. It had been a long, emotional stretch.

The next day, I was back at work at 9:30 a.m. to receive yet more exhibits from other officers who had seized various items from the scene. Included in this lot was a .32 Colt semi-automatic pistol; it was Craig's. We found out later that the gun had been manufactured in a firearms plant in Hartford, Connecticut, back in 1924. A relic with serial number 333-738. Also belonging to Craig was a black overcoat, black pants, a pair of glasses with a leather case, and nine dollars in bills.

Belonging to Jamie was a thick, grey, three-quarter-length overcoat, which had saved his life by absorbing so much shrapnel fire. From the Munros' car, a 1968 Chrysler, there were many .12 shell casings, as well as six padlocks and the accompanying keys. And then there was Michael Sweet's service revolver, a .38 that still carried four unfired shells; one shell had been fired and one chamber was empty. Also included were Sweet's boots, his tunic, and his sweater. There were bullet holes in both the tunic and sweater in the right-sleeve area. These holes were from the bullet that had hit him in the chest and that ultimately killed him.

I reported off duty at 5 p.m., and the next day Dave and I met with Crown attorney Robert McGee, the attorney who would prosecute the case. McGee was the head Crown attorney downtown and well known to us. We had done many murder cases with him. He was a chubby guy with an infectious laugh who absolutely never got flustered. He took on the toughest cases and always did them with flair. His jury addresses were colourful in that he could bring you to tears and then find something humorous to inject. But there was no humour in this case.

On March 24, Dave and I picked up Jamie Munro from the hospital so we could take him to the Toronto East Detention Centre. Jamie, but not his brother Craig, was now medically fit for discharge, even though Jamie was the one who had suffered the worst injuries. At the hospital, we told Craig he was in violation of his parole and that we were now executing the warrant for that violation. I remember that Dave asked Craig, who was still in his hospital bed, how he was feeling.

He said tersely, "No comment."

Then Craig turned to Jamie and told him to hang in there, to remember everything he had told him, and to call their lawyers so they could get their "suit" going.

Craig then asked me what my name was and if I was the one who had "threatened" him. I had no idea what he was talking about. I told him my name and asked him what accusations he was making.

"Yeah fine," Craig said. "I'll fix you too."

What I most remember about Craig Munro were the cold, cold eyes of a psychopath. They were all steel and ice. I had seen such a look before, but only in killers. And of all the killers I've ever seen in my life, he had more of that look than any of them.

I felt I was on a roller coaster. I had been working in homicide since 1975, five years by that time, and Michael Sweet's murder was one of maybe two dozen cases I had personally investigated. But that didn't mean there was anything routine about it. We were police who had a job to do and we were determined to do the best we could, as we did with every homicide we investigated. But at the back of my mind, the thought wouldn't escape that this was a police officer, a young man and father, and now he was gone. It could have been me.

The visitation for Michael Sweet—for the *body* of Michael Sweet—took place on the evening of March 16 at the Jerrett Funeral Chapel in

Scarborough in the east end of Toronto. I was working on the case and didn't get to go, but many officers I know did. It's a very sombre kind of thing. The wreaths. Two police officers in uniform with their white gloves standing guard on either side of the coffin. Draped across the coffin a Canadian flag, a pair of white gloves, and the dead officer's official police hat bearing the badge number. For Michael Sweet that number was 4794.

It has always bothered me that I couldn't attend Michael's funeral. Dave Boothby couldn't go either. We were just too busy working on the case, but that's how it is when you're in homicide. However, I did know a lot of people who went and there was no getting away from the extensive media coverage.

On the morning of March 18, a Mass of the Resurrection was celebrated for Michael at Precious Blood Catholic Church in Scarborough. I know that the place was packed, so full that hundreds of people who couldn't get in had to watch the proceedings on closed-circuit television from the church's parish hall, while another *thousand* people who couldn't get into the parish hall stood outside the building, huddling in the cold, listening to the mass over loudspeakers.

Reverend Kenneth Robitaille, who was the Monsignor at St. Michael's Cathedral, one of Toronto's biggest Catholic churches, delivered the eulogy. He had become the chaplain for the Toronto police not long before, and this was his first mass for an officer killed in the line of duty. I was told that during the mass, when he mentioned how Sweet lives on in his wife, Karen, and their three little girls, many in the congregation began to weep openly. Including police officers.

I have been to many police funerals in my time, across Canada and across North America, and it's like losing a member of your own family. A lot of people don't understand that and even some politicians don't understand that. This becomes clear when you hear their rhetoric about too many officers attending police funerals. At a police funeral, there are always lots of cruisers with their bright red flashers going and the flashers are always shrouded in black cloth. It is a very moving event.

As I said, Sweet's funeral was massive. More than two thousand police officers from all over Canada and the United States attended. They came from local municipal police forces, the Ontario Provincial Police, and the Royal Canadian Mounted Police. They came from as far away as British Columbia on the west coast of Canada, and from Newfoundland on the east coast. They came from Quebec and from such American cities as Chicago and Minneapolis. The procession itself was more than a mile long with over two hundred and fifty cars.

Many dignitaries were also present. Among them were Police Chief Harold Adamson, who was soon to retire, and incoming chief Jack Ackroyd, the man we all knew as Kojak. And politicians. Lots of politicians. Cabinet ministers from the government of Ontario, members of Toronto Council, and mayors of local municipalities. But conspicuously absent from the group was the man who was mayor of Toronto. John Sewell.

Sewell was a long-time community activist, who had first been elected to council in 1969. Before becoming mayor he was the acknowledged leader of the so-called reform wing, which represented left-of-centre politics on city council. He carried around the image of an environmentalist who would ride his bicycle to city hall and show up in blue jeans. He was elected mayor in 1978 and would serve only one term, but relations between him and the police force had been frosty even before the Michael Sweet shooting.

Sewell once made a speech about the number of people shot by the police in the city—over a period of thirteen months eight people had been killed by the police—and when he was mayor he said the police should not be going around shooting people. We were all furious with his remarks and even more furious when he didn't attend Sweet's funeral. Newspaper reports at the time said he had stayed away because of a doctor's appointment. Later, Sewell admitted that he just didn't like to attend police funerals.

Sewell's absence at the funeral didn't sit very well with me. When a person who keeps the peace and order in your community is shot and killed in the line of duty, and the mayor, who after all is chief magistrate of that community, doesn't bother showing up for the funeral, you have to wonder what funeral the mayor would show up for. I wasn't there either, but I had a legitimate reason. The mayor didn't have a legitimate reason. This wasn't just about Michael Sweet. It was a time of great trauma for the whole police department and those police had to be supported. That is the mayor's job. There are many reasons for a mayor to attend a police funeral that go above and beyond pure symbolism. It's about identifying with what that singular act of murder represents, namely, that lawful authority has been destroyed in the most egregious fashion possible. And it's more than whether you like or don't like the police. You have an inherent duty. After 9/11, New York City mayor Rudy Giuliani went to a lot of funerals and I remember what he said: "Weddings are optional but funerals are mandatory."

Incidentally, today John Sewell is involved with an organization called the Toronto Police Accountability Coalition. According to its website, www.tpac.ca, it is "a group of individuals and organizations in Toronto interested in police policies and procedures, and in making police more accountable to the community they are committed to serving." That is all fine and good, but in my view Sewell remains what he has always been. Anti-police.

Michael Sweet was buried at Holy Cross Cemetery. Fittingly, or perhaps ironically, a great many police escorts were required to guide the long winding cortege through the streets from the church where the service was held to the cemetery just north of the city limits. The next day, the Toronto newspapers were full of coverage of the funeral. Family photographs of Sweet with his wife, Karen, and their three children were plastered all over the pages of the city's dailies. On its front page the *Toronto Sun* ran a photo of police officer Stephen Craig, who was identified as a former partner of Sweet's, crying on the shoulder of a friend. On the inside, it ran a full page of photos with the headline in big bold capital letters.

2,000 COPS BURY A BUDDY

I read every one of those stories and felt terrible for Sweet's family and what they were going through. His young wife. His three little girls. His parents. His siblings. And his fellow police officers, who were now wrestling with the fact that they couldn't save him. The death of Michael Sweet, a man I never knew, affected me deeply as a police officer, but it also affected me deeply as a citizen of the community and as a human being. I can't forget those headlines.

Friends, relatives, strangers mourn for slain policeman
Metro pays tribute to one of its finest
The sad farewell
Brave widow's homage

The photo of his little girls that ran in the *Toronto Sun* on March 17, 1980, was enough to break your heart. One of the girls was six, another was four, and the smallest was just sixteen months. Along with those stories and photographs were columns, editorials, and letters from readers. There were many letters and every one of them expressed a profound sense of grief. And outrage.

·8·

Hell on Earth for Me

IN 1991, I LEFT THE TORONTO POLICE AND BECAME CHIEF IN London, Ontario. A quiet prosperous city of 350,000 people, London was known as a university town and a haven for old money. One reason I took the job was that, after spending over twenty years as a police officer in a big city, I thought this would be a chance to gain new insights into policing a smaller jurisdiction. London had a fraction of Toronto's population and a much slower pace of life. After all my experience with organized crime, drugs, and murder, I figured it would be a welcome change. The downside was that I lived just north of Toronto, so taking the London job meant getting an apartment in town and commuting home on the weekend, and that's what I did. It meant very long days.

I spent seven years as chief in London, and while it was much different from Toronto, without the relentless hustle and bustle, it did give me a new perspective on policing. And it also gave me something else. Project Guardian. This would be hell on earth for me.

Not until the mid-1980s did Canada's Criminal Code include any offences involving child abuse, and in the early '90s there was still no law prohibiting the possession of child pornography, even though other countries had such laws. I had been pushing for this after becoming chief in London. I once attended a conference where one of the presenters was an official with the United States Postal Service. He talked about all the seizures they were making of cassette tapes and magazines depicting child pornography. Child pornography was a huge problem all over the world and, as the Internet grew, it got worse. Yet another legal failing in Canada was the lack of laws dealing with the growing problem of sex tourism. Sex tourists are people who travel abroad to such places as Thailand and have children procured for them. For sex. These people are pedophiles. I remember meeting a high-ranking police official from one of these countries and telling him his country should put laws in place to protect children. His reply knocked me back on my seat. He said: "My country would not have a problem with children being abused if you kept your tourists at home."

At the time, Lloyd Axworthy was Canada's minister of foreign affairs and he was at that same conference. He made a passionate speech about Canada's commitment to protect children. Before you knew it, out came Bill C-27. It was supposed to be the "fixer" that would prosecute any Canadian who went abroad to sexually abuse children. We told justice officials the legislation wouldn't work because police agencies couldn't afford to send investigators to all these faraway places to secure evidence that could be tendered in a Canadian court. Nevertheless, the bill passed in 1997, and in all the years since then I know of only one prosecution under that law; a Canadian man coming back from an overseas trip had videotapes of him abusing children, so this case literally fell into the laps of the local police. You need resources to enforce a law like Bill C-27 and the resources weren't there. But nobody would listen to us.

I wanted to devote more attention to this area and joined an Interpol committee called the Standing Working Party on Offences Against Children. I was the only Canadian police chief on that committee and made many contacts with law enforcement people in the FBI and around the world. Louis Freeh, the director of the FBI, was passionate about this issue too, and put a child pornography investigative unit into every FBI field office across the United States. Every single one of them. Finally, on August 1, 1993, Canada passed Bill C-128. It made the possession of child pornography a criminal offence punishable by up to five years in jail.

According to Canada's Criminal Code, the age of consent is eighteen where the sexual activity involves exploitative activity such as prostitution or pornography, or where there is a relationship of trust, authority, or dependency. For other sexual activity, the age of consent is fourteen. Canada's age of consent has been unchanged since 1890, when it was raised from twelve years to fourteen, but in 2006, the government of Prime Minister Stephen Harper introduced a bill to raise it to sixteen. This would mean that most adults who have sex with boys or girls aged fourteen or fifteen could face criminal charges. The bill has still not been passed.

Still, by making the possession of child pornography a criminal offence, Bill C-128 was a major change in Canada. A month after it became law, two residents in London, Ontario, who possessed homemade child pornography decided to destroy their collection. They had a friend dump their incriminating videotapes in a bag in the Ausable River, just north of the city. A boy fishing in the river found the bag of tapes, took them home, and dried them up. His mother put one of the tapes in the VCR and then called the police. There were tapes of children being sexually abused. Three officers from our vice unit viewed them, and when they told me what they saw, I said we had to identify these children, find out where the tapes were made, and go after these guys. The investigation was called Project Scoop and it started off as a child pornography case. We eventually seized ninety-three videotapes from the river.

Our officers made still photographs from the tapes and showed them to both current and retired police officers, social workers with the local Children's Aid Society, and staff from area group homes. One of those people was able to identify a young person from a photo. That person was approached by our police and interviewed, and pretty soon we were on to other youths and suspects and the whole network started to unravel.

I saw some of these tapes myself and they were disgusting. There are no redeeming features about any activity that involves the exploitation and victimization of children. You see this kind of thing and you immediately think about your own kids and wonder how any adult person could be so cruel. But, obviously, some people are that cruel.

The first two suspects in London were arrested in November 1993, and over the next few months we arrested many more. As our investigators started digging around, one kid talked about another kid who talked about another kid and the thing just snowballed. Our investigation grew and it soon became obvious this was about more than pornography. One point that must be clarified right here is that any situation involving child pornography also involves child abuse. These videos were of kids having sex with adults. So we formed a task force and I asked the government of Ontario to fund a joint-forces project that would involve the London police, the Ontario Provincial Police, and also the Toronto police, and that's what happened. The London police became the lead agency and the investigation was renamed Project Guardian. It began in May 1994.

We worked closely with local agencies like the Children's Aid Society and the London Family Court Clinic, and also the Crown Attorney's Office and the Ontario Ministry of the Solicitor General. Then we found out one of the suspects was HIV positive, so we got the Middlesex London Health Unit involved. In a nutshell, Project Guardian was a joint investigative task force designed to, first, identify and disrupt the illegal activities of anyone who was involved in the sexual exploitation of children and youths, and second, to rescue those children and youths.

The children involved in this investigation were as young as seven and eight, and they were being exploited by adult males in return for money, alcohol, drugs, clothing, lodging, and shelter. Many of the children and youths were from broken homes and lacked traditional families. They had witnessed family violence, had been physically abused or sexually abused, and had parents who struggled with drugs and alcohol. As for the offenders, they were everything from Boy Scout leaders to soccer coaches. Some were active in community service clubs and volunteer work, which allowed them to meet single mothers who, in turn, provided an opportunity for access to their children. These guys were very skilled at finding ways of gaining access to young people.

One of them knew all the telephone numbers of the pay phones in the downtown area where youths hung out. He would sit in his car and watch the pay phone until a group of kids gathered, then he'd call the pay phone on his cell and start talking to one of them. While still on his cell, he would drive up and invite the kid who was talking to him to join him for a beer and cigarettes. After a few times, he would introduce the kid to sex.

Offenders would offer such enticements as bicycles, running shoes, and jackets, as well as contraband such as tobacco, drugs, and alcohol. Or they would just pay the kids anywhere from $5 to $100 for a "job." These offenders included a teacher, a school principal, an Anglican priest, and a real estate agent. Project Guardian eventually involved sixty-two complainants and sixty-one suspects. If that's not a "ring," I don't know what is. The ages of the complainants ranged from seven to seventeen years with 50 per cent of them being thirteen years of age or younger, while the average age of the suspects was forty. When it was all done, 535 criminal charges were laid against sixty-one suspects, and the charges included sexual interference, sexual exploitation, anal intercourse, maintaining obscene material, possession of child pornography, making child pornography, paying for sexual services of a person under eighteen years, sexual assault, and extortion. Of all the offences, 39 per cent involved anal intercourse and 49 per cent involved fellatio. What's more, 58 per cent of the complainants/victims had been plied with alcohol before the sexual assault and 27 per cent had been given drugs beforehand.

The conviction rate for Project Guardian was 86 per cent. This is an astounding figure, which is almost unheard of in the criminal justice system. Compare that to Canada's national conviction rate of just under 21 per cent. That's all it is. So this was more than four times that. As things turned out, 71 per cent of all matters were resolved by guilty plea and 29 per cent went to trial. The average sentence handed down was four years.

One pedophile said he had molested more than 200 boys since he had been a teenager. The Victim Impact Statements we collected from the victims tell a sorry tale. We had statements from kids saying how scared they were about getting AIDS, how they had nightmares of being raped, and how they had lost their self-esteem. One of them said he had almost committed suicide after learning that the first person he was sexually involved with was HIV positive. Another said that the man who assaulted him "liked young meat."

The first two men charged were Gary Gramlick, fifty-eight, who was sentenced to ten years after pleading guilty to nine sex-related charges for directing and videotaping sex acts involving children; and Edward Jewell, thirty-six, who was sentenced to fifteen years after pleading guilty to five counts of sexual interference, two counts of anal intercourse, and one count each of possession of child pornography, making obscene material, and invitation to sexual touching. But both men appealed their sentences. At the appeal, Gramlick's sentence was reduced from ten years to five and Jewell's was reduced from fifteen years to seven. Of course, this was very frustrating for the police officers who had devoted so many hours to the investigation, but at least we got convictions.

The fact that something like this was going on in a city like London was remarkable, but then again it wasn't. We were all naive since this problem existed everywhere. We discovered that London had a thriving, child-sex trade run by a group of pedophiles and that there was a connection between London and Toronto; the press called it "a kiddie porn pipeline." Children were being taken from London to Toronto and given to men who used them for sex and/or filmmaking. Some Toronto men were also convicted. We got calls from police as far away as California who had tapes in their possession and who thought some of the people in those tapes might be children and men from London.

Newspapers called Project Guardian the "largest child pornography investigation in Canadian history" and they continued to describe it this way even after it was clear this wasn't only about child pornography. It was also about child sexual abuse and that's a big difference. The fact is, some of these tapes had been made long before we got hold of them, so a victim who was fifteen at the time of the investigation may have been ten or younger when he was abused. And therein lies the problem. *Denial.* People didn't want to confront this for what it was—the perverse abuse of children—and this issue of denial is a huge obstacle that we as police confront every day. As I said before, there is an abused child in any video that shows adults having sex with children.

We made an information brochure about Project Guardian that described it as "a criminal probe into the sexual exploitation of children." In the brochure, I referred to this exploitation as a "pervasive and predatorial network of criminal sexual exploitation of young children, of which child pornography is a component." An official with the Children's Aid Society said the whole thing was about the "abuse of an adult's power within a sexual context." One of the sentencing judges said of an accused: "The accused left many impaired lives in his wake. Enticed them to his home, without any concern for the damage he was doing to the boys. Introduced them into sexual acts that included mutual masturbation and sado-masochistic spanking."

Unfortunately for the police, Project Guardian became an uphill battle because once the critics came out they went right for the jugular. Our jugular. Their campaign, and a campaign it was, was based on a self-serving agenda full of misinformation.

Buryl Wilson, a high-school English teacher in Toronto, wrote vicious letters about the police and about me personally and then sent them to people in government. He wrote to everybody. He is the man who wrote to Prime Minister Jean Chrétien and who got a very nice response from the Prime Minister's Office. Wilson later became a convicted pedophile. Activists in London's gay community said I was a homophobic police chief and we had to go out time and again to explain ourselves. Frankly, it made no sense to me. I figured everyone in the community should embrace any initiative to protect children, and while the great majority of people in London were solidly behind the police and what we were doing, there were some with an agenda who created mischief, made a lot of noise, and got lots of ink.

Then came the morning of March 11, 1995.

We were working on a joint forces project with the Toronto Police and Ontario Provincial Police in pursuit of gangsters called the Balaclava Bandits. These guys had killed the owner of a gun store in Oshawa, Ontario, and had also killed an innocent man for his car. They had committed a number of robberies in which guns were used. So on this particular Friday, we managed to take them down. They had just gone into a National Grocer's outlet in St. Thomas outside London and had shot one of the employees. Our police officers made a high-risk stop of their vehicle and arrested them at gunpoint. The next day, Saturday, we held a news conference in the boardroom at London police headquarters. All the guns and bullets that had been seized were on display, and we were on a real high because we had finally caught these guys. At the end of it, a reporter asked me about the article in that morning's edition of the *Globe and Mail*. I didn't know what he was talking about, but I soon found out. The article was a vile, vicious attack on Project Guardian and me. It was called an "Analysis" and the headline was "The kiddie-porn ring that wasn't." The article claimed that while there were young male prostitutes in London, there never was a child pornography ring. The writer was a man named Gerald Hannon and the article began like this:

> This is the story of an Ontario city in the grip of a police-constructed moral panic. It is the story of Project Guardian, a province-wide investigation authorized by the Solicitor General that is based on a lie. It is the story of a gay community under siege.

The article continued with headlines like "Porn haul proved to be Abbott and Costello." It claimed Project Guardian was about getting "much-needed dollars into the London police budget." It made reference to my being a Catholic and apparently this was why I was so appalled by the videotapes that had been seized. It concluded with Hannon making reference to an alleged conversation about me between two people whom he didn't even identify.

A well-known London journalist, who wanted to remain anonymous, told me he'd had a long conversation with an equally well-known London lawyer. The lawyer felt that, if Project Guardian continued to unravel the way it was doing, "Fantino would crash and burn within the year."

I was shocked that a respected national newspaper like the *Globe and Mail* would run such a story. I filed a complaint through the Ontario Press Council because the article was an opinion piece and anything but an analysis. When I lodged my formal complaint, I said the article lacked honesty, fairness, objectivity, and balance. Later, the Ontario Press Council upheld my complaint against the *Globe and Mail* and agreed that the piece should have been labelled as opinion, not analysis.

At the time Hannon wrote that article, he was teaching journalism at Ryerson University in Toronto. Long before then, he had written articles for a gay liberation publication called *The Body Politic*. The November 1977 issue of *The Body Politic* had run his article called "Men Loving Boys Loving Men."

On November 25, 1995, eight months after Hannon's piece about Project Guardian appeared in the *Globe and Mail*, the *Toronto Sun* ran a front-page story about him called "Ryerson Prof: I'm a Hooker." In that story he disclosed that he had been working part-time as a male prostitute since 1987. The day after that article appeared, Ryerson University suspended Hannon with pay. The university terminated his contract at the end of the school year and later a financial settlement between the two was reached.

The trouble was that the *Globe and Mail* was Canada's national newspaper and widely read from coast to coast. The week after the article appeared, people like London mayor Tom Gosnell, who was also a member of the London Police Services Board, wrote to the newspaper complaining about the piece. Gosnell said that Hannon's article was unfair and that it had an obvious bias against the police. Newspapers like the *Toronto Star*, which is the biggest in Canada, made hay out of all this and published stories with such headlines as "London porn inquiry angers gay activists." That ran on June 4, 1995. Voices in the gay press and in Toronto alternative weeklies such as *NOW* magazine went on the offensive. So that initial article by Hannon led to a wave of interest, with other media jumping on the bandwagon. It included radio talk shows and panel discussions.

Even the *New York Times* got into the act. On May 29, 1995, the *New York Times* published a story called "Sex Tapes of Children Stir Anxiety" and picked up on some of the earlier media coverage by calling Project Guardian "the largest child pornography investigation in Canadian history." It also quoted Hannon, who said that London was "in the grip of a police-constructed moral panic." While I didn't relish seeing that, it was reassuring to read in the same article the comments of a London radio station host who said that, when I was on his program, calls ran four to one in favour of the police.

Then there was the CBC, the Canadian Broadcasting Corporation. Not long after Hannon's *Globe and Mail* article appeared, CBC Radio and CBC Television aired programs that impugned the integrity of our investigation. One of them in particular I found extremely nauseating and a monumental waste of taxpayer's money. It was called "After the Bath" and was broadcast on CBC Newsworld. National television. It was May 13, 1995. This program featured gay activists making a statement about the gay community being under siege—which wasn't true—and had interviews with people like Charles Roach, who was the lawyer of my old letter-writing friend Buryl Wilson, the convicted pedophile. When asked about me, Roach said I was a cop who knew how to get things done "not necessarily following conventional means." In the program, it was alleged that I had created Project Guardian "as part of a high-profile bid" for the Toronto police chief's job. It also referred to my "perceived homophobia." In short, it made me and my police force out to be the bad guys. The program ended with this statement:

> I found no smoking gun in London. Instead, I found a police force, a newspaper, and a social service agency that can't or won't distinguish between consensual gay sex and abuse. I found a gay community under siege and torn apart by paranoia and rhetoric. I found my hometown in the grip of a moral panic.

This program had nothing to do with protecting children. It was totally about attacking and discrediting the police. Not surprisingly, one of the people involved in it was Gerald Hannon. His name was in the credits. It was part of a well-organized campaign that somehow got Canada's national television broadcaster to serve as its conduit. Naturally, we, the London police, complained to the CBC, but we got nowhere.

Without a doubt, Project Guardian was *the* case that made child abuse such a big issue with me. My officers were attacked every day and we took a lot of heat. But I was the one who faced the media and I was the one who faced all the critics. I didn't send anybody to deal with these people. I did it myself. I am also the one who took the issue forward to the provincial government at the outset. We wanted funding so we could do a comprehensive investigation, which we did, but we were under constant attack. I never realized there could be such a pushback and such influence. I was shocked that the CBC could be co-opted into this kind of nonsense, knowing full well that we were dealing with a very serious problem, the sexual exploitation of children. Looking back, I think of that entire campaign as the most vile, unfair, unethical treatment of police that I have ever seen in my career in law enforcement. To this day, I find it hard to believe that taxpayer's money was spent as it was on that CBC program. What it tells me is that those who influenced the expenditures of taxpayer's money must have had a sympathetic ear for pedophiles. All we were trying to do was ferret out those individuals who abused children and investigate legitimate, bona fide complaints from victims. We weren't going after homosexuals. We were going after pedophiles, and the two are not the same. There was a lot of misinformation and a lot of disingenuous reporting.

I am not anti-gay or homophobic and never have been. Frankly, I don't care what someone's sexual orientation is as long as they don't break the law. It would be impossible for someone who is homophobic to be chief in a city like Toronto, which has one of the largest, most flourishing gay populations in North America. You just wouldn't get the job. You wouldn't even be considered for the job. However, I am very much against anyone who abuses kids or young people, and as long as I'm in law enforcement, I will go after these characters with everything I've got. You can bet on it.

· 9 ·

Throwaway Kids

C HILD PORNOGRAPHY AND THE SEXUAL ABUSE OF CHILDREN is a rapidly growing problem all over the world. In the 1990s, I attended a number of conferences in different countries, and if there is one issue that really gets my blood boiling, it's this. I went to those conferences on behalf of Interpol and met people—not only police officers, but also customs officials and professionals with various agencies—who were on the front lines and who felt very frustrated. This feeling of frustration and not being supported was universal. Without fail, these people had experienced the same lack of support from their governments as we had. We were all trying to move the yardsticks forward and get governments around the world to address this issue head-on. But just like with Project Guardian, it has been an uphill battle.

Still, we have made progress, but then, so has the pedophile movement. Technology is the pedophile's best friend. Today it is no longer a matter of videotape cassettes and magazines going across borders and being seized. Now it's a borderless world where all this stuff is done in a secretive way and is much harder to detect because of the Internet. I fear we don't even know half of what is going on because of the difficulty detecting it. When physical things go across borders, they can be intercepted. Police and customs officials know what to look for. But now people encrypt files. This is a problem that has grown exponentially and we haven't kept up, even though most major police departments have a unit dedicated to such investigations. When I was chief in Toronto, I gave a lot of support to this unit, which meant time, money, and manpower. I plugged into Interpol with the committee I was on and learned just how big a problem child pornography was becoming. Soon we began holding conferences and training seminars of our own to get our police up to snuff on the issues. These were things we hadn't done before.

The Toronto unit achieved a name for itself not only across Canada, but around the world. Detective Sergeant Paul Gillespie ran it for years and was dubbed "Canada's top child-porn cop" by the media. He did a fabulous job, and later I'll talk more about him and the great work he did with the support of Bill Gates and Microsoft. That is a terrific story.

But make no mistake, these are heart-wrenching investigations for the police because of what they must view. In Project Guardian, the London officers who viewed those tapes and the officers who interviewed the victims were deeply affected by the experience—professionally and personally. I viewed the tapes myself and it wasn't an easy thing to do. None of us had ever seen anything like this before. I look at my own grandchildren and can't imagine someone abusing a child like this. It makes your heart weep. But then you see some of the things people do. To little children. To *babies*. Pedophiles have been known to father children just so they can abuse them. The whole thing is a sordid, sick, perverted crime.

Unfortunately, the Internet has made the networking of producing, distributing, and exchanging child pornography seamless. There are no borders to worry about. No parcels. No packages. Nothing to carry around. It has enhanced the ability of people to collect child pornography and some people collect child pornography the way the rest of us collect stamps or coins. To qualify to join some of these clubs, you need thousands of pictures; the members can be contributors as well as receivers. The biggest problem with the Internet is that it allows all these pedophiles to find each other.

The long-standing child pornography section of the Ontario Provincial Police is called Project P. Before the Internet took off—in the early to mid '90s—that unit investigated perhaps two cases of child pornography each year. In 2000, it had 200 investigations on its plate and, the year after that, 410. However, because of all the time and legwork required, those 410 investigations resulted in only thirty-seven arrests.

When I was chief in Toronto, I always made a point of supporting Inspector Bob Matthews of the OPP, who ran Project P. He and I worked together to try to get politicians to enact legislation, like making possession of child pornography an offence.

With the Internet, a pedophile only has to make a few clicks on a computer screen to enter a bottomless well of child pornography. Any pedophile who is somewhat sophisticated on the computer will probably avoid detection. The Toronto unit once discovered a man who was receiving up to 300 movies and 1,000 pictures *every day* as part of an Internet swap program. He received a conditional sentence, which is essentially house arrest, meaning no jail time.

Every picture of a child being abused is the actual victimization of a child, but many people don't perceive it that way. It's seen as just another video or photograph. Some judges don't appreciate what is being portrayed on these videos and can't connect what is on the video with the actual act of brutalizing a child. The result? The severity of the crime is not reflected in the lenient sentences handed out. Pedophiles often receive conditional sentences or house arrest or are told to stay away from their computers. Sometimes the sentencing judge doesn't even want to see the photographs or the movies because they are so disgusting and then that same judge will pass sentence without having seen the evidence.

In 2003, Randy Weber, a forty-three-year-old business executive, was convicted of possessing and distributing images of small children who were tied up and raped. When this case went to court, the York Region Crown prosecutor, Michael Demczur, showed right in the courtroom a video of a four-year-old girl who was being sexually assaulted by a man while she cried and struggled with him. He also showed the court an image of an eight-year-old girl who was tied up and hung upside down. Nevertheless, the judge, Justice Roy Bogusky, sentenced Weber to house arrest on the condition that he receive psychiatric counselling, stay off the Internet, and have no contact with anyone under eighteen years of age unless there was adult supervision. He also ordered three years' probation. So, no jail time. When prosecutor Demczur asked the judge about Weber not having access to computers, the judge ruled that Weber could not have access only to the specific computer he had been using. Just that one. When this case went to the Ontario Court of Appeal, the panel of appeals court judges upheld Bogusky's decision.

Canada is at the low end of sentencing in this area. In the United Kingdom, an offender might receive years of jail time, and in a U.S. state like Texas, maybe decades. What is typical for Canada, however, is house arrest. In Canada, the province of Alberta tends to give stiffer sentences than does an area like Toronto. In the Greater Toronto Area, 48 per cent of those who are convicted of possession and distribution receive conditional sentences.

Some judges just don't get it.

Toronto's Sex Crimes Unit grew to become the largest such unit in North America and one of the most recognized in the world. It all started back in December 2000, when a U.S. investigation called Project Avalanche identified a couple in Dallas who were generating more than U.S.$1 million a month by selling subscriptions to child pornography websites. This was a huge international operation involving 35,000 people, and 2,300 of them were in the Toronto area. Of those 2,300 people, 241 used a credit card to subscribe. Detective-Sergeant Paul Gillespie was quickly put in charge of the Child Exploitation Section of the Sex Crimes Unit for the Toronto police. In 2002, the Ontario government gave that unit a grant of $2 million and the unit grew to twenty full-time people. That group was dedicated to this kind of work and achieved international recognition as it managed to identify and rescue child victims of computer-facilitated, sexual abuse. From 2002 to 2006, the unit was involved in the identification and rescue of eighty-four children around the world, and was featured on CNN, NBC, and CBS, and was widely praised by the FBI and Interpol.

Those people did outstanding work but, as always, the sentences meted out for offenders were often a joke. A man named Joseph Downey of Elora, Ontario, was a target of Project Avalanche; in Canada, the investigation was called Project Snowball. Police found more than 500 pieces of child porn on Downey's computer. His sentence? Fourteen months of house arrest, which again meant no jail time. It's true that possessing or even distributing such material does not mean the person is physically abusing children. But studies have shown that one out of three people who possess or collect this stuff are abusers themselves and some studies put the figure as high as 80 per cent.

Peter Collins is manager of the Forensic Psychiatry Unit with the Ontario Provincial Police and an associate professor at the University of Toronto. In 1999, he accompanied me to an Interpol conference on child pornography in Lyon, France. With regard to pedophiles, he says, "We can treat them, but we can't cure them." He also agrees that we must take a harder line on sentencing. Collins is a leading expert on this subject and is privy to lots of studies that have been done. Results of one notable study done by Michael Seto, James Cantor, and Ray Blanchard, who are all with the Centre for Addiction and Mental Health in Toronto—Seto and Blanchard are also affiliated with the Department of Psychiatry at the University of Toronto—were published in the *Journal of Abnormal Psychology* (Vol. 115, No. 3) in 2006. They concluded with this: "Our results indicate that child pornography offending is a valid diagnostic indicator of pedophilia."

In 1999, when I was chief of the York Regional Police, British Columbia justice Duncan Shaw ruled that possession of child pornography should not be a crime because *laws against it violate the Charter of Rights and Freedoms.* I thought this ruling was perverse and said so in an article published in the *Toronto Star* on January 25, 1999. In fact, the possession of child pornography has absolutely nothing to do with the "intrusion into freedom of expression," as quoted by Justice Shaw. That ruling was out of touch with reality and the upshot was that it gave apologists and proponents of adult-child sexual encounters a licence to prey on children.

Canada Customs once seized a publication called *Answer Me*. It included graphic drawings and stories involving the mutilation, rape, and degradation of very young girls. A man in Richmond, B.C., was charged with possession, but the judge ruled that the material was *political satire* and acquitted him.

Another big problem is that many resources in law enforcement that had been looking at this issue have since been diverted to terrorism, so now there isn't the same kind of capacity to fight child pornography. There is only so much money to go around and priorities are priorities. While Toronto has a viable unit dedicated to this cause, many cities with a million people or more are struggling along with one or two officers working on this. People have no appreciation for the time involved in these investigations. In 2005, the Toronto unit had over 600 investigations, but made only forty-one arrests because of the very onerous task involved in doing the investigations.

There is no question that we must do more to protect children. In Canada, making the importation and possession of child pornography a criminal offence was a step in the right direction, as was getting a representative from Canada Customs on the Interpol Standing Working Party on Offences Against Minors. In 1989, the United Nations Convention on the Rights of the Child, which set out the rights of children, was adopted by the United Nations General Assembly. It generally defined a child as any person under the age of eighteen, unless an earlier age of majority is recognized by the country's law. The articles in that Convention were about protecting children from neglect and abuse, economic exploitation, sexual exploitation and abuse, and illicit drugs. They were also about the right to be protected from abduction, sale or trafficking, and all other forms of exploitation.

This Convention has been ratified by almost every country in the world, including Canada. Strangely enough, there has always been a problem getting the United States on board. In 1995, Madeleine Albright, then U.S. ambassador to the United Nations, signed the

Convention, but the U.S. Constitution requires treaties to be approved by two-thirds of the U.S. Senate, and some U.S. states still authorize the execution of persons as young as sixteen, so this has been an obstacle in getting the U.S. to ratify the Convention.

Back in 1995, the Parliamentary Joint Committee of the National Crime Authority in Australia released a report called Organised Criminal Paedophile Activity. It went into detail about the history of pedophile networks and referred to a 1986 United States Senate subcommittee which said that organizations advocating adult sex with children had been operating in the U.S. and Europe since the 1960s. According to this U.S. Senate subcommittee, one American group had a slogan of "sex before eight or else it's too late." The North American Man/Boy Love Association, which was founded in 1978, still has chapters all over the U.S. today and publishes a newsletter that is distributed around the world. The Paedophile Information Exchange was a group founded in the United Kingdom in 1974, but it went out of existence when some of its leading members were arrested. Such European countries as the Netherlands, Belgium, Denmark, and Germany are known to have pedophile support groups operating through the Internet. The Australian Paedophile Support Group was formed in 1983, and there have been other groups in that country as well, like the Australasian Man Boy Love Association.

In August 1996, on behalf of Interpol, I attended the World Congress on the Sexual Exploitation of Children in Stockholm, Sweden. That conference was a real eye-opener for me. I chaired a workshop on the problems of law enforcement and identified the biggest problems faced by police internationally. The top five problems were:

1. Corruption on all levels,
2. Denial and a lack of appreciation of the issues,
3. Lack of resources in terms of human resources, training, and support,
4. Lack of information gathering and sharing, and
5. Inadequacy of laws.

Among the things we called for at that conference were the following: the training of police and judges; agreement on a common age of consent for sexual encounters; the rights of a child victim taking precedence over the rights of an offender if they are in conflict; a centralized database relating to the movements of pedophiles; an international Central Register of Missing Children; and public recognition that the commercial sexual abuse of children is big business.

Bjorn Eriksson, who was president of Interpol at the time, said there were 30,000 pedophiles in organized groups throughout Europe. He said that most of them were linked through the Internet, and that some were guilty of the kidnapping, trading, and even murder of children.

An American presenter at that same conference had surveyed 165 countries and said that only thirty-one of those countries had specific legislation prohibiting the production, distribution, and possession of child pornography. Even today most countries have no laws against child pornography, and in those that do the sentences are often pathetic in terms of leniency.

I recall that a member of the Child Pornography Panel at the conference talked about the control pedophiles wield over children. He mentioned a man who worked for an aid agency in Bangladesh and who had abused up to sixty children in a single village. Apparently, not one of those kids told on him. Then he related the story of another man who had abused and murdered young girls in the United Kingdom, France, and Germany. This person was said to have abducted a baby when he was only nine years old and to have abused a child when he was fifteen. Said the presenter: "The authorities did not recognize the need to give him treatment but hoped he 'would grow out it'." The man later received ten life sentences for child murder and, according to the presenter, this is what he said upon sentencing:

My choice of holiday destination was partly determined by my sexual interest in children. Initially to Denmark and Holland. At the time of my arrest, I was saving for a trip to Bangkok,

Thailand...countries which have liberal pornography laws...
especially access to child pornography was also a leading factor.

How bad a problem is this? Well, in my travels I have learned about
Latin American countries that tax legal brothels and about the fluid borders between such countries as India and Nepal and between Cambodia
and Thailand, a situation that perpetuates the exploitation of children. I
have heard about some Asian cultures where child prostitution is not
considered to be morally wrong. At one of the conferences I attended, an
official from Nicaragua said that street children in her country did not
view their exploiters as exploiters, but kept returning to them for love
and affection. This woman said she did not feel the term "pedophilia"
could properly encompass such a phenomenon.

An organization called End Child Prostitution, Child Pornography
and Trafficking in Children for Sexual Purposes (ECPAT), was originally
called End Child Prostitution in Asian Tourism. In 1996, its name was
changed to reflect the organization's geographic expansion and broader
mandate. It has done excellent work to try to protect children from
predators. Its newsletter is prime reading, but some of that reading isn't
very pleasant. When I was first introduced to this organization back in
1997, I pored over every word of the newsletter. Here is an excerpt from
issue no. 20, from July 1997:

> The scourge that we are speaking about is child sexual abuse. It has
> accounted for probably more misery and suffering than any of the
> great plagues of history, including the bubonic plague, tuberculosis
> and syphilis. Its effects are certainly more devastating and wide-
> spread than those of the modern-day epidemics which currently
> take up so much community attention and resources: motor vehi-
> cle accidents, heart disease and, now, AIDS. Yet the public response
> to child sexual abuse, even now, is fragmented, poorly coordinated
> and generally ill-informed. Its victims have no National AIDS
> Council to advise governments on policy and research issues. They

have no National Heart Foundation to promote public education as to the risks of smoking and unhealthy lifestyles. They do not have a Transport Accident Commission to provide comprehensive treatment and rehabilitation services for them.

You get the idea.

According to ECPAT, in the city of Cartagena, Colombia, girls as young as twelve have been readily offered to groups of men from Italy, Spain, Germany, France, and *Canada*. At one time, says ECPAT, it was believed that 21,000 under-age prostitutes were at work in Colombia alone. It adds that every summer hundreds of Egyptians bring their young daughters to one of three villages near Cairo and offer them to Arabs from the Gulf states, in return for gifts. ECPAT also reports that hundreds if not thousands of children living on the streets of Bucharest, Romania, readily sell themselves for sex to pedophiles from such countries as Germany, Italy, France, and Britain.

According to ECPAT, sex tourism began in a big way in eastern and central Europe after the collapse of the Soviet bloc. Pedophiles, especially those from Finland and Sweden, were quick to make the scene in the new Baltic republics. Russia attracted a broad range of nationalities with open soliciting in hotels in St. Petersburg and Moscow. Not surprisingly, organized crime was involved.

These operations can be very sophisticated. For example, one of them involved two Czechs who ran a casting agency in Prague that recruited young males for films and photos shot locally. The cassettes and cartridges were sent to Cologne for development and editing before the final material went to Dusseldorf for distribution throughout Europe. Production was segmented in order to avoid police raids and prosecution. Just as in North America, police in Europe have been severely hampered by paperwork and cross-jurisdictions.

According to ECPAT, during the one week of that 1996 conference in Stockholm, more than *one million Asian children* were spending their evenings providing sexual services for adults, and before the week was out those children would receive *10 to 12 million adult male customers*. At the end of the conference, a man named Trond Waage, who was the Ombudsman for Children in Norway, announced that an international body had been set up to monitor the Internet. An organization called Norwegian Save the Children hired fifteen expert computer hackers to work with child welfare agencies, national police forces, and Interpol to surf the Internet for pedophiles.

Needless to say, when I returned to Canada from Sweden, I wanted to alert the Canadian government about the international problem of the sexual exploitation of children. I prepared a report on the conference and included material about Project Guardian, which by that time was completed, and also included recommendations. One of them was that Canada should implement a National Strategy on the Safety of Children. My report was sent to Lloyd Axworthy, who was minister of foreign affairs, to Allan Rock, who was minister of justice and attorney general of Canada, and to Herb Gray, solicitor general of Canada. The only one who ever replied to me was Herb Gray. But Phil Murray, then commissioner of the RCMP, took immediate action and assigned Assistant Commissioner Cleve Cooper to head up an integrated, multi-disciplinary committee to investigate these issues.

A few months after I was in Sweden, the 65th General Assembly Session of Interpol was held in Antalya, Turkey. The session resulted in a number of resolutions: countries should enact legislation (if they had not done so) to make the production, distribution, importation, or possession of child pornography criminal offences; they should make assistance and incitement punishable in the context of such offences; they should consider enacting legislation to allow the seizure of assets derived from such offences; and they should improve international co-operation among police to combat offences against children.

In March 1997, I attended the International Conference on Crimes Committed Against Children in Buenos Aires, Argentina. Once again, I did a presentation on Project Guardian and took part in a workshop about recommendations. On my return to Canada, I prepared a report

for the same threesome as before—Lloyd Axworthy, Allan Rock, and
Herb Gray. I told them about the work of such police units as the
Metropolitan Police Organized Crime Group in England, the
Paedophilia Unit of New Scotland Yard, the Child Exploitation Squad in
Australia, the Paedophile Intelligence Unit for the United Kingdom, and
United States Customs. I again urged these federal government officials
to consider the need for a National Strategy on the Safety of Children.
Again, Herb Gray was the only one who responded to me.

At the time, Canada's police community was trying to make government authorities wake up to the severity of this issue. In the summer of
1997, the Canadian Association of Chiefs of Police met in Fredericton,
New Brunswick, and we agreed that the Internet was proving to be a
nightmare because of the opportunities it offered criminals. At that
meeting, the chiefs called for a national sex registry that would include
the names of anyone in the country who had been convicted of a sex
crime and also of anyone who had been a suspect or who had been par-
doned or discharged of such a crime.

Later that year, a conference was held at the Ontario Police College in
Aylmer, Ontario, that resulted in the Aylmer Declaration. It recognized
that children in Canada were not safe and explained that they weren't safe
because the country wasn't doing enough to protect them. In the United
Kingdom, pedophiles were being tracked by satellite tags, but that sort of
thing would have been considered a major "rights" issue in Canada.

Some companies, such as Microsoft Corporation, which has been the
private sector's greatest friend in the fight against child pornography,
have done yeoman's work. Microsoft even closed all its chat rooms in
order to help curb the pedophile menace.

What should be done at the national level? Plenty. Here are a few recommendations:

1. Enact specific Criminal Code legislation to eliminate the defence of
    "artistic merit." There is no legitimate reason for anyone to possess
    this kind of material.

2. Make it illegal to facilitate the distribution of child pornography, and this would apply to any individual or organization, including Internet Service Providers and credit card companies.
3. Take DNA samples of *anyone* who is charged with a criminal offence, not only those who are convicted of child pornography charges.
4. Force accused persons to reveal the keys to their encrypted computer files seized during child pornography investigations. The United Kingdom is already doing this, but not Canada.
5. Allow investigators to view a *sampling* of child pornography materials seized as evidence. What happens now is that hundreds of thousands of pictures and movie frames must often be viewed by investigators, which obviously takes a lot of time.
6. Require Internet Service Providers to maintain client information records and logs for a minimum of two years, if not longer. This is standard procedure in most countries, but still is not law in Canada.
7. Raise the age of consent from fourteen to sixteen. Recently, this legislation was introduced in Canada, but for me it's a no-brainer. It should have been done a long time ago.

Interpol is based in Lyon, France, and I have attended a number of meetings there to give talks and develop strategies about child pornography. At one meeting, I said I was embarrassed and ashamed of Canada's criminal justice system because it had put the rights of pedophiles ahead of the rights of children. I said that pedophiles had become the poster boys of the usual network of civil libertarians. I expressed distress with a justice system that provided what I considered to be obscene protection to pedophiles to the detriment of their intended victims.

In 2006, a highly organized child porn ring involving people who swapped pictures and live video of children being sexually abused and raped was busted. Two of the administrators who helped run the Internet child porn trading post were based in Canada—in Edmonton, Alberta, and Longueuil, Quebec. Toronto's Child Exploitation Unit played a crucial role in cracking that case. It all started when a woman in Edmonton overheard a conversation between two children at a sporting event. One of the children talked about being abused by an adult. The Edmonton police got involved, arrested the offender, and found out he was part of an Internet chat room. The Edmonton police called the Toronto unit, who then infiltrated the group in an undercover capacity. While this man was in jail, police took over his account and pretended to be him online and managed to trace everyone in the chat room. The operation turned out to be worldwide. It involved brutal images of child abuse and shared live-streaming video of molestation and rape. Some of the victims were even children of the accused.

On March 15, 2006, U.S. Attorney General Alberto R. Gonzales gave a press conference in Chicago announcing that criminal charges had been laid in the case. Tony Warr, a senior officer with the Toronto Police Service, and two members of the Toronto unit were on hand in recognition of the role that unit had played. In fact, the Toronto unit coordinated the investigation. This is what Attorney-General Gonzales said:

Over the past few months, undercover investigators infiltrated a worldwide Internet chat room that was being used to facilitate the trading of graphic images of child pornography—including live streaming video of adults sexually molesting children and infants. As of today, twenty-seven individuals in the United States, Canada, Australia, and England have been charged in connection to activity in a chat room called 'Kiddypics & Kiddyvids.' The charges brought by the United States occurred in nine different U.S. Attorney districts and include possession, receipt, distribution, and manufacture of child pornography, as well as conspiracy and other offenses. As a result of this operation, seven victims of molestation have been identified.

The youngest was less than eighteen months old.

The chat room in this case was monitored by "hosts" who established rules for participation, some of which it appears were designed to hide their illegal activities from law enforcement.

Some participants of the chat room used minors to produce images of child pornography and then made those images—including live shows—available to other members through the Internet. For example, according to the indictment announced today in Chicago, in the last year a defendant who used the screen name "Acidburn" allegedly produced live streaming video of himself sexually molesting an infant.

The behavior in these chat rooms—and the images many of these defendants sent around the world through "peer-to-peer" file sharing programs and private instant messaging services—are the worst imaginable forms of child pornography.

Eventually, more than forty people around the world were arrested in that ring and ten of them were Canadians. Carl Treleaven, a forty-nine-year-old man in Edmonton, was sending out images all over the world from his twenty-gigabyte collection. Treleaven, who had earlier convictions going back to the '70s for indecent assault and gross indecency against girls, pleaded guilty to distributing child pornography and was sentenced to three and a half years. Believe it or not, I believe that was the longest jail term ever imposed for such an offence in Canadian history. And let's not forget that three and a half years can mean parole after fourteen months, and day parole after only seven months.

While that was a major case and a great success for all the investigators involved, the fact remains that organized networks of pedophiles thrive in every corner of the globe. These people occupy respected positions in society. They are teachers, professors, clergy, doctors, lawyers, journalists, and politicians. They are also in law enforcement. They use their positions to manipulate public opinion.

Two things remain crystal clear to me when it comes to the issue of child pornography. The first is that the child is always the innocent victim. The second is that those who produce, distribute, or consume the product are exploitive mercenaries and should be recognized for what they are. Brutal criminals.

· 10 ·

The Trial of the Munros

THE TRIAL OF CRAIG AND JAMIE MUNRO BEGAN ON JANUARY 14, 1981. During the ten months since their arrest they had been incarcerated at the Toronto East Detention Centre. For any court appearance, they were always under heavy police guard since they were considered high-risk. Which they were. As the two investigators on the case, Dave Boothby and I interviewed more than a hundred people, and the list included police officers, forensic experts, witnesses, and patrons who had been at George's on the night of Michael Sweet's murder. Our preparation for the trial was a huge undertaking. We had to prepare a report for each and every one of those witnesses, so the workload was steep, but that was how we helped build the case for the prosecution. Piece by piece. During those ten months, Dave and I were also involved in other murders because crime never stops in a big city.

We fully expected the Munros to plead not guilty and they did, and while we were confident we had a strong case, no one was naive enough to think that convictions for first-degree murder for these two brothers was a sure thing. Both of the defence counsel were highly esteemed attorneys whom we knew well from other cases. John Rosen was defending Craig Munro, and Earl Levy was defending Jamie Munro. They were both very good lawyers. These guys were thorough, demanding, and excellent at cross-examinations. The Crown attorney, Robert McGee, was also a top lawyer and an absolute first-rate prosecutor. He would lead the prosecution team. The judge was Mr. Justice Frank Callaghan, who had a reputation as a no-nonsense kind of guy, but at the same time he was known as a judge with a big heart. He really knew his business and could cut through any legal argument. He was a big imposing man and in his robes looked every bit the authority that he was.

Early in the proceedings, Craig Munro complained he couldn't hear what was being said, so the judge arranged for him to get a hearing aid. An appointment was hastily made with the Toronto General Hospital hearing clinic and Craig was moved to the front of the queue—even ahead of people who had been waiting months for their examinations. He was given a test unit on loan that was supposed to be returned after the trial. But the hospital never got it back.

In his opening address to the jury of nine women and three men, McGee, the chief prosecutor, spoke for almost an hour as he set the scene for what had happened at George's Bourbon Street in the early-morning hours of March 14, 1980. He explained how Craig and Jamie Munro had attempted to rob the tavern and had taken several hostages before the confrontation in the basement with police officers Doug Ramsey and Michael Sweet. He said that as many as nine shots were heard in the exchange of gunfire and that Ramsey heard his fallen partner say to the Munros, "Okay, okay, stop, I'm dead. Don't shoot anymore. You've got me."

McGee also told the court that, while negotiations were going on for more than an hour, Jamie was allowed to leave Sweet's side on two occasions—the first time to fetch a few bottles of liquor from the bar, and the second time to be escorted outside onto the street where he could retrieve a package of heroin from his car. And all the while his brother Craig had his gun on Sweet, who was slowly bleeding to death. McGee told the jury that police agreed to these requests after Craig had threatened to finish off Sweet with the words: "If my brother isn't back in two minutes, I'll kill him."

McGee then described how police had stormed the passageway after deciding "enough was enough." Those were the words he used. Then, as the wounded Craig was being taken to hospital, McGee said Craig had told Constable Barry Doyle that he would have killed more police officers if he'd been able to get his hands on the sawed-off .12 shotgun. According to McGee, Craig had told Doyle, "If I had got to that fucking shotgun, I would have got a few more of the bastards."

The next day McGee began calling his witnesses and one of them was Patricia Morgan, a bartender and waitress at George's. She testified that Jamie Munro had been at the tavern on the day before the attempted robbery. That was March 13. She said a man had approached her at 2:15 that afternoon claiming to have lost his wallet containing $200 in cash as well as credit cards. She said he claimed to have left his wallet on a table during lunch and now he wanted to know the manager's name and phone number. She also said that the man was verbally abusive to her, swearing and yelling at her when she refused to give him the manager's home telephone number. She said she recognized Jamie's photo in a newspaper the day after the shooting. Three other witnesses corroborated her story.

Another witness was Officer Nelson Lee Train, who told the court how his attempts to get the two suspects to surrender were met by a bullet that deflected off his wristwatch. Train said he told the suspects, "It's the police. Put down your weapons. We don't want anyone hurt." He said the next thing he knew, a bullet was fired through the back door of the building. Train said he heard a voice from inside say they had a shotgun and two handguns and that they wanted a bottle of whisky. It wasn't long after that, he said, when he heard a series of rapid shots followed by a single shot from inside. Then he said the voice gave him a warning. Train told the court, "If I entered the building they would blow Mike's head off and shoot themselves." Train said that when he finally did enter the building after Eddy Adamson, Gary Leuin, and Barry Doyle went in, he helped pick up the wounded Jamie Munro off the kitchen floor and drove him to the hospital in a cruiser.

Aside from the Munro brothers, the person closest to Sweet when he was shot was Officer Doug Ramsey. When Ramsey took the stand he faced three hours of testimony, including relentless grilling by defence counsel John Rosen. But first it was the turn of prosecutor McGee to question him. McGee asked Ramsey to relate exactly what had happened that night at George's. This is what Ramsey said:

> We arrived at the scene at the front of the building in a police car. As we arrived some civilians came out the front door. I spoke to one of them, as a result of which I got into the car and relayed information to the dispatcher. Constable Sweet entered the restaurant. I subsequently entered the restaurant. I stood in the foyer at the door to the reception area and had a clear view of the restaurant. I saw Sweet behind the bar, between Table No. 2 and the bar. [John] Latto and [David] Wieland were by the swinging doors, one on either side. I could hear Latto shouting.
>
> I advised Sweet I was going to check the basement. I went down first. He followed. He had a cap on. He was wearing his uniform. My cap was off. We were both wearing nylon pea jackets. We both had our guns out. We checked the rooms as we went down the passageway.

Ramsey told the court how he and Sweet searched the basement of the building and heard loud shouting. He said someone came bolting down the nearby stairs, and that he and Sweet realized it was almost impossible to escape unseen because of the light from a room beside them. So, Ramsey said, they stepped back into the shadows behind a refrigerator and crouched down low as a figure hurried past them. That was Jamie Munro. Ramsey said he then heard another person coming towards him, so he moved to get a better view, and that was when he saw Craig Munro crouching and moving cautiously until he disappeared from view behind a pillar. A short time later, Ramsey said he heard shots ring out. And that was how he set the scene just prior to the gunshots:

I was looking east between the pillars. The first footsteps moved quickly, proceeded down the hallway past the table and opening to the southerly entrance to the food preparation area. I then lost sight of him. It was a man in a crouched position, not too low, with a shotgun leveled at his hips, moving in a southerly direction. Sweet and I had been in our positions three to four seconds until he went by. I had a side view of his head. He glanced from left to right. I saw his face. There was no mask on. He was not a clear view but I can identify him.

Ramsey stopped and pointed to Jamie Munro. He continued.

He passed out of view down the passageway. I heard a second set of steps. They were a slower pace. I moved further north so I could see over Tables 3 and 2. At this point I was directly behind Table No. 5. I could see the second party from the shoulders up, proceeding at a much slower pace in a crouched position. The second suspect had no mask. I couldn't see his hand.

Ramsey said he was partly blinded by the bright flashes from the guns and couldn't tell who was talking but that he distinctly heard three different voices. One of them he described as "weakened," another as a "strong soft voice," and the third as "rough, quite blunt."

When Dave Boothby took the stand he recounted the conversation that had taken place between him and Craig Munro in the hospital. I was there with him at the hospital when this conversation occurred. Dave said he told Craig he was under arrest for the murder of Michael Sweet and Craig told him, "We had to do it. It was either him or us."

The day after Dave's appearance came key medical testimony from Dr. Rilva Ilyes, a chest specialist who had examined Sweet at Toronto General Hospital an hour and a half after the shooting. It was Dr. Ilyes who had pronounced Sweet dead at 6:08 a.m. on March 14. Dr. Ilyes said that when Sweet was brought to the hospital he had no blood pressure and his heart was in fibrillation, which meant it was quivering. He said Sweet was in a state of shock from loss of blood, and that after attempts to stimulate his heart, it failed. He said the bullet track he discovered in Sweet's body had entered the right side of the chest, passed through the right lung, and lodged in the vertebral column. He said he put his finger on it and that this bullet had caused the lung to collapse, resulting in internal bleeding.

When Dr. Ilyes was finished, it was my turn to take the stand. I've been in court so many times to give evidence that I've lost count, but I have always made it a point to act professionally and to be truthful and up front. Some days defence counsel can give you a hard time on the stand and other days they don't. But the way I looked at it, they might be defence counsel today but a judge tomorrow, so I wasn't about to play games with any of them. At this trial, however, I wasn't there so much to be cross-examined as to enter Crown exhibits, and there were hundreds of them. So all in all the experience was pretty straightforward for me. Those exhibits included bullet fragments, two blue masks, and the clothing found at the scene. It took an entire day just to introduce those exhibits. Much of the next day of the trial was devoted to examining all those bullet casings and fragments that I had entered as Crown exhibits.

Then, Ontario forensic pathologist Dr. John Hillsdon-Smith, the man who had performed the autopsy on Sweet, took the stand. He said the cause of death was internal hemorrhage or internal bleeding due to a gunshot wound to the right lung. Dr. Hillsdon-Smith said that at the autopsy he found only one and a half litres of blood in Sweet's chest cavity. There was no other blood in the body, he said. He added that a normal body for a man Sweet's size would contain six to seven litres of blood.

Finally the Munro brothers themselves testified. They took the stand on February 2, and each of them related how they had planned to rob George's so they could net enough money for Craig to pay his $1,000 fine from an earlier conviction and stay out of jail. Jamie said they had been led to believe that a "gang of crooks" playing cards after the club's closing hours were the intended victims of the robbery. He said he himself had been a reluctant participant who had been recruited by his older brother at the last minute because he could get a car and because another man who was supposed to take part had backed out.

Then Craig took the stand. He was dressed in a suit and looked immaculate. Like a businessman. But his eyes were still cold and lifeless.

"It was supposed to be simple," he said. "It was supposed to be nice and easy."

When questioned by his lawyer, John Rosen, Craig told the court how he had been convicted of possession of a dangerous weapon and sentenced to pay a fine of $1,000 or spend six months in jail. He said at the time of this conviction he had been under mandatory supervision for a series of offences dating back to 1978.

Craig said he had approached friends and family to get money for the fine, but no one would give it to him. He also said he had tried to sell some personal jewellery, that it had great sentimental value to him, and that he was "pretty insulted at the prices that were being offered." Then he said he had approached "some criminal types" about having them "front me $1,500 for a card game" and these people also refused. After that he said he had planned a robbery of a heroin dealer, but that fell through and then someone suggested robbing George's.

Jamie took the stand again and told the court that in the standoff with police he and his brother had wanted to surrender but were afraid the police would shoot them when they came out of the building. He added that if they didn't get shot right then, they feared being tortured at police headquarters later.

The next day saw more testimony from Craig and, from my vantage point, it was an Academy Award performance. He appeared so cold and matter-of-fact, it was almost as if he wasn't even a protagonist in the whole thing. But as things turned out, he didn't convince any members of the jury. He said he didn't know whom he was shooting at when he fired his handgun. He spoke only about "a light that was firing at me." He said he was feeling his way along a dark hallway in the basement when "there was a fast shot and a flare and I felt a sting on my back." Then he said he turned and "just impulsively and instantaneously started shooting towards the flares."

Craig said he lost his balance and fell to the floor after firing his gun and emptying it of bullets. He added that he usually wore glasses to correct impaired vision in his right eye, but that on the night of the attempted robbery at George's, he wasn't wearing his glasses because he had a mask on his face. Then, when he recounted his version of what had happened that night, he mentioned the injuries he had suffered on the tip of his nose, his ears, and the palm of his left hand. He said all these injuries lined up to show that he was, in fact, in a state of surrender when he was shot. He even held up his hands as if he was surrendering. So, in his version of events, he got shot in cold blood. But he did admit that he was the one who had shot Sweet.

I was the one who shot the police officer. I told my brother I would ultimately . . . I'll take the rap. I'll go up and tell anyone what had happened, that I had shot someone who I'd been told was a police officer. I had no intention of shooting anybody at that time or any time.

But Prosecutor McGee wasn't about to let him off so easily.

"You knew it was a policeman you were firing at, didn't you?" McGee asked him.

"I wasn't firing at the policeman. I was firing at the bottom of the door and I was on the step."

"Well, who did you think was out there? Mr. Kita, one of the patrons?"

"All I knew was there was police officers out there, but I fired towards the bottom of the door, not to hurt anybody."

McGee asked Craig if he knew that his brother Jamie was in the basement. Craig said yes.

"Well, how was it that you didn't think maybe this person you were shooting at was your brother?" asked McGee.

"I don't think my brother would shoot at me," Craig replied.

"Well, all the witnesses that gave evidence here indicated that the lighter calibre gun fired first. Can you explain that?"

"I can't explain how any of the witnesses would pertain to what sound was first because I couldn't even distinguish the sound there. It was so fast and so loud. I couldn't even distinguish them myself and I was right there."

"Well, you've heard the evidence."

"Oh certainly I heard it."

"And some of them said they heard five light calibre shots and one heavy calibre shot, in that order."

"Well . . ."

"And some of them said they heard three light calibre shots and one heavy calibre shot, and then three more light calibre shots, in that order. Is that right? Do you remember that evidence?"

"Yes. A lot of the witnesses seemed to be very confused about the order, and how many shots were fired. You're right."

"But there's not much doubt about their evidence, is there, that the first shots that were fired in that basement were the light calibre gun, which would be yours?"

Throughout the trial McGee didn't pull any punches. We had known him as a sharp and very intelligent prosecutor and he didn't disappoint in this case. He was well prepared. He had done a lot of homework and had many consultations with us. He had looked at every exhibit and had examined every last detail. He is definitely one of the best Crown attorneys I have ever known, and nowadays he is in private practice. McGee was going for the maximum conviction—murder in the first degree—for both Craig and Jamie. However, as I said before, you can never be sure what will happen inside a courtroom.

During his closing remarks, McGee told the jurors to imagine themselves at home watching television or reading the newspaper, and then he said, "You may have seen some senseless act of cruelty or violence . . . you may on occasion say, 'What are they doing about it?' This time, in this case, You are the 'they'."

That prompted a sharp outburst from Jamie's lawyer, Earl Levy. "Your Lordship, I object," Levy said. "I find this very inflammatory. It's inflammatory and I know what's coming."

But Judge Callaghan told him to sit down and he let McGee continue.

"You may use that phrase 'What are they doing about it?'" McGee went on. "Well tomorrow, after his Lordship's charge [to the jury], confining yourself strictly to evidence in this case and only to that evidence, you are 'they'. And the only proper verdict, I submit, on the evidence in this case, is guilty as charged."

In his final address for the defence, Jamie's lawyer urged the jury to acquit his client of first-degree murder. He said Jamie was a victim of misguided loyalty to his older brother and for that he had been seriously wounded and had already spent a year in jail.

As for Craig, his lawyer, John Rosen, said the jury's only realistic verdict was to return a conviction of second-degree murder unless the Crown could prove that at the very moment Craig fired his pistol in the basement of George's, he knew he was shooting at a police officer.

"If you have a reasonable doubt on that issue, you can go no higher than second-degree murder," Rosen said. He said Craig was trapped in the basement and scared and didn't know a police officer was there. Then, when he heard a noise "in his blind hysteria and stupidity, he continued to pull the trigger of his gun."

But McGee quickly countered that argument. He asked who Craig thought he was shooting at.

"Well, who did he think it was," McGee said to the court. "If it was as dark as he said it was, how did he know he wasn't shooting his brother?"

Finally, Judge Callaghan began his charge to the jury and it would last five and a half hours and stretch over two days. After thanking the members of the jury, he went out of his way to stress the importance of the task at hand. This is what he told the jury:

This has been a most difficult trial. Any homicide involving the death of a member of the community is extremely difficult and when the victim is a police officer the difficulty is compounded. You have been most patient and attentive in giving your undivided attention to the evidence over the past sixteen days. I know you have all suffered personal inconvenience as a result of that, to come here and serve as jurors. However, I am equally sure that you recognize that you are engaged in the most important duty a Canadian citizen can be called upon to perform.

You occupy a position in the administration of justice which is the equivalent to my job as a judge on the Bench. You stand as judges between the public and those who commit crimes of violence and you are, in your present position, legal guardians of the rights of the community in which you live and of which you are members. The public must be kept in safety and security. Life and liberty must be protected and offenders must be fairly but strictly dealt with. You are especially the legal guardians of the rights of the accused persons. You have a duty to see that the accused are properly charged and to ensure that an innocent man should never be found guilty in this country of any crime he has not committed.

As the evidence went in, I am sure your minds were 'boggled'. Neither you nor I have an opportunity of knowing what evidence we are going to see or hear. I think I should tell you, as I'm sure you realize, that there is no scientific method or legal device for precisely reconstructing past events. There is and only has been, in this community of ours, the fair and impartial human judgment of the men and women of a jury in evaluating the evidence presented to the Court and determining issues of guilt or innocence.

At the end of the testimony which you have heard you have the same task as every other jury has had in this community for century upon century, and that task is to determine as best you

can, in accordance with the law as explained by me, what the facts
are, and to render the verdict prescribed by law for those facts. In
doing that you bear the solemn responsibility of assuring that justice, which is the great goal of our legal system, is done for every
person in every case.

It is true to say, as one of the counsel said today, that our
whole society rests on the foundation of justice under law. There
is no higher duty or finer public service any citizen can perform
than to participate, as you are now, in that system as a member of
a trial jury.

Judge Callaghan then instructed the jury to erase from their minds
"all prejudice or partiality." He acknowledged that the trial had received
widespread publicity and said the jurors must "put from your minds anything that you may have heard or read about the matter" and consider
only what transpired in the courtroom. "Your job is to try the accused on
the indictment before you," he said. "You are not here to remedy all the
ills in society or take into consideration any other offences that may have
happened in the past."

I was very impressed with Judge Callaghan's work in that trial, especially his charge to the jury. He had to instruct lay people on how to
interpret, how to assess, how to evaluate, and then how to come to decisions. It was not an easy task, but I thought he did an excellent job.

The court was adjourned at 4:39 p.m. on February 5, 1981. It recon-
vened at 9:44 the next morning. A Friday. Judge Callaghan continued
with his charge to the jury and wanted to make sure they understood the
nature of the charges against the Munros and the differences between
first-degree murder and second-degree murder, and between those two
charges and the lesser charge of manslaughter. But when he mentioned
the word "kidnapping," Craig Munro interrupted him.

"Excuse me," Craig said.

Craig's attorney, John Rosen, told him he wasn't allowed to interrupt.

"I'd like to say something," Craig continued.

"You just sit down or you'll be put out of the courtroom," Callaghan told him.

"I'd like to know why you said 'kidnapping'," Craig went on. "I think you meant something else. Well, I never heard a kidnapping charge mentioned at any time in this trial so maybe Your Honour made a mistake."

If someone had gone to central casting to recruit a judge for this trial, it is unlikely a better fit could have been found than Frank Callaghan. He was widely respected and looked every bit the seasoned, firm but fair judge he was supposed to be. But he was also a man who didn't put up with any shenanigans in his court. And he didn't. He instructed the jury to leave the courtroom and when they were gone he wasted no time with Craig.

"Mr. Munro, stand up. I'm going to read you Section 577 of the Criminal Code and you'd better listen very carefully. 'The court may cause the accused to be removed and to be kept out of court where he misconducts himself by interrupting the proceedings so that to continue the proceedings in his absence would not be feasible.' That section entitles me to put you out of this courtroom if you interrupt my charge to the jury and if you say another word in the course of my charge to the jury you will be put out of this courtroom."

"Well, can I ask Your Honour a question?" said Craig.

"No, you can't. You can't."

"I can't ask you a question?"

"You can't at this time."

"Well then, I'll get my lawyer . . ."

"You can have your counsel ask questions, but not now. I'm telling you, you just be quiet through the course of my charge or you will be put out of this courtroom."

"Well, I just got confused, Your Honour, when you said 'kidnapping' because I never heard it mentioned at any time."

"Well, it happens to be one of the underlying offences which you're charged with. Bring the jury back in. You open your mouth once more and you're out."

"You don't have to talk to me as if I were a five-year-old kid," Craig said. "I think I've got your words clear."

The jury came back and Judge Callaghan continued with his charge. He went into a detailed discussion of homicide and culpability. He reminded the jury of much of the testimony they had heard from key witnesses and quoted Section 214(4) of the Criminal Code: *Murder is first degree when the victim is a police officer acting in the course of his duties.* He continued:

> The real issue upon which the defence of Craig Munro is based is whether or not he knew that Michael Sweet was a police officer. This is one of the key issues in the case. You will have to decide, as a question of fact, whether or not Munro, in fact, knew when he shot Michael Sweet that he was a police officer. If he didn't know it, or if you have a reasonable doubt after considering all the evidence on the issue, then that doubt, of course, must be resolved in favour of an accused person and the Crown will have failed to prove murder in the first degree. If, on the other hand, you are satisfied beyond a reasonable doubt that he knew Michael Sweet was a police officer when he shot him, and you are equally satisfied that the other elements I've mentioned have been proved beyond a reasonable doubt, then you are obliged to bring in a verdict of guilty of murder in the first degree.

Judge Callaghan then spoke about Jamie Munro.

> As to James Munro, if you have a reasonable doubt that he knew or ought to have known that Craig Munro would use the weapon on a police officer, your proper verdict is guilty of second-degree murder. If you have a reasonable doubt that James Munro knew or ought to have known that Craig Munro would use the weapon if needed, he has no criminal intent and your proper verdict is not guilty.

When he was finally finished, the jury left the courtroom to begin deliberations, which lasted for more than six hours. But it wasn't a continuous six hours. Several times they came back to ask questions. Once they were back to receive instructions on the charge from the judge and another time to ask about the difference between being a party to a crime and "aiding and abetting."

Judge Callaghan told the jury it had to consider two main issues. The first was whether Craig Munro knew he was shooting a policeman and whether Jamie Munro knew or ought to have known that his brother would use his gun during the attempted robbery. The second issue was whether the brothers' forcible confinement of Sweet caused his death. Judge Callaghan also told the jurors to consider whether the Crown had proved beyond a reasonable doubt that Jamie had been a principal in the shooting and not just a party to it. He explained that only the actual shooter could face first-degree murder, which was Craig, and that Jamie, not being the actual shooter, could only face second-degree murder.

At 9 a.m. on February 7, 1981—it was a Saturday—the jury went out for the final time to deliberate. They returned at 11:45 a.m. to announce their verdicts and the courtroom was teeming with anxiety. There is always anxiety at a time like that because you never know for sure what a jury will do. Still, I have always had a tremendous amount of faith in the jury system. That day there were a lot of police officers besides Dave Boothby and me in the courtroom, and when the jurors emerged all of us tried to get a reading of their faces. You always want to try to figure out the verdict before it's announced. But again, you can never be sure.

I have always found the moment before a verdict is announced to be a difficult time. The wait before the jury comes back is excruciating. As an investigator, your work has been done, but your mind starts racing about other things you should have done or could have done. It just keeps replaying over and over. Then, when the jury arrives, you get a bit of a rush.

After this long and worn-out trial that had dragged on for a month, the two Munro brothers were told to stand in the prisoner's dock. Their feet were shackled wide apart.

"Would the forelady please stand," the registrar said and the woman speaking for the jury rose. "Have the members of the jury agreed upon their verdict?"

"Yes, we have."

"What is your verdict for James Scott Munro?"

You could have heard a pin drop.

"The members of the jury find James Scott Munro guilty of murder in the second degree."

I wasn't surprised. I was relieved.

"Craig Alfred Munro?"

"We find Craig Munro guilty as charged."

That meant Craig was found guilty of first-degree murder, and I felt very gratified about that. For me, the only thing missing was the order to have this guy executed.

Earl Levy, counsel for Jamie, immediately asked that the jury members be polled. All jurors indicated that they agreed with the verdicts as stated. Then Judge Callaghan spoke.

Members of the jury, you have convicted James Scott Munro of second-degree murder. Under the Criminal Code there is a mandatory term of ten years that must be served by a person who has been convicted of second-degree murder before he can be paroled. On the recommendation of the jury who try the case this period can be increased by me up to twenty-five years. You have heard the circumstances surrounding the killing and I must ask you to retire at this time and consider if you wish to recommend that the period be increased beyond ten years.

The jury left the courtroom and then Judge Callaghan spoke to Craig, who had just been convicted of first-degree murder.

"Mr. Craig Munro, you have heard the verdict of the jury. Do you have anything to say before I pass the sentence that the law requires me to pass?"

"Yes I do. I'd like to say that it was a foolish and desperate robbery. I was personally under a lot of pressure at the time and the case wasn't exactly as the Crown put it forth. I don't believe it was a fair trial. I believe that both the verdict on myself and my brother is not a fair verdict because I know myself personally in my own heart of what actually did happen. And I'm sorry the whole situation happened for all concerned, with regards to the public and the members of all families concerned, around the constable and around my brother and myself. And I will state for the record at this time that there will definitely be an appeal launched. And I hope that, morally, this next trial that will come up will not be a political trial but will be a fair and just trial under the moral rights of God, not man."

"All right. Craig Alfred Munro, the law requires me to pronounce a sentence of life imprisonment on you, without eligibility of parole, for twenty-five years. Remove Mr. Munro, please."

That sentence meant Craig wouldn't be eligible for unescorted temporary absences and day parole until March 16, 2002, and wouldn't be eligible for full parole until March 16, 2005. There was absolutely no latitude as far as Craig was concerned. But Jamie was another matter. As things turned out, the jury would recommend that Jamie be considered for parole *before* the ten-year minimum sentence was served. But Judge Callaghan would explain to them that their only choice was to recommend a confinement period ranging from ten to twenty-five years or to make no recommendations at all. Still, the jury recommended mercy for Jamie.

When the verdicts were read, Jamie's twenty-year-old wife, Rose, started weeping. Connie DiChristofero, who was twenty-one, was Craig's common-law wife and the mother of the couple's seven-month-old son; the boy had been born while Craig was in the detention centre awaiting trial. At first, she was without expression, but then she too burst into tears. Later, she told a reporter that it wasn't a fair trial and that the verdicts were what they were only because Sweet had been a police officer.

The day after the verdicts came down, the headline "25 YEARS MINIMUM FOR MURDER OF POLICEMAN" blared across the front page of the *Toronto Sun*. There was a photo of Craig Munro in handcuffs with his head bowed and another one of Jamie sitting in the back of a cruiser, a numb expression on his face. The *Toronto Star* devoted a full page to the trial with the headline "Killer apologizes to constable's family." It had a photo of me escorting Craig Munro from the courthouse.

The trial over, there was an element of closure for me on this case. The bad guys got convicted. Justice was done. In a way, it was gratifying but, at the same time, there was no closure for Michael Sweet's family.

It was another five days before Jamie was sentenced. Chief prosecutor Bob McGee was pressing for Jamie to serve at least fifteen years before being eligible for parole, and in his submissions to Judge Callaghan he stressed that Jamie had worked hand in glove with his brother and that nowhere in any of the evidence presented during the trial was there an indication that Jamie had tried to talk Craig out of doing the robbery. McGee also pointed out Jamie's criminal record prior to the Michael Sweet killing, and his numerous convictions since marrying his wife.

On Thursday, February 12, 1981, Judge Callaghan dealt with Jamie.

"James Munro, do you have anything to say before I pass sentence on you?"

"Yes, my Lord. When people used to ask me, 'How do you feel about this incident?' I used to just lower my eyes and drop my head in shame because I felt there were no words that could express how very sorry I felt for the officer and his family, and also mine. I wish there was some way I could undo this whole thing but unfortunately I can't. Thank you, my Lord."

If he seemed contrite with this little speech of his, it sure didn't work for me. As far as I was concerned, it was crocodile tears.

At that point Judge Callaghan thanked counsel for both the defence and prosecution. He also went out of his way to mention the "very professional, careful, thorough and fair investigation of this incident by Staff Sergeant Boothby and Sergeant Fantino," which he said was in accordance with the highest traditions of the Metropolitan Toronto Police Force. Dave and I appreciated that. It was a nice gesture that the judge recognized all the hard work we had put in on this case.

Then he addressed Jamie.

As to your character, Mr. Munro, you are only twenty-two years of age. Your criminal record indicates to me that you do not really qualify right now as a person of good character. While I would hesitate to say that you are embarked on a life of confirmed criminality, your record and the nature thereof would indicate that you are disposed to criminal conduct. There are convictions for violence, convictions for use of weapons, all incurred at a young age and some incurred while you were married.

Callaghan said he had to take the jury's request for mercy into consideration but added that if they had not made such a comment the sentence he was about to impose would have been much more severe.

Suffice it to say that after listening to that evidence, I can only conclude that this was one of the most callous killings of a police officer this municipality has seen for many years. To have let Michael Sweet lie on the floor of that tavern and bleed to death while you and your brother bartered for time, liquor, and drugs was a gross criminal act and one that I cannot overlook in determining the appropriate sentence.

Judge Callaghan told Jamie he would be imprisoned for life without eligibility for parole until he had served twelve years.

Appeals were filed for both Craig and Jamie, and in 1983 they were rejected. But for all intents and purposes, the trial of the Munro brothers was over on Saturday, February 8, 1981, when their guilt was there for a whole city—and a whole country—to see. That was the day Dave and I escorted the Munro brothers out of the courtroom and on to jail. It was the finale to a long, arduous, difficult, and traumatic case. It was gratifying to me and to Dave and to Eddy Adamson and to all of us who had worked so hard on this case.

But if it was a victory, it wasn't a pleasant one. To this day I believe justice would have been better served if we'd had capital punishment. Craig Munro, if not his brother as well, deserved it. You are talking about two guys who planned to rob a tavern using guns. They broke into the place, took hostages, threatened to kill them, and then shot a police officer and allowed him to bleed to death as he begged for his life. Then, while he was dying, they negotiated to get some liquor and heroin. I firmly believe both of them deserved the death penalty. But at least they were convicted. Now, I've never said this before, but if the Munro brothers had been acquitted of Michael Sweet's murder that day, I would have turned in my badge. No question about it. That would have been it for me. If those two had gotten off, my faith in the justice system would have been totally shattered.

I would eventually learn that truth in sentencing was a long way from what actually happens. And little did I know that my battle with the Munros wasn't finished. In fact, it was just beginning.

· 11 ·

Walking in the Shoes
of the Dead

WHEN I JOINED THE TORONTO POLICE DEPARTMENT IN 1969, my goal was to be a detective like my mentor, Frank Barbetta. In 1975, I became a detective and was transferred to 12 Division. I was there only six months when I was asked to join the homicide squad. Prior to that time I had assisted homicide investigators as an interpreter, but joining this squad was something else. They were all senior officers. The top investigators on the police force. The elite. We called them "the tea cup squad" because they had this aura of prestige about them.

Homicide investigators work in pairs and I was partnered with Wally Tyrrell, a man with a great reputation in the department. We were on call around the clock and in those days there were no pagers, cell phones, BlackBerrys, or computers. In the first couple of months, we didn't have a murder case of our own and I was getting itchy. Then one night Wally called me and said, "We have a murder."

It was a domestic killing. A young woman had been stabbed by her husband, who was later apprehended and arrested, and Wally and I had to go to the house. The crime scene was under guard and left intact. Everything as it was. That was when the reality of the job set in for me because now we weren't only reading material about a murder case; this

166

was *our* case. The woman was obviously dead and there was a lot of blood. What hits you right away is that you're dealing with the violent death of a human being, who not long ago was living and breathing.

Wally knew he was dealing with a novice and walked me through things, taking time to explain investigative techniques and the forensic sciences. He showed me what must be done to present the best possible case for court. Investigating murders is demanding work and draws on your emotions, and Wally, a seasoned homicide detective, understood that. But the thing that really struck me on this, my very first murder, was how everything seemed to move in slow motion. I thought we should be doing things much faster. I learned that the investigation is done this way because you only have one chance to do the job right. There are no reruns.

The autopsy and forensic examination was a traumatic experience. I found the matter-of-fact way the pathologist did his work strange because this was new to me and emotionally draining. But it was routine for him. He conducted a thorough examination of every inch of the external body, followed by every inch of the internal body. He removed and weighed all the organs, including the brain. I watched and listened to how his saw cut through the skull to expose the brain. It was like a dream to me. It just didn't seem real. The sights, the sounds, the smells were so different from anything I had ever experienced, and by that time I had seen a few things. But not like this. I can still remember the smell of the blood that had pooled in the chest cavity, a condition caused by internal bleeding from the stab wound. I could actually smell the blood. I remember his taking precise measurements and notes. Then photographs. He dissected and retrieved samples of organs and body fluids to be examined in more detail later in the laboratory at the Centre of Forensic Sciences. What I couldn't erase from my mind was that all this was a waste, a tragedy, and the only thing that remained of this woman was a decomposing corpse.

This was what a murder looked like.

I kept thinking throughout the whole ordeal—and the first time it was an ordeal—that it could have been me or a member of my family on that stainless-steel table. But in time you learn to rise above all that and just do the job.

Not anyone can be a homicide investigator. Forensics and autopsies aside, you need special skills because you are dealing with the most tragic outcome in society. There is no more tragic outcome than one human being killed by another. You need excellent investigative skills so as not to discount anything. You have to probe and pursue everything and always try to determine some kind of answer or explanation for what happened. You need acute powers of observation, but must also know what to look for and be able to distinguish what is relevant evidence from what isn't. I'm talking about hairs, fibres, blood stains, and even the composition of blood stains.

This is why knowledge of the sciences is important, because a lot of work is done in the laboratory. A homicide investigator must know how to identify any potential evidence that will be examined by forensic experts. The objective is to produce matches made with other evidence in order to substantiate a theory or relationship between a crime scene and suspect. The study of blood is vital. Years ago blood grouping was a fairly primitive affair based on the A-B-O system of blood identification. Now it's all about DNA testing, which is a powerful, scientific, investigative tool that can not only help to convict the guilty, but can also exonerate an otherwise innocent party who is a suspect. Similarly, an investigator needs to know about firearms in order to work with experts who analyze fired bullets and shell casings to trace them back to a particular gun.

Initially, everything at a murder scene is sheer chaos. Very often the scene shows evidence of violence. A lot of violence. Things are messy and disruptive and running a mile a minute and this is why the investigator tries to slow everything down. That means taking charge, delegating, identifying priorities, giving direction, and making sure everything gets recorded. Invariably, the suspects have left the scene or are in custody, but it's still important for the investigator to take control and slow things down, and that's how you manage.

Of course, a homicide investigator must know the judicial system inside out. This is crucial. And you carry around all these smarts as you work with a partner, which is why teams always involve two people who must be compatible with each other. There is no other way.

The first thing a homicide investigator must do is identify the deceased, and sometimes the only option is to have a family member come in. This is truly heartwrenching and requires a great deal of compassion. I have often helped with the identification of a murder victim and it's difficult because you can't just detach yourself from the human element. The undertaker will try to make the deceased as presentable as possible, but let's remember that a homicide can be a very violent death. The absolute worst thing of all is seeing the bodies of murdered children and that's even more difficult when you have children of your own. Seeing the remains of a brutalized child . . . the obvious signs of abuse . . . a body burnt with cigarettes . . . fractured bones showing how a little boy or little girl was beaten. It's all so traumatic, and one can only imagine what the parent is going through.

What can you say about the battered and bruised corpse of a child? People who do this are monsters and sometimes they are even the child's own parents. It makes me think of all the people who can't have children of their own, who would love to have a child, and who go to faraway countries to adopt one. And then you see something like this.

Before an identification, I always sat down with the people and tried to prepare them. You explain why the identification is necessary and important and try to give them courage. But at the same time, you agonize over it because it's hard to find the words. These people have lost a loved one. They are traumatized. They are crying. They never come alone, so you pick the strongest person to talk to. But many times people break down when called to do an identification and this is why we have gone from direct contact with the deceased to doing it on camera, which can help relieve some of that anxiety. This practice started during my time in homicide. Once, an entire family—the mother of the murder victim and other relatives—went into a total meltdown and collapsed during the identification. Every single one of them. When that happens you must show compassion and caring. Regrettably, those of us in homicide got awfully good at this sort of thing because it had to be done, but at the same time I always had to work hard to keep my feelings in check. Of course, even long after the identification is over you stay in touch with the family and support them in the months and months leading up to a court case. Naturally, you develop a strong bond with the victims and their families.

Over a period of eight years, I was in and out of the homicide squad three times and dealt with about a hundred victims.

In any homicide, the investigator has to prepare a brief, which is essentially a book with the whole story in it. The brief—it's called a Crown Brief in Canada—has an executive summary of who did what. It contains the highlights of the case, scale drawings of the scene, photographs, and exhibits, and includes who will introduce those exhibits and also the continuity of the exhibits, which means reconstructing the chain of events. The brief also contains background information on the accused and on the deceased, a list of witnesses and their evidence, and the statement of the accused. Then there are scientific reports. Lots of them. There's the autopsy report and a report from the Centre of Forensic Sciences, and also reports from toxicologists and biologists. These Crown Briefs were printed on long-bond paper—foolscap size—and sometimes ran hundreds of pages. When I was in homicide, they were typed on a manual typewriter, and later on we used an electric typewriter. So this was some of the work that went into preparing a case for court.

We made copies of the Crown Brief for the Crown, of course, and also for the defence counsel. Long before the Supreme Court decision about disclosure, we in the homicide squad were already disclosing our cases openly. In those days, defence counsel never abused the confidentiality of some of those items. It's a little different today with disclosure rules and the potential for abuse, and this can often result in lengthy trial delays.

A lot of training goes into being a homicide investigator. You attend seminars at the Ontario Police College in Aylmer, Ontario, and at the

Canadian Police College in Ottawa. These seminars would be presented by senior homicide investigators, forensics people, and pathologists. So you learn about the forensic sciences and rules of evidence. This was much different from police college for new recruits, which provided only a general grounding for police work. Training for homicide is far more in-depth, but then anyone selected for homicide has already proven themselves. Or else they wouldn't be here.

As a homicide investigator, I myself often trained and lectured about how to prepare cases at the Ontario Police College and the Canadian Police College, as well as at other accredited police-training facilities. I liked doing that because it meant elevating the expertise of police officers. Wally Tyrrell, who had first trained me in this work, later brought me in to be the on-the-job training officer for the homicide squad. I would take newcomers and work with them on the job, just as Wally had done with me. This training was more practical than theoretical. These were real cases. I also did some training outside the country, and being familiar with other jurisdictions isn't a bad thing because homicide investigators sometimes have to testify elsewhere.

It happened to me a few times and one case sticks out because it involved jurisdictions in two countries—Canada and the United States. It was in the late '70s and concerned a man I had arrested in Canada. While in Canada, he confessed to a murder that had been committed in New York City. He went back to New York for trial and I had to give evidence. There was an issue about whether he had been given the Miranda rights, which police must do in the United States. In the U.S., police have to inform the suspect of his/her Fifth Amendment rights to remain silent and Sixth Amendment rights to have a lawyer present during questioning. But this is U.S. law and I hadn't given him any Miranda rights because I'd arrested him in Canada under Canadian law, for possession of a handgun and for illegally being in the country. However, this character had confessed the murder to me.

We ended up in court in the Bronx, and I'll never forget it because there were sixteen courtrooms all going at the same time, most of them handling murder cases. What was different about that place was how they ran things. It lacked the decorum I had been used to in the high court where our murder trials were held. The judge wore judicial robes, but aside from him, everyone was very casual and informal. The New York City Police Department (NYPD) homicide investigators testified without jackets or ties. What did that tell me? That this was a very busy production line, that they had a lot of cases, and that they didn't take the same time to look after all the niceties. The judge was a gruff character, an older guy with a bad back who would come down off the bench and walk around to stretch. And he did all this while the court was still running!

When I testified, the public defender for the accused interrogated and gave me a rough time because I hadn't informed his client of his Miranda rights. He was trying to make the case that I was operating as an agent of U.S. authorities—of the NYPD—and had obtained the confession on their behalf. Therefore, he claimed, the arrest was unconstitutional. This lawyer got on the judge's nerves as he threw these legalities at me, so the judge told him that I was a police officer. Not a lawyer. He said the things the lawyer was asking me he should know himself because he was a lawyer. Then the judge said, "Besides, everybody knows the law in Canada isn't much different from the United States. It's only in Quebec where it's different. Isn't that right, Detective?"

Well, I didn't know what to say to that, but luckily for me I didn't have to reply because the judge didn't wait for a response. He just told the public defender to get on with it and he did. The judge eventually ruled that I wasn't operating as an agent of the American authorities at all and didn't have to inform the man of his Miranda rights. The guy was convicted.

During my years in homicide and afterward when I was chief in Toronto, there were some particularly brutal murders. In 1979, an eighty-four-year-old woman who lived alone and who was trying to remain independent had her home broken into. It was totally ransacked. This poor woman was beaten, bludgeoned, and sexually assaulted. Later, a youth of fifteen was arrested. A lot of coins had been stolen from her home, so we canvassed local shops and heard about this lad who had come into one of them with these coins. Completing all the applications to bring him to adult court involved an enormous amount of work; the Crown Brief was about 500 pages long! So, even in those days, much of the work was tedious, labour-intensive and very demanding, and today it's worse. But that case seemed to go on forever.

In homicide, we also did investigations involving incidents where the police had shot someone. If a person was shot or killed by a police officer, or if a person had died in police custody, the case went to an inquest and we looked after those inquests. But in all the cases I investigated, a police officer was never convicted because in every instance where a gun was fired it was justified. And in every case that went to an inquest jury, which comprised six citizens, the officer was invariably commended by the jury for the actions taken.

One really ugly case involved two killers—Anthony Speciale and Robert Charles Miller—and a mob-related drug deal that went bad. Early one morning in July 1977, I got a telephone call at home from my partner about a triple homicide. Three men were dead in an apartment and a fourth person, a woman, had been wounded. In addition, another shooting was connected to this one. In the second shooting, two more people were wounded, so the total tally was three dead and three wounded in two different locations. One of the deceased was found with a .38 revolver in his hand. The gun was empty and, as it turned out, he never did have a gun; it had been put there by one of the accused. We managed to contain the apartment with the three dead men inside and arrested Speciale and Miller on the spot. As for the deceased, one of them was found on the balcony, another in the hall, and a third in the bathroom. They had been chased around by the gunmen and were frantically running through the apartment. The wounded female was in the bedroom and she's the one who called the police. She had been shot and the tape of her call is just riveting. Speciale was the main guy in all this and when he was arrested he said, "I don't really know anything about the murders" and then he said he was a "scapegoat." Later, he and Miller were both convicted of second-degree murder.

Years later I wanted to see Speciale, who was serving time in prison, about another case I thought he might be involved in. I told the prison guards not to tell him who was coming. I showed up, he took one look at me, turned around, and went back to his cell.

I was interviewed about that case in the June 1980 issue of *Toronto Life* magazine. The cover story of the magazine was called "Life Behind the Badge" and several members of the city's police department were quoted. I was the one they picked from homicide. I was thirty-eight years old and in my fifth year in homicide and this was the same year Michael Sweet was killed. In that article, I talked about Anthony Speciale and how we found him reloading his gun right in front of the woman he had just shot and how he was about to shoot her again and finish her off. I said I felt like stringing up the bastard right then and there. And why did he shoot her and these other people in the first place? Because he needed some money and either they didn't have it or they wouldn't give it to him. And we're supposed to rehabilitate someone like that?

Another thing that always bothered me when I was in homicide were the so-called expert psychiatrists who would testify in court. One day they would appear for the prosecution and the next day they'd appear in a different case for the defence. For that reason alone, I wondered why anyone would put much stock in what they said.

It's always satisfying for investigators to get a conviction, and even if a plea bargain takes place, which happens often, at least you've got your man. But then there are cases that are never solved. One that sticks out for me was the murder of an entire family. Their name was Airst and it happened on October 1, 1979. The husband, wife, and their son were found bludgeoned to death in their home. It was a Sunday, I was visiting my in-laws, and was dressed in casual clothes. The homicide squad called for help and I wasn't dressed properly for work, so I had to rummage through my father-in-law's closet to find a shirt, jacket, and tie. His wardrobe wasn't up to snuff and I ended up with a very large tie—it was more like a bib—and if that wasn't enough, it even had polka dots on it. When I appeared at the crime scene, cameras were all over the place and what got into the newspaper the next day was a photograph of me wearing that polka-dot tie as I escorted the bodies out of the house. You can bet I got ribbed for that photo. That case remains unsolved to this day. We did a tremendous amount of work on it, and while there were theories as to who might have done it, theories don't get you very far in court.

By far the worst murder scene I ever saw was a quadruple killing that happened the night of July 26, 1980. In fact, another team of lead investigators was involved, but after they went in and saw what they were dealing with they called for help, so we had two teams of investigators on that one. It started out as a home invasion. The four victims were a married couple, a boarder, and a friend. The principal was the manager of a tavern and what happened was that two guys went into the house, bound and gagged two of the occupants, and took the tavern owner to the bar so he could open the safe. Eventually they came back to the house and a fourth person showed up. But the two guys didn't want to leave any witnesses behind, so they killed the people. All four of them. It was the most horrific scene I've ever laid my eyes on and it wasn't only the fact that these people were murdered, but how they were murdered. They were bound and gagged, then beaten, shot and stabbed, and their throats were slit. The bodies were stacked on top of one another like pieces of meat.

After doing a lot of interviews and legwork on that case, we arrested three men—Vincent Macdonald, Charles Fish, and a third party who was an accessory after the fact and who had helped the other two dispose of the clothes and gun. The accessory got seven years. Macdonald and Fish were both charged with first-degree murder and pled guilty to second-degree murder. They each got life with no parole for sixteen years. The way I see it, they got four years per victim. Macdonald later died in jail, but Fish is still doing time today.

I've kept tabs on two murder cases over the years—the one involving the Munro brothers, who killed Toronto police officer Michael Sweet, and this character Macdonald, who was involved in the quadruple homicide. Macdonald has been out on temporary absences many times, but in 2006, a parole hearing was held for him. That's right, an application for *full parole*; a man is convicted of four murders and he's still eligible. You figure. Anyway, I was allowed to sit in on the hearing but couldn't say anything because I wasn't a victim. What's interesting is that at the hearing Macdonald was represented by another lifer who was speaking on his behalf. That's how it works. It's like Alcoholics Anonymous. The hearing was all about Fish and his anger-management problems and his drug-abuse problems while in maximum security. They wound up giving him unescorted passes but no full parole. Fish, incidentally, had already been out on more than forty escorted passes by that time.

From day one, I let the National Parole Board know that I wanted to be advised of any activity on that case and they've been very good about it, from his first application for day parole back in 1994, which he got, to the first time he applied for full parole in 1997, which he was denied. The reason I kept tabs on these multiple murderers Macdonald and Fish is that some of the witnesses who helped convict them feared what might happen if these two men ever got paroled. What's funny is that when I went to Kingston to attend that parole hearing, the guards treated me like royalty. They were chuckling and I asked what was so funny, so they said they had bet with the lifers whether or not Fantino would show up to attend the hearing. The lifers thought I wouldn't. The guards won the bet.

On August 4, 1998, Toronto police officer William Hancox was murdered. At the time I was chief in York Region, just north of Toronto. I mention this case because of the unique circumstances that took place after the sentence was passed. Hancox had been conducting surveillance on a known break-and-enter specialist and was in his unmarked police van in the parking lot of a plaza. That night his team members received a garbled message from him on their police radio. The two officers went to the scene and saw Hancox beside his van with the radio microphone in his hand. He told them he had been stabbed and then he collapsed. He had suffered a large stab wound to the chest and was rushed to hospital where he died. The investigation found that two women—Elaine Rose

Cece and Mary Barbara Taylor—had stabbed him while trying to steal his van. Both of them were found guilty of second-degree murder and sentenced; one got eighteen years and the other sixteen years.

What upset me most was that these two women—the convicted killers of a police officer—were allowed to share a cell. In fact, the two were lovers who wanted to remain together after they went to prison. Incredibly, the authorities granted them this right! I was so incensed that after I became chief in Toronto, I wrote to Lawrence MacAulay, who was then Solicitor General of Canada. In my letter I told him about these two being in joint custody at the Joliette Prison for Women, a place we called "The Love Shack." I told him that they had plunged an eight-inch knife into the chest of a police officer and that his government allowing them to continue their relationship in prison was "an affront to the credibility of a system of justice where a modicum of common decency and respect for the public interest must prevail long before those who murder and victimize are rewarded for their sordid crimes." I asked for some justification for his government's action, but I don't remember getting a response to that letter, and for all I know those two could still be sharing a cell today.

This is the sort of thing that really irks me and I've seen it time and again—authorities bending over backwards for convicted murderers. But, as upsetting as that one was and as horrific as those other murders were, the two cases that left their deepest mark on me both involved children. They occurred when I was chief in Toronto and they came one after the other.

· 12 ·

Two Little Girls and a Trail of Broken Hearts

O N MAY 12, 2003—IT WAS A MONDAY—TEN-YEAR-OLD Holly Jones went missing. She was last seen walking a friend home in her neighbourhood, and her sudden disappearance prompted an Amber Alert. An Amber Alert is the quick-response, public-alert strategy that goes into play when a child kidnapping is suspected. Our officers immediately conducted a massive search, and the next day her parents made a public appeal for her safe return. That same day human remains—body parts—were found in two bags on the shore of the Toronto Islands, just off the city's mainland. One of the bags had been weighted down with a barbell. Later that afternoon, DNA testing confirmed that the remains belonged to Holly.

This shifted our investigation from a kidnapping to a search for her killer. It was now a homicide. Our police divers searched the waters in and around the Toronto Islands, in fact, the whole waterfront of the city. Planes and helicopters were also involved. Two days after Holly went missing, flowers, cards, and gifts were being dropped off on the front lawn of her family's home. We were receiving countless tips from the public, and the entire community was in a heightened state of anxiety. People were afraid for their children.

This case, which traumatized the whole city, was handled by our sex crimes unit and our homicide squad. Things were such that we had to turn away on-duty and even off-duty officers who wanted to work on it, which means we had people on this case who weren't getting paid for all the time they put in. Lots of them. They didn't care. I don't think the public realizes this aspect of police work, that sometimes a case will come along and you just want to get involved. You feel compelled to get involved. This has happened to me many times, like the time when officer Jimmy Lothian was killed. None of us cared about going home. Nobody wanted to go home. We just wanted to stay with the case and work around the clock to find out who did it, and that's what we did.

I really infused myself in the Holly Jones case. Of course, when something like this happens, anyone who has anything to do with the investigation is completely devastated and I was devastated too. I made sure we got the absolute highest priority from the Centre for Forensic Sciences. And right from the outset, I wanted to make sure that both the sexual assault squad and the homicide squad were in on the investigation together. We suspected there was a sexual component here and the people we had in the sexual assault squad were a very talented bunch. Normally, it would have been just the homicide squad handling the case, but I wanted a blend of the best talent and the best experience from both those squads to work on this case. Gary Ellis was unit commander of the homicide squad and Bruce Smollett was unit commander of the sexual assault squad. Throughout the investigation both of them gave me a steady, blow-by-blow account of everything that was going on. The other thing I wanted was direct, ongoing contact between our investigating unit and the family. Bruce Smollett took on this responsibility, helped the family through this very difficult time, and even shouldered some of the media issues for them. I visited with the family a few times as well.

Our investigators were family people themselves. They had children of their own. They knew what it meant to have a child.

Right off the top we knew there were 200 sex offenders living within three kilometres of Holly's house. This was the Parkdale area of Toronto.

It was an older, densely populated community by the lakeshore in the west end of the city. It was mostly residential, but along with the older homes and factories was the rail traffic heading into the downtown railway yards. In its early days, Parkdale was the destination for many immigrants from eastern Europe. When I joined the police force in 1969, the area had an overabundance of saloon-type beer halls, seedy hotels, and cheap wine stores that attracted quite a bit of indulging and a lot of quality-of-life concerns for the police. While much of that has since disappeared, Parkdale has had more than its share of problems with prostitutes, vagrants, and drug activity, which often results in major sweeps by police. It also had several halfway houses where parolees resided and many of those parolees were sex offenders.

The crazy thing is that, with all these known sex offenders running around, we still didn't have a national, sex offender registry, and only minimal DNA legislation. All we had was a provincial registry for the province of Ontario. I don't know that having a national registry would have prevented this horrible crime, but it would have been another scientific tool available to police investigators. DNA is like a fingerprint, and while the United Kingdom had laws allowing police to take DNA from suspects, as did many states in the U.S., there was only limited access to this kind of thing in Canada. The fact remained that sex offenders were getting out of prison on a regular basis and the police didn't have DNA for many of them.

This was one of those defining cases that raised both the ire and compassion of the community. For forty days, some 300 police officers and civilian members of the Toronto Police Service pored over the 2,300 tips that came in. However, there was a problem with the video surveillance cameras down by the waterfront. I was very angry when I was told about businesses being reluctant to turn over videotapes that could have helped us with the investigation. The lawyers for some of those businesses said we needed search warrants before we could study the videotapes. If that wasn't enough, some of those video cameras weren't even working. So all I could do was tell our investigators to follow due process and persevere.

In Canada, there is often an overreaction about protecting people's privacy in the public domain. Frankly, I don't understand why any person wouldn't want to co-operate fully with the police in a case like this. Yet, some people seem very concerned with an already overworked Canadian Charter of Rights and Freedoms. I never believed the Charter was designed to invent unreasonable and truly mind-boggling schemes to protect criminals, but to a large degree this is exactly what has happened. In many instances, it has turned our system of justice upside down. We got into a Charter issue with the Holly Jones case, too.

At the beginning of the investigation, I was mindful of a case in the U.K. where the police had gone door-to-door asking males to volunteer a sample of their DNA, which eventually led to that case being resolved. Actually, it was Gary Ellis who came up with the idea of getting DNA samples from men in Holly's neighbourhood. This hadn't been done before in Canada, so he ran the idea by me and I said go ahead and do it. There was nothing illegal about it. Gary did his research, and so did I because I knew I'd have to defend this decision. As it turned out, I could have written the script myself. I knew what was going to happen.

We felt in this instance that the killer or killers must have been in the area and that they knew the area. So we had our people do an organized, meticulous canvassing of the local community. In addition to asking for DNA samples, we wanted to identify the origins of some carpet fibres found on the body that led us to believe we were looking for a certain colour of carpeting.

There was no law that prevented us from asking for DNA on consent—although by law, people didn't have to provide it—so our officers went door-to-door and the overwhelming majority of men who were asked to provide DNA did so. Taking a DNA sample isn't like taking a quart of blood. It's a non-intrusive swab of saliva on a Q-tip. No big deal. But one guy, Michel Briere, didn't let us take his DNA, so we targeted him. Eventually, he discarded a can of Coke into a garbage can and our people recovered it. We were then able to match his DNA with blood found under Holly's fingernails. And that played a large part in how we got him.

When it became known that we were requesting DNA samples from men in the area, however, a number of police critics came out of the woodwork. Alan Gold, a well-known defence lawyer in Toronto, was interviewed on CBC television about whether a DNA request from police is truly voluntary. I knew Alan Gold. He was a very good lawyer and I've always had a lot of respect for him. In fact, I once retained him on behalf of the police when the *Toronto Star* alleged that we were involved in racial profiling. On the CBC, he talked about the "enormous pressure" to comply with the police and said, "To call it consent is a little disingenuous." So he was taking the approach that this was a slippery slope. Also on the CBC was Alan Borovoy of the Canadian Civil Liberties Association, who said, "It asks too much to say to the public, 'just trust us.' Democracies don't function that way." The implication was that our requesting DNA from men in the area was improper behaviour on the part of the police and an abuse of our power and authority. Another voice was that of lawyer Clayton Ruby, a guy who never passes up on an opportunity to criticize the police for being power-grabbing and for overstepping the bounds. But we weren't breaking any laws. We did our homework, and I believe to this day that it was the right thing to do.

As a police officer and as a chief, I have come to learn that there are always some voices out there who will do nothing but criticize. But the fact is, if the rhetoric from such people was the law of the land, the Holly Jones case may never have been solved and neither would many other cases.

Michel Briere was a thirty-five-year-old software developer with no criminal record. He lived alone in an apartment a few blocks from Holly's home. He seemed innocuous. Nobody knew him. He pled guilty to first-degree murder, was convicted and got life, meaning twenty-five years with no chance of parole. Of course, he was still eligible for the so-called faint hope clause, which allows even lifers the opportunity of a hearing after fifteen years. In our investigation, we learned that he was attracted to child pornography. He admitted this to us himself. What happened was that one day after watching child pornography on the Internet, he saw Holly, grabbed her by the neck, took her to his apartment, raped her, and strangled her before stuffing her body in his fridge. Then later he used a handsaw to dismember her. Over the next three days, he disposed of her remains. One day he carried her torso in a gym bag—right on the Toronto subway—and dumped it in the harbour. The next day he was riding the subway again, carrying another bag with more body parts, and dumped that somewhere else. The day after that he stuffed more of her remains into garbage bags and left them on the curb outside his apartment for the regular garbage pickup. He stayed awake all night watching until the bags were collected.

One of the things I directed our investigators to do was to collect all the garbage in the neighbourhood. We were looking for evidence. We knew the girl had been murdered and dismembered, and with the evidence discarded, we sure didn't want to miss anything. So we did some extraordinary things with this case, and picking up all the garbage in the local neighbourhood was one of them.

All this happened after Briere had downloaded child pornography off the Internet. When he confessed, he said how easy it was to find such material. He said you could search for the word "baby" and find all kinds of stuff. He also told our investigators about his fantasy.

> I always had the fantasy of having sexual relations with a little girl. So I just got carried away and I walked outside and Holly was . . . I didn't know her. I'd never seen her before. If she wouldn't have been on the street corner I probably would have just walked the street and just gone back home.

During that case, I went to the family's home several times, and let them know we were providing as much support to them as we could. When you see the family in their home, they are often concerned about whether the killer is going to be caught or whether the police are going to be diverted to another case. They are worried that *their* case will go on a back burner. I gave them assurances that solving this case was the most important thing we were doing. And it was. Staff Inspector Bruce

Smollett, who was in charge of our sex crimes unit, was really wonderful in his care and conscientious regard for the family. Holly's mother, Maria, who became involved in victims' rights and the protection of children, handled this whole thing in a very noble way. She made a point of raising awareness about the safety of children, and she exposed her grief, her family, and her home to the media and everyone else. And I think she did it for all the right reasons. It wasn't about notoriety. It was about sharing the tragic loss of a daughter with the rest of the city. At a time when most people in that situation would have secluded themselves, she became very public. The backyard of the family home was made into a memorial to Holly and it was heartwrenching to see it. No matter how many times I think about this case, I can't help but wonder how anyone could do such a thing to a child.

In 2005, the sex crimes unit of the Toronto Police Service helped locate a six-year-old American girl who had been a victim of horrible abuse. Toronto investigators found hundreds of pictures of this girl on the Internet. There were images of her being beaten, raped, and held in a dog cage. Detective Sergeant Paul Gillespie led that unit and told me these were the worst child pornography pictures he had ever seen in his life. The unit pored over all the pictures and used image-enhancing technology to focus on a wristband on the girl's arm. They were then able to make a connection to an amusement park in the U.S. They were also able to focus on her Girl Scout uniform and her school uniform. After connecting her to the Raleigh-Durham area in North Carolina, they began working with the FBI and it didn't take long to find the girl's school. The FBI made an identification and a forty-one-year-old man, Brian Shellenberger, a former software developer and the father of three children, was charged with possession of child pornography. He admitted to making the pictures and to torturing the girl. And also a baby boy.

In October 2005, Brian Shellenberger was sentenced to 100 years. If this case had happened in Canada, he might not have gone to jail at all and, if he had, not for long. In Canada, Shellenberger may have received a sentence of five years, if that, and almost certainly would have served half of it before being paroled. At the time that Shellenberger was convicted in the U.S., a new child pornography law was being passed in Canada. It carried a minimum sentence for possession of child pornography.

Fourteen days.

Holly's mother, was interviewed on TV about Shellenberger and offered her thoughts on Canada's justice system. Maria said that a person who physically rapes a child would likely be placed behind bars, but as far as Canadian law was concerned, "It's okay to watch." Which is pretty well how it is.

The Holly Jones investigation cost $1 million, and after we arrested Michel Briere, 10,000 people signed a petition calling for tougher sentencing for pedophiles. Many times I have spoken out about this issue and about Canada not having a national, sex offender registry. But the fact of the matter is, the federal government of the day was far more interested in decriminalizing pot than in protecting children.

Not long after that case, we had another one and this hurt even more because of Holly Jones.

During the night of October 19, 2003, nine-year-old Cecilia Zhang was abducted right from her own bedroom in the family home. It happened in a good, middle-class area in north Toronto. Cecilia was the only child of a couple who had moved to Canada from China in 1998. They discovered she was gone when they went to her bedroom to wake her up for school in the morning. Right away, it appeared to our police detectives who arrived on the scene that a window had been tampered with.

Cecilia was a Grade 4 student. Four feet eleven inches tall. Seventy pounds. From the beginning, we felt this was an inside job involving someone or some people who knew the girl and the layout of the house. We still believed she was alive, of course, but the case went on for so long. Two days after she was reported missing, we issued a statement saying we had no reason to believe this was a random attack by a predator. We went door-to-door through her neighbourhood and hundreds of tips came in. We had hundreds of officers working on the case, including fifty detectives. Cecilia's parents held an emotional news conference on TV, pleading with the kidnappers to release their daughter. We set up a website and made another appeal.

This quickly became a national story and even an international story. The family's neighbours set up a fund offering reward money to anyone who gave tips that would lead to Cecilia's safe return. The mother appealed to three Chinese-language newspapers, and on November 1 she appeared on the TV show *America's Most Wanted*, which taped right inside the home. It had an audience of over ten million viewers. The case would be featured on that program again. The next day, I appeared on television and urged the kidnappers to call me directly.

As with the Holly Jones case, I got deeply involved in this one. I went to the house, examined the scene, and tried to analyze it in my own mind. I talked to the investigators and met the parents. Everything pointed to an inside job, so we felt it was important to get a sense of the relationships in the family. I sat down with the parents and they came across to me as decent, hard-working, loving people. I was satisfied after my first meeting with them that they had nothing to do with this. We all felt someone else had abducted their daughter, so on November 12, we announced that the parents were not suspects and released videos of Cecilia with the hope that someone would recognize her and help bring her back home. We also announced a $50,000 reward for her safe return.

In December, as the weeks rolled into months, police in the United States and China became involved in the search for Cecilia. We asked the abductors to come forward with a ransom demand. In January, after this investigation had been going on for three months, Cecilia's father said he would mortgage his house and offer $200,000 for his daughter's safe return.

Never before in the history of Toronto and anywhere in Canada, for that matter, had there been such an extensive search for a missing child. Thousands of taxicabs displayed Cecilia's photo, as did virtually every Toronto Transit Commission bus, streetcar, and subway car. As well, thousands of posters were distributed all over the place in English, Cantonese, and Mandarin. And, of course, the media were on top of the case every day.

On and on it went. It was very frustrating. In any investigation you have to play out every lead and 99 per cent of the time you wind up chasing down leads that take you nowhere. This is extremely time-consuming and adds to the sense of frustration. You spend so much time chasing down loose ends and sometimes might get really pumped up about what you're doing and then there's a letdown. At the same time, we in the police community know that every crime is solvable. It can be only a phone call away. Somebody knows something.

During the investigation, we kept hoping Cecilia was alive, but the downer came on March 27, 2004—161 days after the abduction—when a hiker found human remains, a skeleton, in the woods in Mississauga. The next day, we confirmed it was Cecilia. The woods were about fifty kilometres from her home in north Toronto. I made the announcement at a televised news conference and urged the killer or killers—now we weren't dealing only with kidnappers—to come forward and surrender. I promised we wouldn't give up looking for them.

A few days later, the Peel Regional Police took over the investigation as the lead agency because the remains had been found in their jurisdiction. But the Toronto police were still very much involved. Noel Catney, who was Peel chief at the time, was a good friend of mine whom I had known for many years going back to our detective days. We both knew there wouldn't be any problems working together to solve this case. Right away we ironed out the rules of engagement between our two police forces, so it would be a joint investigation, and that's how it operated. Seamlessly.

I will never forget my visit to the Zhang home after we learned Cecilia had been murdered. I was just returning from a meeting of the International Association of Chiefs of Police in the U.S. and went from the airport straight to their house. On my way into the house, neighbours of the Zhang family handed me some flowers and a teddy bear. I found it hard to control myself. I told the parents how sorry we were and assured them we had done everything possible to bring their daughter home safely. The fact that we hadn't been able to do that was weighing very heavily on all of us.

Some time later the family had a gathering at their home with Cecilia's schoolmates and her schoolteachers. It would have been her tenth birthday and I was invited. I thought from the very beginning that Cecilia's parents were a wonderful couple. But what can you say to them? Your heart sinks. They had just lost a child—their only child—so I tried to console them, which is as much as one can do.

During those 161 days when we were looking for Cecilia, our people worked flat out. We may have had fingerprints from the scene, but that doesn't mean much if you can't match them with anything. Police put a lot of pressure on themselves in a case like this. Police have families, too, and they are involved in the community. In fact, the police are probably more involved in the community than any other profession. What's more, they care. They care a lot. A great many things on this case happened outside of regular schedules, and by that I mean people working overtime and volunteering endless hours. Believe me, we wanted to crack this case more than anything, and after it became a murder investigation, we wanted to catch the culprits and bring them to justice. I think "driven" is a good way to describe it. Sergeant Jim Muscat was our media spokesman and one day he talked about how police are taught early in their careers not to get emotionally involved with victims and to keep them at arm's length. But the day he appeared on TV standing next to Cecilia's mother, he confided to me how he could feel the pain just oozing out of this poor woman.

On July 22, 2004, the Toronto Police Service and the Peel Regional Police Service held a joint news conference. There were massive numbers of media in attendance. Peel chief Noel Catney and I announced that a twenty-one-year-old man, Min Chen, who was a visa student from China, had been arrested and charged with the first-degree murder of Cecilia Zhang. This was an emotional news conference for both of us and it was Noel's call as to how it would unfold. He wanted me there, but it was definitely his lead. My intent was basically to applaud the efforts made by the investigators and also to applaud the family for their courage and steadfastness in doing what they could to help us. So, at the news conference, Noel announced the arrest and went through the alleged events leading up to Cecilia's disappearance. He explained how the case had become global in nature, involving police in mainland China, the FBI, and other police agencies throughout Canada and the United States. But then he called Min Chen a murderer, and I knew right away this would cause heat. Noel was very passionate and charged up about the case and he let his feelings be known. I can't fault him for that, but I remember thinking as I sat beside him that this isn't going to go down very well. And it didn't. The next day I was at a function with Major-General (retired) Lewis MacKenzie. It was called Ride for Vets and involved hundreds of motorcycle enthusiasts raising funds for war veterans. At this event, the media was on to me right away about Noel's comments. Noel took the heat, as I knew he would have to, but I supported him. Let's face it, the guy is a human being just like any other police chief and you can't help but get emotional about a case like this one. Police are hands-on, front-line people dealing with these tragedies, and from time to time it's bound to get to you.

Min Chen came up on the investigators' radar screen when evidence pointed to a man having known or having had contact with the Zhang family and their home. The Zhangs had rented out rooms in their home to visa students from China. The room where Cecilia slept had once been occupied by a female visa student from China, and this woman was an acquaintance of Chen's. During the year and a half that she had lived in the Zhang home, she had received several visits from Chen, who was even introduced to Cecilia's parents. When the woman moved out of the house, Cecilia moved into that bedroom.

A lot of work was done to trace anyone who had either direct or even remote contact with the home—literally hundreds of people—and eventually everything pointed to Chen. He was also tied to the scene of the abduction by his fingerprints. They matched the prints taken from the scene. But the problem was the state of decomposition of Cecilia's body, since so much time had passed since the murder. There was no scientific evidence of sexual assault. We thought her body had been in the woods for several months but couldn't prove it. The post-mortem examination failed to determine the cause of death because of the decomposition of the body.

Good old-fashioned police work is what caught Chen. A detective in the Peel Regional Police Forensic Identification Bureau got Chen's fingerprints, along with those of many other people, and matched them to fingerprints found at the crime scene at the Zhang home. The investigation then zeroed in on him. Police conducted a very thorough investigation and were able to determine that he had acted alone.

On July 12, 2004, another Peel detective met with Chen and told him he was the prime suspect and that police were arranging a forensic examination of his car. Surveillance was continued. Two days after that meeting, Chen left the trunk liner of his car with a car-care specialist so it could be cleaned, then he went to a gas station and vacuumed the trunk. Peel police seized the trunk liner that had been removed and replaced it with a similar one to avoid detection. A few days later, on July 22, Chen was arrested and confessed to the murder of nine-year-old Cecilia Zhang.

In the spring of 2006—the day was May 9—Chen avoided trial by pleading guilty to second-degree murder. It was a plea bargain. He was sentenced to life with no eligibility of parole for fifteen years. Considering the lack of forensic evidence due to the state of the body and other complications—there was no evidence in the immediate area where the body was found—that was the best we could do. If he had pled not guilty and the case had gone to trial, it might have resulted in a conviction for manslaughter. Not murder. The sentencing judge said Chen would likely be deported to China upon his release.

And what was Cecilia's abduction all about in the first place? Chen was a visa student from Shanghai who had come to Canada at great expense to his parents. He was failing in his studies and worried that he'd lose his immigration status and have to return to China. One of his friends had arranged a marriage of convenience at a cost of $25,000, so he could obtain permanent residency in Canada. Chen wanted to do the same thing for himself, but he needed the money. As mentioned earlier, he had been in the Zhang household several times because the family rented out rooms to foreign students and a friend of his had been a boarder. So the Zhang family knew him. On the night of the abduction, he broke into the home only to find Cecilia in the hall outside her bedroom with a towel around her. He grabbed her around the head and neck and put his hand over her mouth to prevent her from screaming. She struggled and he kept a tight hold on her as he carried her out of the house.

According to the Agreed Statement of Facts for the case, in the morning when Cecilia went missing her father had found the kitchen window open with the screen bent outwards. There was a visible shoe print on the kitchen counter. That window, which was at the back of the house about eight feet off the ground, was believed to be the point of entry into the household. During the investigation, Forensic Identification Service officers discovered fingerprints on the edge of the window screen where it had been pulled out of the frame. They also found a fingerprint on the outer surface of the window. Our detectives identified eight latent fingerprints and also partial palm prints that belonged to Chen. In criminal investigations, a "latent" fingerprint is one that is scarcely visible but is visible enough to be developed for study. As for the point of exit, the side door to the house was left open. It was Chen's intent to keep Cecilia for a short time in the trunk of his car, make his ransom demand, and receive payment all in the same day.

It didn't work out that way. By the time he had reached his car with Cecilia, she had stopped struggling. She wasn't moving. She wasn't breathing. He admitted that, by placing his arm around her neck and holding his hand over her mouth and nose, he had caused her bodily harm by smothering and choking her. He then put her in the trunk of his car and drove off. Thinking she was now dead, he decided to dispose of her body in a heavily wooded ravine he knew in Mississauga. He had planned to bury her there, but the ground was too hard, so he left her body in the woods.

This was a really difficult case for all of us. Cecilia, just like Holly Jones, had become everyone's child. What made it even more personal for me was that a mere two months before Cecilia's abduction, I became a grandfather for the first time. Does it make a difference when you do this kind of work and have grandchildren of your own? Yes, it does. A huge difference. I would look at my grandchildren and other children and think of those two little girls. Holly and Cecilia. To think that someone would grab a child off the street or come right into their home and snatch them is beyond belief.

I have always been very protective of children, both on the home front and in the public domain, but knowing what I know and realizing that children can be preyed upon has made me an extremely protective grandfather. Child murders and the vicious abuse of children have much deeper meaning to me than the evening news because I have seen the handiwork of these animals up close, which is why I believe some cases cry out for capital punishment. It wouldn't bother me to pull the switch, open the trap door, or give a lethal injection to such killers of children. Predators must know there will be a certain and severe consequence for their actions.

Holly Jones and Cecilia Zhang I will take to my grave. These two little girls belonged to all of us. They were part of us and they are gone because some evil was injected into their lives through no fault of their own. And so, I reflect on my own grandchildren all the time. It makes me think that there but for the grace of God go they.

· 13 ·

Keeping the Guilty
Off the Street

URING WORLD WAR II, THE NORWEGIAN AIR FORCE trained at a small airport in Canada. Norway was occupied by Germany, and the little Scandinavian country flew as many fighter planes as it could out of a runway that was located in the picturesque Muskoka region of Southern Ontario. It was near the town of Gravenhurst, about 200 kilometres north of Toronto. Many years after the war, the Canadian government thought this would be a good place for a new experiment in corrections, so it set aside 350 acres of woods, rock, and swamp—right beside the airport—and built the Beaver Creek Penitentiary. It was the country's first, minimum-security, federal correctional institution.

The word "penitentiary" is not a fitting description for this place. The low-lying buildings are made of wood, not concrete, and there is no exterior wall. There are no fences and no guards brandishing guns. On the grounds are a baseball diamond, a tennis court, and two putting greens. Though the facility doesn't have a hockey rink, inmates are allowed to form a team of their own and play in a local league. Beaver Creek doesn't look like a prison and families sometimes drive onto the grounds thinking it is a campsite.

In 1998, a medium-security institution was opened next to Beaver Creek. It was called Fenbrook and didn't look like a prison either. Built on twenty-three acres in cottage country, it encompasses fifteen build-ings and houses 400 offenders. The total staff complement is 270, of whom 160 are correctional officers.

As Canada's newest federal prison and the first one built since the early '70s, Fenbrook was designed along the lines of a residential subdi-vision so inmates wouldn't feel that they were locked up. It has "streets" with names like Forest Circle, White Pine Trail, and Tamarack Way. Four low-lying buildings, each accommodating a hundred offenders, are divided into ranges or floors with eight to twelve offenders living in each one. The actual sleeping quarters are two to a room and the rooms are similar to a university dormitory. Offenders receive a set food alloca-tion—money—and pool their resources to buy groceries from Fenbrook's corner grocery store. Thus, there is no prison cafeteria and no "central feeding kitchen." Offenders are encouraged to cook their own meals, and if they like steak and veal and it's within their budget, so be it. Likewise, if it's within their budget, they can have a colour televi-sion. Apartments are wired for cable. One thing that is prohibited is Internet access.

Authorities say the idea of the group arrangement is "to instill living skills." Fenbrook has an inmate canteen where junk food can be bought after hours. It has recreational fields with a baseball diamond and soccer pitch, and a place to play horseshoes. There is also the Program Building. The Program Building is equipped with a gymnasium, a hobby craft area, a woodworking shop, and a library, which is part of the local municipal library system. Alas, no wall runs around the grounds, just a fence with barbed wire at the top. But there are cameras, of course, as part of the "perimeter detection system;" the one escapee who did make it out of Fenbrook was quickly apprehended.

Any offender in Canada's federal correctional system must be assessed for risk before being placed in maximum-, medium-, or minimum-security institutions. At Fenbrook, the whole setup embodies what is called the "community model" so that offenders feel they are living in a community. Private family visits are courtesy of seventy-two-hour stays in any of the six cottage units on the grounds. The inmate applies for the visit, and as long as a unit is available, he gets the wife or girlfriend, kids, or the whole extended family.

Fenbrook doesn't get into the news very much, which might be a good thing. But in 2005, Correctional Services Canada was ordered to pay one of its inmates, Vlado Maljkovich, who was serving a life sentence for the 1995 murders of his wife and daughter, $5,000 in damages for exposure to second-hand smoke. No surprise then that the following year the entire correctional system adopted a universal no-smoking policy at all its institutions. Authorities say the policy has been less than successful.

Two years before that happened, in 2003, the offenders at Fenbrook staged a magazine drive and began taking delivery of porn magazines. According to Randy White, the Canadian member of Parliament who first addressed this issue in the House of Commons, inmates were receiving *Playboy*, *Penthouse*, *Hustler*, *Only 18*, *Amateur Porn*, *Wet Dreams*, and other publications. Correctional officials responded by saying that adult magazines available in stores were, in fact, allowed in their prisons, too.

In police circles, Fenbrook isn't known as Fenbrook. It's called *Club Fed*. Today one of its inmates is Craig Munro. When he was convicted of first-degree murder in the death of Michael Sweet—which in the vernacular of the Canadian criminal justice system means "life"—he became eligible for unescorted temporary absences and day parole on March 16, 2002. He became eligible for full parole on March 16, 2005. His time in prison has not been without incident.

From his initial apprehension at George's Bourbon Street in the early-morning hours of March 16, 1980, until February 20, 1981, Craig Munro was housed in the Toronto Jail. He was kept in what is called Administrative Segregation for security and safety reasons. That's because he was considered dangerous and a threat to escape. On one occasion he spat and threatened his escorting officers, and on another he physically attacked two corrections staff. He was later moved to the Regional Reception Centre in Kingston, Ontario, and was assessed as an inmate who needed counselling. His Parole Eligibility Report said, "he showed very little interest in anything except his appeal." He was kept in segregation, then moved to the maximum-security Millhaven Institution, also in Kingston, where he found himself in a Special Handling Unit.

While Craig Munro showed no interest in vocational training at Millhaven, he did maintain contact with his family and common-law wife, Connie. In May 1981, he joined the regular prison population, but didn't participate in the Case Management process. He was moved to another maximum-security institution, Laval, which was in Quebec, and while there was charged with "Disobeying the Rules and Regulations." For that he received "five days of off privileges." Another time he was charged with possessing contraband. He pled guilty and got a warning. Another time still he was charged with fighting with another inmate. To this he also pled guilty and received what the corrections system calls "thirty days disassociation"; that means he was placed in a segregation unit apart from other prisoners.

On December 14, 1984, Craig married Connie and took advantage of the Private Family Visiting program, which would include his wife and young son. But since his family lived in Toronto, he asked for a transfer back to Millhaven, which was closer to home, and got it.

In June 1986, during one of those family visits, he and Connie got into an argument—prison staff said he slapped her—and the Private Family Visiting program was suspended. No institutional charges were laid and the program was reinstated six months later. Craig was taking two school courses—Introduction to Computers and Consumer's Studies—and attending the Wednesday Bible Study group, the Salvation Army program, and the John Howard Society group. In October of that year, he was charged with failure to obey the rules. He pled not guilty, was found guilty, and given a warning.

In January 1987, his wife lost their second son in childbirth. Later that year, Craig's Case Management Team recommended him for transfer to the medium-security Collins Bay, but this was overturned by the warden because of "institutional charges and behaviour problems" during those family visits.

Craig asked for a transfer to medium-security Joyceville Institution, which again was closer to home, but his Case Management Team would only go as far as Collins Bay. Not Joyceville. The warden supported this, but regional headquarters didn't and Craig became a candidate for the Dangerous Offender Program in British Columbia.

He didn't help his case much on February 24, 1988, when a urine test came back positive, indicating drug use. In August 1989, he was moved to the Regional Psychiatric Centre in British Columbia. Two months later, Connie gave birth to their third son. It was recommended that family visits be continued if travel for his wife and sons could be arranged, but Craig was still described as having a high potential for violence. On November 20, he was charged with being disrespectful and threatening to staff. He pled not guilty, was found guilty, and received "thirty days disassociation." On April 24, 1990, he was transferred back to Millhaven in Ontario, where he resumed with his family visits, now involving a wife and two sons.

In August 1990, his Case Management Team okayed him for transfer to Joyceville, but after he was found intoxicated during a family visit, the transfer was denied. In April 1991, his Case Management Team again approved him for transfer to Joyceville, as did the warden, but regional headquarters said no.

Then, on August 28, 1991, while in segregation, he asked for more medication. It was denied. He was placed on close watch and was later seen standing on some furniture with a sheet tied around his neck. According to the official Incident Report, the episode was considered an "attention-seeking device" to get more medication.

A private family visit in November ended in a shouting match with Connie "accidentally" spilling boiling water on Craig. The couple were considered good candidates for marriage counselling. Craig completed his Grade 10 equivalency, but continued to spend time in segregation for being intoxicated "from time to time."

In October 1992, his Case Management Team supported a transfer to Collins Bay, and the next month that was approved. But a few weeks later, there was yet another incident; in a family visit, Connie had suffered a cut foot. Support for the transfer was withdrawn and Craig wound up back in maximum security.

He was recommended for an anger-management group and, in July 1993, the family visits were approved once again. In March 1994, he was reclassified to medium security, but on May 16 was again placed in segregation for "being under the influence." The family visits were suspended and back he went to maximum security. Eventually, he returned to medium-security Collins Bay.

During the two years he spent in the maximum-security Millhaven—from 1992 to 1994—Craig was charged *seven different times* for being intoxicated, and once each for possessing contraband, refusing an order, and refusing to provide a urine sample. The punishments meted out for these misdemeanours included two to fifteen days' "disassociation," in two cases a $10 fine, and for the contraband charge—the contraband turned out to be a $20 bill—he was just asked to return the money.

When he was moved to Collins Bay in February 1995, he was rated "moderate" as an escape risk and "moderate" in terms of public safety concerns. What about his chances for reoffending? A document called the General Statistical Information on Recidivism report scored him a minus 3; that level means one out of two offenders, or 50 per cent, are not expected to commit an indictable offence after release, an indictable offence being a serious criminal act.

This is moderate?

His papers said he had a continued problem with substance abuse, showed poor insight into his offences and criminal history, and "displayed no remorse over the death of Officer Sweet." Nevertheless, his case management worker at Collins Bay still described his behaviour as "totally satisfactory."

Several times throughout his incarceration, Craig Munro has applied for various types of release. According to Section 745 of the Canadian Criminal Code, any lifer can apply for a review after fifteen years. His hearing for Section 745 was scheduled for early 1997 and was to take place in the same Toronto courthouse where he and his brother Jamie had been convicted in 1981. Crown attorney Paul Culver was to argue against the release, and for Culver, whose father was a police officer, this would be his third such hearing and the second one involving a police killer. In 1988, he had argued against the early release of Rene Vaillancourt, a Montreal man who shot and killed Toronto police officer Leslie Maitland in 1973; Maitland had been chasing his suspect after a bank robbery and was shot four times. Vaillancourt was denied his early release.

I have known Paul Culver since the days when he was a junior Crown and I was just an up-and-coming detective. He handled a lot of my cases. At the time, I was chief in London, and Culver advised me about Craig's upcoming hearing, so I wrote to Herb Gray, who was the Solicitor General of Canada. I told him about Craig's many charges and run-ins with authorities while in prison over the years. In the letter, I asked why this offender was allowed so many privileges when in maximum security and how he was able to consume intoxicants on a regular basis. In his reply, Gray said only that Correctional Services Canada did not tolerate drug or alcohol abuse and that it had a National Drug Strategy in effect. While I'm sure that my letter didn't help Craig's cause for early release, the nail in the coffin for him was an article by Christie Blatchford in the *Toronto Sun* with the headline "Let the cop killer rot." That story ran on May 1, 1997, and the media attention that followed was such that Craig advised his lawyer to abandon the hearing altogether. The very next day, another article ran in the *Toronto Sun* that was based on an interview I had given them about Craig Munro and his application for early release. The headline was "Chief is horrified."

What would have happened if that hearing had taken place? In a newspaper interview with Thomas Claridge, who was the courts reporter for the *Globe and Mail*, Crown attorney Paul Culver said that the jury would have heard how Craig had become a model prisoner at Collins Bay, married, and become a father of two children. Claridge also interviewed Felicity Hawthorn, who was the lawyer representing Craig.

In the article Hawthorn said that at the hearing she would have demonstrated that her client was extremely remorseful for his acts and was now a changed man. Said Hawthorn in a quote: "He is quite a sensitive guy. I think his remorse is genuine and I think it would have shown through to the jury."

Craig never got his early release, but in 2001, he applied for an Escorted Temporary Absence. By this time, he had been transferred to Fenbrook. *Club Fed*. And it is in those cottages where he sees his wife and family.

When I first heard about his application for an Escorted Temporary Absence, I again wrote to the National Parole Board and said I wanted to appear at the hearing myself. Once again, I was told that I couldn't because I was not a victim. However, I could prepare a written statement, which I did. In my letter to the National Parole Board, I asked why Craig had been moved to Fenbrook in the first place—Fenbrook had the lowest level of security in the entire system—when at the time he was under investigation for criminal offences. I took pains to remind the National Parole Board about his behaviour while in prison. That hearing, which was scheduled for November, was then cancelled.

However, another police killer, the aforementioned Rene Vaillancourt, was successful in obtaining his various early releases. He first got day parole in 1995 and had other releases after that, but his day parole was later revoked after he was arrested for shoplifting. Vaillancourt had initially been sentenced to hang, but his sentence was commuted to life imprisonment after the Canadian government abolished the death penalty in 1976. He took his case all the way to the Supreme Court of Canada to try to get his sentence reduced.

In 2005, when I was still chief in Toronto, Craig was up for full parole because he had served his twenty-five years. I promptly wrote the National Parole Board and included all my earlier correspondence about him. I said I wanted to appear at his parole hearing. The hearing was scheduled for February 15, 2005, at Fenbrook and, as before, I was told that I could prepare a written statement. But that was all. Also planning to attend that hearing was Steve Sullivan from the Canadian Resource Centre for Victims of Crime.

Craig then asked for a postponement of the review and it was rescheduled for April 12, 2005. Once I found out about this, I wrote to Carol Sparling, the regional manager of Community Relations and Training at the National Parole Board. In my letter to her, I referred yet again to Craig's troubles in prison and said that unless the National Parole Board could give assurances that he has been rehabilitated and was not a threat to public safety, his parole should be rejected. The next thing I knew, Craig waived his right to the hearing.

Over the years, Jamie Munro has fared considerably better than his older brother. He was convicted of second-degree murder and sentenced to life with no chance of parole until he had served twelve years. On July 6, 1988, he sent a letter addressed to the chief of the Toronto police advising that he intended to change his last name from Munro to Marra, which was his wife's maiden name. He said he was looking forward to employment as a hairstylist, and that he expected to be granted day parole by the National Parole Board as part of his pre-release program.

Jamie did legally change his name and was indeed released on parole in May 1992. The following January, he was one of seven people who were being held in custody after a police drug raid resulted in the seizure of heroin and cocaine. One of the other men involved was also on parole and, just like Jamie, was a convicted killer. What happened is that a member of the police Emergency Task Force fired at a guard dog after the animal lunged at police, who had been executing a search warrant. The bullet killed the dog and grazed a man, who was taken to hospital where he recovered. Jamie, who was coated with pepper spray, wound up in the same hospital.

Jamie was charged with breach of parole, possession of heroin, and assaulting a peace officer. He was, in fact, breached for parole violation, which meant his full parole was suspended, but he claimed he was being harassed by police and the assault charge was stayed. Then he arranged a deal. An agreement was made that allowed Jamie—now Massimo

Marra—to obtain a passport in his new name, leave Canada, move to Italy with his wife, who was an Italian national, and never return, at least, not without the permission of the National Parole Board. He was re-released on full parole on April 8, 1994, and on August 31 the National Parole Board granted him permission for voluntary departure to Italy. He left Canada on September 24, 1994, armed with a Canadian passport issued in his new name.

However, in the fall of 1995, we had reason to believe he was back in the country. We had information that Jamie had left a message on the answering machine of an official with Correctional Services Canada. Someone he knew. The official confirmed that the voice was Jamie's. In the message, Jamie said he was in Canada and that his return had been authorized by the National Parole Board. We checked this out and it wasn't true. So an arrest warrant was issued for breach of parole. Police never did confirm his whereabouts, and the police in Italy said they had lost all contact with him, which was no surprise because he had never been under any form of control or supervision in Italy anyway.

On March 14, 1996, when I was chief in London, I wrote to Allan Rock, minister of justice and attorney general of Canada, about Jamie. In the letter I asked how Jamie was allowed to change his name and be issued with a Canadian passport. I also wanted to know how a condition of Jamie's parole, that he not return to Canada without prior authorization from the National Parole Board, could be made when there was no way to enforce a restriction like that. I asked Rock a few other questions, too.

Did the National Parole Board ever make an effort to officially notify Italian authorities that a convicted police killer was being paroled to their country? What was Jamie's destination in Italy and where was he now? On whose authority was Jamie allowed to apply for and be granted a change of name, while serving a life sentence for murder and prior to his parole even being granted? Finally, seeing that Jamie had been convicted of murdering a police officer and was sentenced to "life," I asked Rock how Jamie was being supervised or monitored by the National Parole Board.

The silence from Rock was deafening.

But a response from Herb Gray, Solicitor General of Canada, came six months later. Gray said he could share only limited information about Jamie because of the Privacy Act, but he did tell me that offenders didn't require authorization from Correctional Services Canada or the National Parole Board to change their name. As for Jamie's supposed return to Canada in 1995, Gray said the matter had been looked into by a case management specialist who concluded that he had not re-entered Canada. Thus, on December 11, 1995, the warrant was withdrawn.

In 2003, Jamie requested a return to Canada to visit his mother, who he said was ailing. He said he had never been in the country since leaving for Italy. But according to the Canadian Professional Police Association, there was reason to believe that Jamie had illegally returned to Canada *three times* since his deal and that each time a warrant was issued but later dropped when police couldn't locate him.

Meanwhile, in Italy, Jamie has been operating a gym in Calabria and has apparently become something of a bodybuilding champion. At the 2002 World Fitness Federation World Championships in Northeim, Germany, he placed first in the category of Men's Extreme Body. His name was listed as Massimo Marra and the country he represented was said to be Italy.

In 2004, the National Parole Board said it had made an error ten years earlier by allowing Jamie to leave Canada for Italy. A two-member panel at the board concluded that because Jamie was still a Canadian citizen, he could not legally be precluded from re-entering Canada and living here. So, if the condition was that he leave and could not come back, he should have surrendered his Canadian citizenship. But he didn't. Somebody had made a mistake.

On October 13, 2004, Jamie wrote to the National Parole Board. In his letter he claimed that police reports called him "a gentleman at all times" and that while he was in prison Correctional Services Canada reports stated he had a "calming effect on hostile situations." He also said the last time he'd been stopped by police, they severely beat him, shot and killed his dog, and shot a civilian who was standing directly behind him. And he even singled me out personally. He said I would use my "corrupt police" in Toronto to cause trouble for him should he ever return to the city.

The Munro brothers are far from isolated examples of career criminals who get the kid-gloves treatment from the Canadian justice system, despite a propensity for constant reoffending. And even reoffending after going to prison. Consider the case of Charlie Hart, who is no bank robber or police killer, but who has an obvious problem with drinking and driving. In 1970, Hart, then twenty, was driving while drunk and killed two people. One of them was his best friend, who was travelling with him, and the other was a twenty-three-year-old man coming from the opposite direction. Hart got six months in reformatory for dangerous driving and lost his license for three years. At the time, he could have received a two-year sentence, but the judge gave him the benefit of the doubt. Keep in mind this was 1970, when there was no such thing as Mothers Against Drunk Drivers (MADD).

In 1972, Hart was again charged with drunk driving and yet again *every single year for the next eight years* after that. And many times he was charged with the same offence throughout the 1980s as well. On February 4, 2006, the *Globe and Mail* ran a three-page feature on Charlie Hart because he had the dubious honour of having received the most severe sentence for drunk driving in Canadian history. In 2005, he got one year for mischief and five years for refusing a Breathalyzer test. And what did he do to deserve that?

Thirty-nine convictions for drunk driving.

It wasn't until 1990 that this man did any federal time; that year he was sentenced to four years, but got paroled after seven months, and when he got out, authorities gave him an identification card with the wrong date of birth and the wrong spelling of his name. Hart used that card to get a brand-new Ontario driving license. And what does he have to say about all this? According to that *Globe and Mail* article: "I don't figure I had as much to drink as half the cops do when they're driving down the street."

This man is eligible for parole on December 9, 2008. While Charlie Hart is no Craig or Jamie Munro, he is a prime example of a long-time repeat offender who has been let off all too easily time and again by the courts.

Then there is James Roszko. On March 3, 2005, the Royal Canadian Mounted Police experienced the blackest day in the department's history. That was the day Roszko shot and killed four young constables—Peter Schiemann, Brock Myrol, Leo Johnston, and Anthony Gordon—before turning his gun on himself. Those four officers were investigating Roszko's property near the town of Mayerthorpe, Alberta, after a marijuana-growing operation and stolen auto parts were discovered.

This was just after I had left Toronto as chief and had started my job as commissioner of Emergency Management for the province of Ontario. I was in Israel, in Tel Aviv, on a fact-finding mission with Ontario minister of Community Safety and Correctional Services Monte Kwinter and a few other people. We were there to look at the strategies, tactics, and intelligence of the Israelis for things like security and counterterrorism. I was told about the shootings—it was night there—and I couldn't believe it. I was in my hotel room. I immediately made a call to RCMP commissioner Giuliano Zaccardelli and managed to get hold of him. We spoke and to be perfectly frank, we both got teary-eyed. It was an awful tragedy and he was hurting bad. He was down. When I got back to Canada, I spoke to him again and saw him in Edmonton at the memorial service for those four Mounties. Monte Kwinter and I were there representing Ontario.

James Roszko was labelled a petty criminal and small-town "badass" by Alberta justice minister Ron Stevens when Stevens released a report about this man's criminal past. That report, dated September 23, 2005, and prepared by Calgary's chief Crown prosecutor, Gordon Wong, is insightful.

Roszko had been charged with forty-four offences, but had been prosecuted in only sixteen of them and convicted in fourteen. Depicted after the killings as a gun-loving, cop-hating pedophile, he often got the benefit of the doubt at the hands of the justice system. For Roszko, it began in 1976 when he was seventeen years old and was charged with two counts of break, enter, and theft. He was convicted on one charge and on one count of possession of stolen property. He was fined $150 on each charge and given one-year probation. No incarceration.

Roszko was a first-time offender.

Later that year, he was convicted of theft under $200 and fined $250. That meant no incarceration. In 1978, he was charged with one count of possession of stolen property and another count of break, enter, and theft. He pled guilty to possession and was acquitted on the break and enter. He was given a suspended sentence and put on probation for eighteen months. Again, no incarceration.

In 1979, he was convicted of making harassing telephone calls and three counts of breaching conditions of his probation order. For this he got his first jail sentence—thirty days for the telephone calls and two fifteen-day sentences for breach of probation. Which makes forty-five days in all.

In 1990, he was convicted of uttering threats to cause death or serious bodily injury and fined $200. In 1993, he was convicted of two traffic violations, for which he was fined $25 each, and was acquitted on another charge of using obscene language. Later that year, one charge of assault was stayed. Why was it stayed? According to the report, there were three witnesses to this assault, but on the day of the trial none of them showed up because the subpoenas they had received had the wrong date on them.

In September 1993, Roszko was acquitted on one count of impersonating a peace officer after an essential witness who was supposed to testify didn't attend the trial. In December, he was acquitted of such charges as pointing a firearm, counselling to commit murder, unlawful confinement, possession of a weapon dangerous to the public peace, and assault with a weapon. Why was he acquitted? The key witness was nowhere to be found.

One might glean a pattern here that witnesses subpoenaed to testify at trials involving James Roszko had a tendency to disappear. In 1995,

Roszko was convicted of the sexual assault of a boy over a six-year period. It began when the boy was eleven and Roszko was twenty-four. The report says these acts occurred *approximately once a week*. He was sentenced to five years, but appealed and a new trial was ordered. In 2000, the sentence was reduced to two and a half years. This is what the report stated:

> The Court found circumstances existed, in the reporting of the offence and in the victim's conduct towards Roszko after the sexual acts had stopped, to conclude that the victim had not suffered long-term harm.

As one who has investigated more cases of sexual assault against children than I want to count, I find it absolutely mind boggling how any judge could say such a thing.

Nevertheless, Roszko appealed this conviction too, but his appeal was dismissed. There were many other charges, acquittals, charges stayed, what have you, after this. So why was this man never labelled a dangerous offender? Says the report:

> In general terms, before one can be declared a dangerous offender, the offender must demonstrate a pattern of significant criminal conduct that would lead the Court to conclude that the offender cannot control his/her behaviour and that there is a future likelihood of significant criminal conduct as a result.

Roszko had been flagged as a dangerous offender in 1995. But there was never any possibility of actually declaring him a dangerous offender because, the report says, "there was no history of proven criminal conduct that would amount to a successful application."

The families of those four slain RCMP officers have demanded changes to the justice system: mandatory minimum sentences, reduced parole, and elimination of the statutory release provision that lets most inmates out after two-thirds of their sentence, even if they have been denied parole. These are all things that I and the Canadian police community have been recommending for many years. The fact of the matter is, when it comes to real changes that have taken place in the criminal justice system—be it matters pertaining to sentencing or parole—the changes haven't come about because of the insight of politicians. Not by a long shot. They have come about because victims' groups like MADD, the police, or some members of the media have looked at the system for what it is, seen the flaws, and made a lot of noise. Only then have the politicians reacted. In almost forty years in this business, I don't know of much legislation that was sole-sourced from politicians who moved on an issue without there first being a human cry, constant begging, and other efforts designed to motivate them to change the laws. Politicians, by and large, never have to deal with the kinds of things victims of crime have to deal with. The trauma. The tragedy. And the fact that we just can't rehabilitate some people.

Many politicians are insulated from reality.

In 1993, Peter Whitmore abducted an eleven-year-old boy and sexually assaulted him over a twenty-four-hour period. The next year, he abducted a young girl and held her for three days. For those two abductions and a third one involving another boy, he was sentenced to five years, but served only sixteen months. When he was released in 1994, he kidnapped an eight-year-old girl and forced her to perform oral sex. He did another five years and was released in 1999. He was freed because he was not considered a dangerous offender; dangerous-offender legislation had been enacted two years earlier in 1997. Whitmore wound up in jail again and was released in 2006. He was charged with kidnapping two boys, aged ten and fourteen, which resulted in a Canadawide search that led to the rescue of the two boys in a farmhouse in Saskatchewan. Whitmore is still not classified as a dangerous offender.

Richard Condo, an offender who is considered a psychopath, is another example. In 2006, he was released from prison to a halfway house in Quebec. His most recent conviction was an eight-year sentence for the aggravated assault and kidnapping of his estranged wife. Upon release, he was subject to several conditions. In 2001, the Crown attorney's office tried to have him incarcerated indefinitely as a dangerous offender, but the judge ruled that he didn't fit the criteria. *Even though he had more than 80 convictions.*

The list goes on and on.

In the summer of 2006, the National Parole Board changed its mind about Jamie Munro and gave him the green light to return to Canada from Italy. Then, shortly before his arrival, it did an about-face and said he could not come into the country after all because of his "excessive and strong negative feelings" towards the police. Current Toronto Police Chief Bill Blair has been just as vehement as I have been about Jamie Munro coming back to Canada.

And where is Michael Sweet in all this? Dead but certainly not forgotten. On May 7, 2000, a downtown-Toronto street in 52 Division—where he once worked—was renamed in his honour. As for my personal campaign to keep Craig Munro behind bars and to keep whatever tabs I can on Jamie, there has been a great deal of support from rank-and-file police officers. Said Toronto officer Randy Bested in one of the many notes I have received about Michael Sweet over the years: "For those of us who knew Mike and were involved in that devastating event, it's nice to know that someone still speaks out on our behalf."

I believe, without a doubt, that Craig Munro would be a free man today and out walking the streets if the National Parole Board and Canadian authorities had their way. I am determined to make sure that never happens. But the system being what it is, this remains an ongoing battle.

· 14 ·

The Agony of Police Corruption

I N SOME COUNTRIES AROUND THE WORLD, THE COMMON perception is that police—virtually all police—are corrupt. Several years ago, when the City of Toronto was bidding for the 2008 Olympics, I was in Moscow as part of the team supporting the bid. I was responsible for putting together the security program and had to be available to answer questions. Before the trip, we were given a briefing on how to conduct ourselves in Moscow. We were told that police in Moscow are corrupt and on the take and that people driving in the city are afraid of the traffic police because they always have their hands out. If you get stopped, you must pay them or else they won't let you go. The point was to make sure we had money on us. In the end, we opted not to drive in Moscow. But another time when I was in Mexico, I experienced this form of corruption first-hand. For no particular reason, the car I was in got stopped by a traffic officer. Fortunately, the driver was accustomed to the Mexican routine; he spoke to the officer who then just drove away. When I asked the driver what all that was about, he said the guy, meaning the police officer, wanted to be paid off. I had to accept this was how it worked in some countries.

Things are different in North America, but we certainly aren't immune to police corruption. I used to be a member of the Major Cities

Chiefs, an organization representing chiefs of the biggest cities in Canada and the United States. We met four times a year and I made many lasting friendships with this group. Police corruption was an issue we all faced, but some had more experience with it than others. In 1997, the FBI sent a survey to fifty-one major North American cities to gather data on police misconduct and corruption; thirty-seven of the fifty-one police agencies responded. This didn't mean the other agencies weren't interested; most likely they were too busy to meet the arbitrary deadline imposed on them. The FBI released a report based on results from those responding agencies and found that, on average, a major city police chief can expect to have ten officers charged every year with abuse of police authority, five arrested for a felony, seven arrested for a misdemeanour, three arrested for theft, and four arrested for domestic violence. In the year of the study, 1997, there were several notable incidents. Three Chicago police officers were convicted of robbing a suspected drug dealer. Two Indianapolis police officers were charged with murder in the shooting death of a suspected drug dealer, and one of those officers said the two had been robbing drug dealers for four years. A former supervisor of the FBI's South Florida Organized Crime Unit admitted to taking $400,000 from that agency because he needed the money to pay off gambling debts. In Cleveland, forty-three police officers and jail guards were arrested on charges of providing protection for drug dealers. And a police officer in Metro-Dade County, Florida, was charged with sixteen criminal counts including racketeering, armed robbery, and conspiracy to traffic in cocaine.

While no one, least of all police chiefs, thinks this is acceptable behaviour we must look at the bigger picture. There are 600,000 police officers in the United States and, according to the FBI, less than 1 per cent of them are "bad apples."

Corruption can become a problem when standards are compromised. A good example is the story of the Miami River Cops in the 1980s. It was felt that the Miami police didn't have enough Spanish-speaking officers, so they hired many new people on the fly. But they didn't do proper screening and wound up with cops shaking down drug dealers and even doing killings. A number of officers were arrested and some of them went to prison.

The Rampart Scandal in the Los Angeles Police Department (LAPD) is another example of improper police conduct. The Rampart Division was one of eighteen divisions in the LAPD and served the highest-crime area in Los Angeles. There were allegations about police committing perjury, fabricating evidence, making false arrests, and even stealing drugs and selling them on the street. Before it was over, seventy officers were under investigation.

When I was a member of the Major Cities Chiefs, I discovered first-hand about the anguish faced by some of my fellow chiefs when allegations about corruption surfaced. My friend Bernie Parks became chief of the LAPD in 1997 and put together a unit to investigate the allegations involving the Rampart Division. Parks is a sincere, honourable man with great experience and he was tenacious in his pursuit of law-breakers. He was seen by many of us in the police community as a mentor and someone to look up to as he wrestled with corruption and the damage to the reputation of his police department. In the Major Cities Chiefs, he was open and forthright with his fellow chiefs about his struggles, but despite his noble efforts, he wound up incurring the blame for what happened.

Rampart was a powerful lesson for all of us about the critical importance of front-line supervision and about policies and procedures being followed and audited. It showed us that when people are not held accountable, disaster will surely follow. Of course, this applies to a lot more than policing.

Another chief I knew well was Richard Pennington of the New Orleans Police Department (NOPD). Pennington is a tall African-American who is in excellent shape; he's soft-spoken, articulate, and very friendly. He always struck me as a man who carried a big stick and wasn't afraid to use it, and he certainly did when dealing with corrupt cops on his police force. The NOPD had a reputation for being corrupt and ineffective, and it was. Part of the reason for this was that New Orleans police officers were very poorly paid, with starting salaries as low as $16,000 (U.S.) a year and this was in the 1990s! They had to support their families, so some of them began doing outside work as bouncers in bars and one thing led to another. The FBI came in to investigate and under Pennington's watch more than 200 officers were charged. Since then the NOPD has greatly enhanced what it pays officers. But what a lot of people don't know is that when Pennington started cracking down on corruption in the NOPD, he needed FBI protection for himself because of all the threats he received.

Today, most police officers, at least in Western countries, are well paid. In Toronto, a starting police officer earns over $40,000 a year and a detective drawing overtime and court time can earn $100,000. In police circles, those earning a six-figure income are known as members of the "Sunshine Club." But there is a tremendous amount of work involved and it's anything but a forty-hour week. These people are very busy and work on a lot of cases at once. They spend a great deal of time in court and get involved in things that require a huge commitment, such as murder cases. You can't drop a murder case and say you'll get back to it tomorrow.

When I was at police college in 1969, the director of the college, a superintendent and war veteran, gave us presentations about integrity. One day he came into the classroom and said that three things can get you into trouble on the police department. He called them "rocks in the roadway" to a successful police career. The first of those rocks was consorting with people of ill repute, the second was the mishandling of property, and the third was abusing alcohol. The thought of these "rocks in the roadway" has stayed with me ever since because when you see a police officer getting into trouble, it's usually because of one of these things.

The worst example of corruption that I have ever experienced involved an officer who worked in Toronto's 55 Division. He was doing armed robberies. A few times he even shot at people. I was chief in York

Region when this started, and when I was chief in Toronto we took him down. The whole episode was sheer agony for us. It was a joint investigation by York Regional Police and Toronto police and the guy was eventually arrested, charged, and convicted. He went to penitentiary. But we were on pins and needles throughout the whole ordeal because we knew if we didn't act properly and decisively he might wind up killing someone. This man was very manipulative and he had a position of trust working in plainclothes, and that kind of work lends itself to a non-structured work environment. I know because I've done it. He would leave his partner at the station and go out and do an armed robbery, and do it with police equipment on police time. Some people in the media tried to portray this as standard police behaviour when, in fact, this guy was one of a kind. There was also an expectation in some circles that as chief, I should apologize and take the blame. My view was that you take corrective measures and assume responsibility for systems that don't work, but I've never been one for taking responsibility for the unlawful actions of a police officer. I think it is unfair to directly blame the chief for the dishonesty of people in the organization unless, of course, the chief is complicit.

Sometimes there is a fine line between corruption and stupidity. Police officers have to know that associating with bad guys lends itself to compromise, potential compromise or, at the very least, the perception of compromise. None of these things is good. The fact is, if you hang around with the wrong crowd, you can easily become part of the scenery.

Behaviour not suitable or ethical for a police force is not confined to the rank and file. It can also reach the top. In 1998, I left the London police and accepted a job as chief of York Regional Police. This police force had 850 members, served a population of one million people, and covered a huge area of 1,800 square kilometres. But it had been having a lot of trouble. Morale was low and the previous chief, whom I had known since my detective days, had to resign after being charged with criminal breach of trust. He was accused of accepting a payment from a large corporation that he was planning to work for as a security consultant upon retirement. And the man who succeeded me as chief in London also had to resign eventually when he was charged with breach of trust after pleading guilty to a fraud charge concerning his expense account.

The law enforcement oath of honour for the International Association of Chiefs of Police says:

> On my honour, I will never betray my profession, my integrity, my character, or the public trust. I will always have the courage to hold myself and others accountable for our actions. I will always uphold the laws of my country, my community, and the agency I serve.

When I was chief in Toronto, I had a routine that I performed when it was time to swear in new police officers at their graduation ceremony. I would stand before them and recite the oath of office with them. I did this because their formal training was completed and I wanted to be sure these words resonated with them. I wanted to highlight the importance of their job, the importance of honesty and integrity, and of everything else they are expected to do as they embark on their police careers. I made it a point to remind those graduating recruits—and in front of their families—to always do the right thing even when no one is looking.

If police officers lose the public trust, then everything is lost.

In policing, there are many temptations—money, drugs, and the potential to participate in unlawful activities to achieve criminal means for someone else. There is also what is called "noble cause" corruption where some may feel that, in order to achieve the end result and uphold the laws of the land, they have to break the laws themselves. But police officers cannot become criminals in order to catch criminals.

Think of any police department in a big city. It might have thousands of officers. Then think of all the contacts those officers have, the situations they get involved in, and all the opportunities presented to them. Without the right set of circumstances—proper recruiting, screening, and supervision, as well as accountability, policies and procedures, auditing and inspections—things can happen. But there is no doubt in my mind that the overwhelming majority of police officers—at least, in North America—do their job ethically and honourably without compromise. Still, from time to time you have those who stray. Police officers get approached to do things by people who are looking for a favour. By that I mean people who want help on cases or who want to make a case just "go away" or who want to secure confidential information from police sources.

In my career, I have dealt with corruption in different ways. In the early 1990s, I was an inspector and was asked to investigate allegations about police being approached in Toronto's old Chinatown area by keepers of illegal gaming establishments, unlicensed liquor establishments, and bawdy houses. It turned out that, while some officers were participating in the odd free meal and drinks and things of that nature, the operators of some of these places were actively trying to compromise the police. So a few of us went undercover to investigate. We were quickly approached by some of the operators of these illegal establishments who wanted us to look the other way and they paid us to look the other way. They knew we were police and didn't want us to raid their places or they expected us to pre-warn them if a raid was coming. We went along with it. As time went on, we were paid a considerable sum of money *not* to knock off these places. It was basically paying protection to the police. I personally collected $1,000 a week in cash and this went on for several months. There was also a lot of wining and dining. Eventually the corrupt officers were busted, the case went to court, and we got convictions. But those convictions weren't much, everything from suspended sentences to less than two years in a reformatory. As for the money they gave us, it was all recorded, seized as evidence, and forfeited. But not to me.

One of the raids we did in Chinatown during that undercover investigation was at an unlicensed liquor establishment that was serving liquor openly as if it had a license. We seized a large quantity of liquor as evidence and the bottles were sealed with Centre of Forensic Sciences (CFS) seals. Even before we could process the paperwork to lay charges, I was approached with an offer of money to *not* file the charges and return the liquor. This would result in a weekly payoff of money and meals. To further our undercover investigation, I accepted the offer and we returned the seized liquor, complete with the CFS seals affixed to the bottles. A few days later, we went back to the place to get our payoff and, of course, liquor was being served. Believe it or not, some of the bottles on display at the bar still had the CFS seals on them! That case also resulted in a liquor inspector being convicted, although he got a light sentence.

Some people think police corruption starts with a free cup of coffee, but this is an exaggeration. Corruption is much more than that. I find it hard to believe that a police officer would sell his or her soul, reputation, and badge for a cup of coffee. The police chiefs I know—and I've known pretty well all of them in the biggest Canadian and American cities—are very diligent about making sure they deal with corrupt practices, whether it's prevention or investigations.

In Toronto, we put into place a proactive system that tracks the activities of individual officers when we thought there were indicators or potential signs of problems in the making. I was introduced to the issue of police corruption right after I became chief in Toronto. I was met with a flurry of complaints from lawyers who made serious allegations about their clients being falsely accused or having their money stolen. The complaints focused on one particular group of police officers. The Central Field Drug Squad unit. As the number of complaints mounted and demands for a public inquiry became routine, I felt something had to be done to clear the air about serious and damning accusations concerning corrupt practices, such as ripping off drug dealers and taking their money. I sought legal advice and was determined to carry out an independent investigation and get to the bottom of it.

In 2001, I approached RCMP commissioner Giuliano Zaccardelli to do an independent investigation. He assigned Chief Superintendent John Neily to head it up, and twenty hand-picked detectives went to work. Some voices are always quick to complain about police investigating police but, in fact, there is no more qualified body of people around to do this kind of work and this is true for two reasons. First, police officers are professionals; they are well trained and this is what they get paid to do. Second, no one is more knowledgeable about the issues and systems involving allegations made against police than the police themselves. If we can't trust police agencies to deal with such cases, how can we trust them to investigate politicians or anyone else for that matter? Either way, their work has to be tested by the highest courts in the land. If the police are not up to snuff when investigating their own, why should they have the responsibility of investigating terrorists or organized crime syndicates? Police agencies have highly skilled and well-trained internal affairs people. This is what they do for a living and they are good at it. In the legal profession, lawyers investigate lawyers. In the medical profession, doctors investigate doctors. I don't see why it should be any different with police.

Does the public think the police are corrupt? I don't think so. Whenever a survey or poll about the credibility of various professions is held, police officers are always at or near the very top of the list. But who's at the bottom? The media, politicians, and lawyers. Lawyers are usually right at the bottom. I think this point is important. It shows that, by and large, police have the respect and trust of the public, and I will argue that point with anybody.

In 1990, an independent agency called the Special Investigations Unit (SIU) was formed in Ontario, initially to look into situations where a police officer had shot someone. It soon had the power to investigate two things—officers who were involved in instances where civilians had met with death or serious injury at the hands of police, and allegations of a sexual nature made against police. In the first nine years of its existence, the SIU had nine different directors and was a totally inept organization. It had incompetent investigators muddling through very complex cases and then passing judgment on the actions of the police. Policing was a job this organization knew very little about. One time it hired a former American police officer to investigate Canadian police, but it took a newspaper reporter to find out that he had been released from the U.S.

police agency he had worked with and that was because of misconduct. And this guy was investigating Canadian police?

In 1999, I was still chief of the York Regional Police and also outgoing president of the Ontario Association of Chiefs of Police (OACP). I wrote to Ontario premier Mike Harris after an OACP meeting where all the chiefs had agreed that the SIU should either be abolished or totally revamped. The problem was that, for the most part, SIU personnel were not police officers themselves (at least, not police officers who had left their jobs with distinction as elite investigators) and they operated with the *preconceived notion* that a police officer under investigation must have done something criminal.

The SIU had directors without proper controls who were turned loose on the police community. We sat back and watched SIU investigators muddle through investigations where they actually mishandled evidence. They didn't collect evidence properly. They didn't submit it properly. They didn't deal with the issue of contamination of evidence. They interviewed witnesses inappropriately. The whole thing was just a patchwork of incompetence and it operated from the premise that SIU investigators had to be anything other than police officers. The SIU charged a number of officers for no reason, which rightfully generated a lot of pushback and resentment from the police community. In the overwhelming majority of cases they investigated, the officers under investigation had put their lives on the line in some very dangerous situations. So what you had were true heroes who were being treated like criminals and that was wrong. Any police officers under investigation were basically deemed to be guilty until proven innocent, which runs contrary to our very system of justice. Another thing was that SIU cases seemed to go on forever before being resolved, so these officers were on the hook for a long time. I was very vocal in my criticism of the SIU. Fortunately, it eventually got better and today the SIU is a model. It does excellent and timely investigations. Its people are well trained and the directors of the organization are solid. Finally, the SIU has a number of reputable, former, retired police investigators. So things improved greatly and today there is a good element of trust between the SIU and the police community. Unfortunately, this happened only after a great deal of trauma was inflicted on many good police officers and their families.

When we had this situation in Toronto, with officers under investigation, I had absolute confidence in the ability of the Toronto Police Service to investigate any alleged wrongdoing on the part of our officers. But I decided to go to the RCMP for an independent investigation. This was more for optics and perception than anything else. I knew that, if the Toronto police were leading the investigation themselves, all kinds of critics would have come out of the woodwork.

The RCMP worked at an undisclosed location outside of police headquarters. And in 2004, we held a press conference where I announced that five officers and one retired officer were facing criminal charges. This saddened and disappointed me and I stressed that these were isolated incidents, which they most certainly were. I also said I wouldn't stand by to allow the reputation of the department to be unfairly attacked or exploited by those who were intent on causing mischief, and that I had faith in due process, leaving the ultimate findings to our system of justice. Like every other police organization, the Toronto Police Service has experienced corruption, but let's not forget that this police force arrests some 50,000 people every year and racks up hundreds of thousands of contacts with the public on myriad issues. That presents a lot of opportunities for potential compromise and this wasn't the first time Toronto police were investigated.

When we asked the RCMP to do that independent investigation, we also wanted to take a long look at what we should do so we wouldn't have to go through this agonizing experience again. That's why I approached retired Ontario justice George Ferguson and asked him to conduct a comprehensive investigation of police corruption and, not only with the Toronto police, but around the world. Judge Ferguson was a highly reputed justice and a man of impeccable integrity. I wanted him to look at police corruption across the board—what leads to it, lessons learned, best practices, and how those things can be applied to our own police force.

Judge Ferguson's mandate was three-pronged. The first part concerned the *disclosure* of police misconduct. When must a police department bring to the attention of a Crown prosecutor acts of misconduct involving an officer who will be a witness or who is otherwise involved in an investigation that has led to a criminal proceeding? Now, *that* is a loaded question. To find the answer, Judge Ferguson compared the law in Ontario with the law in other jurisdictions—the United States, England, Australia, and New Zealand. He chose these countries because a lot of information was available and because each of them had already taken steps to address the issues he would examine. He also looked at the privacy rights of police officers. This refers to the information a defence counsel, on a specific case, is entitled to have about the background of an officer who is a witness. In Toronto, defence lawyers were having a field day obtaining court motions pertaining to background information about individual officers and this was causing extensive trial delays. The problem was that there was no standardization as to what information should be provided and what information should be kept private. Defence counsel normally want everything they can get their hands on, but police officers are citizens and have rights too, and I wanted to strike a balance. This was one area where there was a big difference between Canada and the United States. The U.S. had full reciprocal disclosure for both the defence and prosecution. That meant that, while the defence lawyer could ask for the whole drawer of information on the officer, so could the prosecution. Not so in Canada.

The second part of Judge Ferguson's mandate concerned systemic issues. He reviewed Toronto's policies, practices, and procedures and compared them to those of other large law enforcement agencies. He also looked at best practices and lessons learned.

The third part of his mandate was about police informers and agents. This concerned the relationship an officer may have with a police informant. It's crucial that any meetings or dealings between them stand the test of scrutiny and law and, further, that both the officer and the informant are protected.

Judge Ferguson received written submissions from people in the legal community and from organizations such as the Association in Defense of the Wrongfully Convicted, the Criminal Lawyers Association, and such far-flung groups as the Isle of Man Constabulary and the Police Integrity Commission in Sydney, Australia. He held meetings with such people as Rubin "Hurricane" Carter, a man who was wrongfully convicted in the U.S. and sentenced for a murder he didn't commit. Carter was the subject of Norman Jewison's film *Hurricane*. Judge Ferguson also met with police officials from Toronto, New York, London, England, and elsewhere. He studied legislation in Canada, the U.S., the U.K., Australia, New Zealand, and Korea. In short, he looked at countless cases of police corruption.

In 2003, he released his report and it was a gem. In a nutshell, he explained what led to police corruption and how to prevent it from happening. I believe his report contains the best analysis and recommendations of best practices that has ever been put together on this subject, and I consider what he did a great investment because he gave us answers to issues that were forever being litigated.

For example, when a Crown attorney asks the chief of police for information regarding acts of misconduct by an officer who may be a witness or who is otherwise involved in a case, the recommendations from Judge Ferguson require the chief to provide the attorney only with information about convictions, outstanding charges, or any findings of guilt for misconduct concerning that officer. And that's it.

In the area of police recruiting, Judge Ferguson said Toronto's system of background checks for prospective recruits was inadequate. His recommendation? Investigating new hires for the police department should go beyond simple computer checks and include extensive interviews with the person's family, neighbours, associates, and previous employers. He also said Toronto's Employment Unit should be upgraded and should develop a targeted and focused recruitment program to increase exposure of the police in universities, community colleges, high schools, and other educational institutions. He recommended employing two full-time psychologists to conduct psychological testing of potential recruits and said that anyone being groomed for promotion should also be interviewed by these psychologists.

In addition, Judge Ferguson recommended thorough background and financial checks on anyone being promoted to a management or supervisory position and on anyone being transferred to a sensitive or high-risk unit. He recommended that the entire operation of Internal Affairs be moved to a separate, independent location—not at police headquarters—and that this department develop a process to protect whistle-blowers. He recommended that anyone being promoted or reassigned to a sensitive or high-risk area submit to drug testing.

In the area of how to deal with police informers and agents, he recommended adopting the system used by the Metropolitan Police Service in London, England. There, informers are not deemed to be the private domain of individual police officers, but rather an asset of the police service as a whole. The system is called the Source Management System, and everything is closely monitored in a computer database—all contact and all dealings with the informant are approved, documented, and audited as part of due diligence. The idea behind this is that it prevents individual officers from entering unhealthy relationships.

In Toronto, three sticky issues were the aforementioned drug testing for police officers in high-risk jobs, financial background checks of those in high-risk jobs, and psychological assessments for anyone being considered for promotion. When I left as chief in 2005, those issues were still on the table. But those three items aside, pretty well all of Judge Ferguson's recommendations have been implemented, and not only in Toronto, but in other police agencies as well, which isn't surprising because I sent his report to other chiefs upon request. It's even on the Internet.

I still believe that the most professional system of policing anywhere is found in Canada. Unfortunately, much of what you hear is often driven by perception and biases. I'm talking about preconceived biases like "you just can't trust the police." This line of thought also includes the view that you can't give the police semi-automatics because they'll shoot more people, or you can't give them Tasers because they will be abused. But this is foolish. We are willing to give the police bullets and guns that can kill people, but we're not willing to give them Tasers that can actually save people. This is ridiculous.

I am very proud of the work Judge Ferguson did and of his report. And to all the police critics who like to say that this corruption issue happened on my watch, well, that is just dead wrong. The truth is, the *fix* happened on my watch. We had some problems and, as chief, I had to take affirmative action to protect the reputation of the Toronto Police Service and the reputation of all its people who are honest, decent, and hard-working. And that's what I did.

Chief Fantino visits with local police officers in Lithuania in September 2002.

Hockey great Darryl Sittler and Chief Fantino celebrate the eighty-eighth birthday of Toronto legend "Honest Ed" Mirvish in August 2002. Sadly, Ed died in July 2007 at the age of 92.

Shaking hands with actor Michael Douglas at fundraiser in Toronto.

Chief Fantino and boxing legend George Chuvalo at "Honest Ed" Mirvish's annual turkey give-away, Christmas 2002.

Greeting Pope John Paul II at Toronto's Pearson International airport for World Youth Day 2002.

The chief's office at police headquarters in Toronto in 2003.

Julian and Sister Mary Vanitee—his grade 8 teacher—enjoy a walkabout at a community event in 2003.

With Paul Martin in Toronto at the 2003 SARS concert featuring The Rolling Stones. A short time later Martin would be sworn in as prime minister of Canada.

Looking out over a crowd of 500,000 fans for the 2003 SARS concert. Improvising security on such short notice was a major challenge.

Chief Julian Fantino receiving the Commander of the Order of Police Forces from Governor General Adrienne Clarkson in 2003.

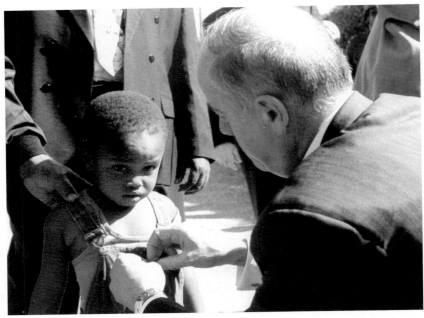

While visiting Kingston, Jamaica, in February 2003, Chief Fantino pins a Toronto Police Service pin on a little boy. [Ian Robertson, *Toronto Sun*]

Once a beat cop—always a beat cop: Chief Fantino making an arrest at Canadian National Exhibition in 2004.

Meeting with the Dalai Lama in May 2004. Left to right: Staff Sergeant Kim Derry (currently deputy chief of the Toronto Police Service), the Dalai Lama, Julian and Inspector Ken Kinsman.

Chief Julian Fantino and wife Liviana, and New York City mayor Rudy Giuliani after 9/11.

Julian introducing Mayor Giuliani at a speaking engagement at the University of Western Ontario Ivy School of Business. At right is Murray Faulkner, chief of the London (Ontario) Police Service.

Julian holding a memento during a visit to Pier 21 in Halifax. To his right is Marie Chapman, Pier 21 senior manager. To his left are his wife Liviana, and two Pier 21 staff members. The woman in front is Ruth Goldbloom, CEO of the Pier 21 Foundation. Ruth almost singlehandedly recovered and developed the Pier 21 project to make it what it is today.

· 15 ·

Being on the Hot Seat

Without a doubt, the most vulnerable person in the police department is the chief. The chief is accountable for everything and I know many of them who have quit because they have had enough. Although you invariably start the job with a honeymoon period, the honeymoon fades quickly and then you get down to constantly juggling bouncing balls. The job description would be something like this: You must deal with an enormous number of expectations from a wide network of constituencies. All the while, you have limited time and limited opportunity to be 100 per cent certain in every decision you make. You don't have the benefit of deferring things and you're on a production line with no on-off or speed switch, so you are event driven. Not only that, but many things are beyond your control since many things impact what you do by virtue of decisions made by other people and by the local politics of the day. Then you've got to deal with the media and with the rank and file in your police association, and on top of that, you must be able to pass the microscope test on everything you do.

The job also involves huge pressures and responsibilities, and it can mean a difficult family life because the job must come first. You are always engaged with and in constant contact with people because you are dealing with human beings and their trauma and tragedy from the cradle to the grave. As well, you can never go anywhere without people approaching you to talk business, even when you might just want to be by yourself or with your family.

In some ways being chief of a big-city police force is like being a CEO. Take the Toronto Police Service. The chief reports to the Police Services Board and everyone else reports to the chief. At the higher levels this includes the deputy chiefs, the legal counsel, the executive officer, and the disciplinary hearings officer. It also includes five large areas of the service: Human Resources Command, Administrative Command, Executive Command, Divisional Policing Command, and Specialized Operations Command. In turn, a whole slew of people and departments reports to each of those command areas.

But while a CEO is basically responsible to the board of directors and the shareholders, the overall responsibilities of a police chief are considerably greater. And so is the pressure. What's the pressure like? I'll tell you.

When I came to Toronto as chief, I had already done my apprenticeship as chief with two other major police forces in London and York Region, but it's different in a big city. In 1988, the G7 Economic Summit was held in Toronto. President Ronald Reagan came from the U.S., along with Prime Minister Margaret Thatcher from the U.K., Chancellor Helmut Kohl from West Germany, President François Mitterand from France, Prime Minister Ciriaco de Mita from Italy, Prime Minister Noboru Takeshita from Japan, and Commissioner Jacques Delors from the European Community, even though that organization was not officially part of the G7. Canadian prime minister Brian Mulroney was the host. Jack Marks was chief of the Toronto Police at the time and he appointed me to head up the criminal intelligence and investigations portion of the police contingent to work alongside the Ontario Provincial Police and RCMP. We had to develop what is called a "threat profile" and, if anything went wrong, it would have been our job to respond. In those days, terrorist groups such as the Japanese Red Army, Italian Red Brigades, and German Baader-Meinhof Gang were very active. Chief

Marks called me in for a meeting that was designed to convey the importance of our responsibility and he did it in a way I'll never forget. He said, "What will Dallas forever be remembered for? I don't want that to happen here."

If anything had happened at that G7 summit, it would have stuck to both the city and Chief Marks. It would have stuck to him for as long as he lived. The G7 leaders were in town for three days and we were on pins and needles every minute they were here. One evening, one of the leaders decided he wanted to go out to an ice-cream shop. Just like that. There were no plans for this, but he and his entourage went anyway. When the leaders left the city after their three-day summit, I heaved a great sigh of relief.

Four years earlier, in 1984, pope John Paul II visited Toronto and I was a staff sergeant in 52 Division. This was three years after the attempted assassination at St. Peter's Square. We were assigned to the Toronto Convention Centre where the pope was having private audiences. We got a call on our police radio that some people saw a man in the crowd outside behaving suspiciously, so we approached him and found that he had a large concealed knife and a papal passport. The papal passport was issued for a private audience with the pope and this one had been stolen. That guy was real weird and ever since then I've always wondered what might have happened if we hadn't stopped him and charged him.

The chief is the one who is on the line for security at major events. When I was chief in Toronto, we had another papal visit in 2002. Because it was the pope, it was a state visit and the occasion was World Youth Day. Almost one million Catholics—most of them young people from around the world—descended on the city for several days. As chief, I was in charge of security and even got to meet the pope. In fact, I met him several times over the years and still have a photograph of me with him on my office wall. I am very proud of that. For the 2002 visit, we worked with papal security people and, of course, the OPP and RCMP, and there was a tremendous amount of planning. It started with the welcoming ceremony at Pearson International Airport, then the Papal Welcoming

Ceremony at Exhibition Place on the shore of Lake Ontario, the Stations of the Cross up University Avenue, and finally the prayer vigil with just under a million people at Downsview Park, which is the site of a former air force base and a huge open area. If anything had gone wrong—anything at all—I would have been responsible.

Just imagine that you're the chief of police and something happens to the pope in your city.

In 2003, when I was chief, the SARS crisis hit Toronto. At the outset, I thought it was strictly a health issue and the police weren't involved. Dr. Sheila Basrur was the city's medical officer of health and she was a tower of strength throughout that whole ordeal. Dr. Donald Low was the expert at Mount Sinai Hospital. Then, all of a sudden, it hit. SARS was traced back to Scarborough Grace Hospital in the east end of the city and they called for a ten-day quarantine. That meant we had to trace every single police officer who had been in contact with that hospital, and there were 170 of them. Police officers are in hospitals every day. When they called for a quarantine, it became a major issue for us as a police force, for those 170 officers, and for the families of all those officers as well. There was fear that police officers could have contracted SARS, so those officers had to go into quarantine, and what scared the hell out of everyone was the unknown. We had never dealt with anything like this before. If we had had an outbreak of SARS in the police department, heaven knows what could have happened. We also had to deal with the fact that some civilians who had been given quarantine orders refused to obey them. That's right. They refused. Who then was going to enforce those quarantine orders? The police, of course. So we put a team together and had to give that team the right equipment and the right information. We also had to put contingencies in place. If some people refused to obey a quarantine order, we sure weren't going to put them in jail. As it turned out, no one was arrested, because the dissenters were paid stern visits by the health authorities and did eventually go into quarantine.

When things started to ease up a bit, Dennis Mills, a local member of Parliament, and Senator Jerry Grafstein got the idea for a concert by the Rolling Stones to help the city get back on its feet. It was planned quickly and the timelines were very tight. The police would handle security, and we were confident because we had done the pope's visit, but at the back of my mind I remembered what had happened to John Lennon. Then one of the newspapers unearthed a crowd-management expert from Chicago and ran an article saying that the Stones concert was a disaster waiting to happen. This expert said there was no time to plan adequate security, and all the media picked up on his comments. Everything was negative. It was a manufactured story without any credibility because this guy didn't know a thing about us and probably didn't even know where Toronto was, but we still had to answer to it. Well, half a million people attended that concert—with every age group you can imagine—and it went off without a hitch. We set up a police barrier between the stage and the crowd—it was like a no man's land—and it worked fine. Everyone was dancing and having a great time. Then we saw this guy who was piss drunk driving around young girls on a stolen golf cart. We charged him with theft of a motor vehicle and impaired driving. That was the only real problem we had.

A couple years later, when I was the Ontario commissioner of emergency management, there was a big scare at a home for the aged in Toronto. A lot of residents got sick and a number of them died. The media descended on the city, especially the American media, thinking that SARS was back. It was eventually determined the cause to be legionnaires' disease, and once that was clear, all the American media lost interest because it wasn't news anymore. Until then, we were being portrayed by the U.S. media as the centre of communicable disease, which was ridiculous, but that's what the reporting was like.

While the job of a police chief comes with great pressures, it also comes with a lot of positives and a great deal of satisfaction. One thing I have always enjoyed, especially in a multicultural city like Toronto, is the interaction with such a diverse community. This involves networking amongst all levels of society and all kinds of people. One day it's the pope and the next day it's the beggar on the street.

The big difference between being a police chief in Canada and in the United States is that in the U.S., most chiefs serve at the pleasure of the mayor or city manager, while in Canada, the chief reports to a commission or a police services board. That's a huge difference. In the U.S., the mayor has ultimate authority over the chief, and mayors often bring in their own staff and their own chief as well. The trouble is, if you politicize the police you run a lot of risks, including the element of corruption creeping in, because you don't want a police chief hanging on to the job based on favours done for the mayor. In Canada, we have checks and balances, and for Ontario jurisdictions, the Police Services Act is very clear about roles and responsibilities.

I believe that in spite of our warts, Canada has the best model and the best police anywhere. I really do. This is readily apparent to me whenever I travel around the world, especially to countries where the police are the army of occupation and are feared by the population. One of the big obstacles Canadian police face is that people come from countries where they may have been terrified by the police and then they must learn to overcome that fear in this country. This can take time.

A case that went to the high court in Canada set a precedent for police chiefs. The chief in a northern Ontario community was being terminated without cause by the police services board, who had overstepped their authority, and he resisted. He went to court, which ruled that, at least in Ontario, the chief is not in a master-servant relationship with the police services board. This meant that a chief had a level of autonomy with which to do the job and was not driven by a special agenda or the politics of the day. I have often had to refer to this ruling in my career.

When I was chief in London, the outgoing mayor was a man named Tom Gosnell. He was a bright young guy, very energetic and highly respected, and then he announced he wasn't running for reelection. He had a young family and wanted to go into business and maybe get back into politics later. The election was between Diane Haskett, who was a member of city council, and Jack Burghardt, who was chair of the police services board. Without prior consultation with me, Diane Haskett put out her "Green Book" and made promises about what she'd do with regard to policing issues after she became mayor. She had visited Edmonton and seen all the community offices they have, so she said London would do that, too. She won the election and I wondered what was going to happen with all those promises she had made. She summoned me to her office and I brought along one of my inspectors, Murray Faulkner, who later became the chief in the city. When Tom Gosnell was mayor, he had footballs in his office and things were very informal. His guests got their coffee in disposable cups. Now with the new mayor we were greeted with a tea service and fine china. As soon as I saw this, I nudged Murray in the ribs and told him we were in big trouble.

The new mayor told me I had to implement all the promises about policing that she had made in her election campaign. I tried explaining that it doesn't work that way, that she had to work through the police services board. She demanded that I set up a community police office in every neighbourhood in the city, but I told her that to do that you need police officers in those offices. She talked about what she had seen in Edmonton, but at that time Edmonton's crime rate was way off the map and London was nowhere near that level. There was just no comparison between the two cities, and for London this idea would have been totally inappropriate. Still, she reminded me that she was the mayor and, being a lawyer, she said she knew the law and was also responsible for public safety. Then she said she'd bring in a retired superintendent from Edmonton to teach us all about community policing. She gave us no credit for the wonderful job the men and women on the London police force were doing. I explained that my employer was the local police services board and that this was not the American system, but she got quite indignant about it. Eventually I said, "Your Worship, you might be the mayor but I'm the only sheriff in town." It wasn't a pleasant start to the relationship. Later, she sat on the police services board, but she had thought as mayor she could boss us around. She couldn't.

In October 2001—one month after 9/11—the International Association of Chiefs of Police (IACP) annual conference was held in Toronto and we hosted the conference. I had become chief in Toronto in March of the previous year. The police association, which was the union representing rank-and-file officers, and I had differences of opinion about some issues, such as roles and responsibilities and how to enforce the line separating the duties of a police chief from the duties of an association. Before my arrival, there had been all kinds of bickering back and forth about the association versus the chief and the association versus the police services board. From the outset, I was trying to establish clear rules of engagement. So, here we were on the first day of this prestigious international conference. The IACP. With my peers. We're talking 12,000 police leaders from all over the world, and it's right on the heels of 9/11 when there was so much trauma after what had happened with so many police officers, firefighters, and civilians who died in New York City. And just then the Toronto Police Association announced that they were going to have a no-confidence vote on me as chief. I don't think it was a coincidence. They couldn't have picked a more devastating time to do this to me and it hurt me and my family deeply. I was a novice in the area of non-confidence votes, but it turned out to be a tactic frequently used to attack and dismantle police chiefs, especially in the U.S.

My fellow chiefs rallied around me with "You too, uh?" and some of them even felt this was a badge of honour. The association announced that the vote was 90 per cent in favour of non-confidence in me. Right away, I was immediately besieged with emails, correspondence, and phone calls from citizens, police officers, and members of the police service who supported me. There was even a thing called The Ten Percent Club started up. I never saw the actual numbers of how many people took part in the so-called no-confidence vote, but I felt it was just a tactic to try to bring me into line. As it turned out, the police services board, which included Toronto mayor Mel Lastman, members of council, and citizen appointees, also supported me and so, I persevered.

It was traumatic for me to be so publicly maligned at such a big conference and it affected my family. In the U.S., 50 per cent of the chiefs who are subjected to a non-confidence vote from their union or association either quit, are deposed, or otherwise leave the job. But I don't think this is as widely practiced now as it used to be. Later on, the president of the association, Craig Bromell, and I managed to work things out and we developed an excellent relationship.

As I mentioned earlier, chiefs of police departments in big cities are under a lot of pressure. When Bernie Parks was chief of the LAPD and tackled corruption issues with the Rampart scandal, he got pilloried in the press and became unfairly identified with corruption himself. The result was that his contract wasn't renewed. One of the L.A. dailies went after Parks relentlessly. Of course, running a police department in a city the size of L.A. is no picnic. I have also known many other big-city chiefs, such as Richard Pennington in New Orleans, who later went to Atlanta. Chuck Ramsay, who was chief in Washington, D.C. Ray Kelly, who was commissioner of the New York City Police Department. Howard Safer, who was in New York before Kelly. And Bill Bratton, who later became chief in L.A. I knew all of these exceptional police leaders because of my involvement in such organizations as the Major Cities Chiefs and the International Association of Chiefs of Police, and also from committees, courses, and seminars we participated in together. In fact, three or four times a year all these chiefs would meet and we developed some very good friendships.

Meetings of the Major Cities Chiefs would have forty or fifty chiefs from Canada and the U.S. sitting down to talk about current critical issues. We would share information, and some chiefs would ask for assistance, and this exchange was the most strategic thing I've ever seen with high-end executives talking very openly in closed sessions. The Canadian chiefs were regarded no differently than the American chiefs, but in some respects we were miles ahead of them, especially on such issues as integrity, policy, and accountability. However, the American chiefs were under more pressure because, as I mentioned above, they serve at the pleasure of the mayor while the Canadian chiefs answer to a board or a commission. Which system is better? As I said earlier, I think the Canadian one is, as long as it works, because there is less politicizing of the police chief's job—although sometimes I wonder—and we are more at arm's length with relation to the political regime. In some cases, police chiefs in the U.S. come and go as mayors and city managers come and go. Today the average tenure of a Major Cities police chief in the U.S. is under three years, which isn't very long.

I remember one meeting of the Major Cities Chiefs when Vancouver chief Jamie Graham talked about a new initiative in his city—the so-called safe-injection site for drug users on the Eastside. Well, everyone's jaws just dropped. This was Graham's first time at the meeting and his presentation didn't go over too well. Vancouver's safe-injection site was made possible with funding from the Canadian government. The feds spent a lot of money to provide drug addicts with a place to shoot up with illicit drugs. I didn't think it was a good idea and neither did the other chiefs. Why not? If people buy drugs illegally and are in possession of illegal drugs, and then the authorities provide them with a facility to use those drugs, that means society is actively promoting the illicit drug market. If that's not enough, it develops a double standard for the police because they are then supposed to look the other way. In short, we are spending public money to facilitate drug use and I think that's wrong. Now, Jamie Graham, who retired as Vancouver's chief in the summer of 2007, was a good guy and a good chief who believed in all this, and that's fine, but the chiefs as a group weren't into it.

The safe-injection site and needle-exchange programs are built around the health issue; drug addicts are expected to turn in their needles. It's supposed to be a needle exchange so they won't be trading needles. The idea is that nobody gets AIDS and other diseases. The problem is, there is no needle exchange because the addicts never bring in their needles. Never. And even in Toronto, some city councillors think this would be a good idea and advocate safe-injection sites. But there is no such thing as the safe injection of illicit drugs. Those who advocate this are sugar-coating things with a palatable, harm-reduction theme so the public will accept it. But the reality is, we are losing the battle and not doing what we should to get young people off these drugs. We do not need safe-injection sites and needle exchanges. What we need is a holistic approach. I'm talking about education and treatment; prevention, *not* facilitation, is the answer.

My first meeting with the Major Cities Chiefs took place in Toronto in 2001 because we hosted that meeting along with the IACP conference and, as I say, it was only a month after 9/11. Not surprisingly, we had lots of security. At the time, many American chiefs were under a no-fly order from their city managers or mayors because of the threat of terrorism. The whole theme of that IACP conference was that we weren't going to surrender to terrorism. I remember that Richard Pennington drove all the way from New Orleans to come to the conference. He told us we had to work together to confront terrorism and then he drove right back to New Orleans. That was his way of making a statement and I thought it was a profound one.

ANY POLICE CHIEF HAS TO DEAL with the media, and I have seen a change in how the media does its business since I first joined the police in 1969. Today everything is about the immediacy of stories, which is made possible with modern technology, and it's very competitive. But I think an evolution has taken place. What used to be reporting the news, which is what the old-timers did, has now boiled down to the quick fix, the sound bite, and the screaming headline. And along with this comes inaccuracies galore.

In the old days, you had seasoned people sitting on editorial boards. Meet with editorial boards now and it's not unusual to see young people with very little life experience writing opinion pieces that rip their subjects apart. They may know little about the ways of the world, and yet they write about policing issues as if they are seasoned police officers who know everything about the job. Some people who try to destroy a police chief haven't walked a minute in the chief's shoes and haven't taken the time to learn exactly what the chief does or how he or she does it.

I think it was better when you had long-tenured, experienced, tried-and-true police-beat reporters who really knew their business. A good example is Gwynn "Jocko" Thomas, who for the longest time was the police reporter for the *Toronto Star*. This guy was a legend. He had contacts and developed a reputation for being trustworthy because he had intimate knowledge of how policing is done. People like that were on the street and had ways of checking and validating what they were reporting.

I can't say I've known a police chief whose career was ruined by the media, but I've certainly known media people who have tried to ruin mine. They didn't succeed because, at the end of the day, the good sense and decency of common, ordinary people will sort out truth from fiction. One alternative weekly, *NOW* magazine, has done nothing but viciously attack and criticize me, and has even altered pictures of me to make me look inhuman. Once they published my home address, a photograph of the house, and even a map with directions on how to get there! This immediately exposed my family to enemies and crackpots.

You expect better from mainstream media, but I've gone to editorial boards of big newspapers to deal with whatever they want to discuss and to give my side of the story only to learn that some people on those boards have their minds made up in advance and want me there only to cross-examine me. When the *Toronto Star* claimed that the Toronto Police Service was involved in systemic racial profiling, I pushed back. I spoke with some of their senior people, but I think they had their minds made up. I don't have any ill feelings toward the *Toronto Star*, but I don't read it. They had made up their mind that they didn't want me as chief from the outset, and then worked very hard trying to prove their point for the next five years. But I don't think they succeeded. Some media regard themselves as another level of police oversight. They create controversy when none exists. They are driven by declining readership and the result is more manufactured hype and controversy.

When I was an inspector in Toronto, there was a national postal strike and in those days things were volatile on the strike lines. The police had a good relationship with the union reps on the strike line and made some concessions to let them do their thing, but at the same time, a lot of tension was in the air. One night there was quite a bit of violence on postal strike lines in other parts of the country, so the next morning, all kinds of media showed up at our location. They expected a flare-up at the huge postal plant on Eastern Avenue. That was the second-biggest mail-sorting plant in the world. Union agitators—we called them "flying squads"—came in to stir things up and a CBC television reporter wanted to tape an interview with me since I was the situation commander and the one who was doing the interviews. His lead-in was that there was all this violence going on and that the police were using brutality on the strikers and what did I have to say about it. I corrected the reporter and said we had no violence, and no police brutality was taking place at my location, but still he kept going on and on about police brutality. I knew where he was coming from, so I told him, right on camera, that this was the most ignorant and despicable interview I'd ever done and that he was trying to fabricate a story. Well, he never aired one sound bite from that interview because I didn't give him what he wanted.

I have learned to hold the media accountable and not to engage in a pissing contest with people who buy ink by the barrel and paper by the ton. So I pick my battles. From time to time, I have gone to the Ontario Press Council to lodge a complaint and even initiate legal proceedings to be vindicated. The fact is, there are professional cop-haters in the media who figure the police never do anything right. They always want to second-guess us. I think they are irresponsible and it all goes back to the screaming headlines. There's an old saying that "if it doesn't bleed it doesn't lead" and very often it's the critic who gets top billing. The story about the crowd-management expert from Chicago who said the Rolling Stones concert was going to be a catastrophe in Toronto is a good example. This sort of thing happens when stories aren't balanced and don't convey accurate information. At the same time, the media has a lot of classy people, too. They are the ones who dig, do thorough research, and prepare real investigative pieces.

The media performs an invaluable function not only in reporting the news, but in informing the public about critical issues and allowing people to make up their own minds. But in terms of policing issues, there is a huge difference between informing and educating the public on the one hand and seeing yourself as another layer of police oversight on the other. The latter are people who operate from the preconceived notion that police lie, fudge, and cover things up, that they are self-promoting, are a closed shop, and must be exposed.

Of course, then you've got those who just have an axe to grind. John Barber is a writer with the *Globe and Mail* who covers city council and civic issues. When I was leaving as chief in Toronto, I held a press conference. At the press conference, Barber said something about me and my record not being "perfect," to which I replied that he should know something about that because many of his columns were also less than perfect. Ever since then, he has never avoided a chance to take cheap shots at me. For example, his column from January 27, 2007, said this:

> I really wish reporters would stop describing Mr. Fantino as "no-nonsense." Whether he is stirring up ancient and unsolvable gay-sex crimes, painting patrol cars black, embracing friendly felons or sabotaging competitors for the attention he craves, he is all nonsense—nothing but. The tremendous progress a reinvigorated Toronto Police Service has made since his ouster from the top job here is the best testament to his seriousness and competence as a leader. Chief Bill Blair, his successor, has quietly and simply shown him up. In the history of the force, Mr. Fantino's tenure will be known as an openly political and ultimately failed attempt to block overdue, inevitable reforms. The reformers' subsequent triumph has been dramatic.

Bill Blair, the current chief of the Toronto Police Service, is a good friend of mine, an excellent police officer, and a very fine chief. We can only chuckle when this sort of thing gets into the press. But none of us did much chuckling with the series the *Toronto Star* did in 1989.

At the time, I was the superintendent in charge of 31 Division in the Jane-Finch area of Toronto. The Toronto media is always going on about "the Jane-Finch corridor." This is an area of 75,000 people in the north-west end of the city. It is one of the city's most stressed areas because of the socio-economic conditions with eighteen public-housing develop-ments—there are lots of high-rise buildings—along with an inadequate infrastructure to support many new arrivals, many of them from Third World countries. But the term "Jane-Finch corridor" is a slight on that community which, for the most part, is a decent, law-abiding commu-nity which certainly does have issues and pressures. But those people don't live in a "corridor." They live in a community. That term was coined by the media and it's very unfair.

However, that area did and still does have a considerable amount of crime, much of it violent. Back in 1989, there was tension between the police and certain elements in that community. At the time, the political jurisdiction of Metropolitan Toronto involved six municipalities—the City of Toronto and five boroughs or "cities" as they liked to call themselves. One of them was North York. On December 15, 1988, when I was a staff inspector working out of 31 Division, I attended a meeting of the North York Committee on Community, Race and Ethnic Relations along with Wally Tyrrell, who had been my first partner in homicide many years ear-lier. Wally was then staff superintendent of 3 District, which was responsible for policing in North York. This committee had been criticized in the press and was floundering. At that meeting, there was a discussion about the negative relationship between the police and black youth, and I was asked to gather information about the state of crime in the Jane-Finch area and how that related to police contacts. So I manually retrieved all the data and immediately got concerned about how it would be perceived because so much of the interaction between black youth and police in that community was negative. I called the executive director of the committee to express my concerns about the information and he said, "Tell it like it is." Then I went to Wally Tyrrell and he said our presentation of all this data would be at a closed, in-camera meeting of the committee. It was supposed to be a private meeting. I still have the statement that detailed the request:

> That the police of 31 Division gather information with respect to the social-economic-racial status of those whom they charge with criminal offences and provide appropriate data to social-recreational service organizations as a way of supporting community activities aimed at improving the quality and capacity of social-recreational services.

On February 16, 1989, Wally and I appeared at that committee again to give our presentation on "The Jane-Finch Crime Picture: A Comparative Analysis." In that presentation, I mentioned the geographic and demographic characteristics of the area, the high population density, the numbers of single-parent families, the large concentration of recent immigrants, and the large concentration of subsidized-housing developments. Then I explained about all the programs the police were doing in the community. That was followed by a crime profile according to stats generated from the year 1988. The stats showed an inordinate number of serious crimes involving blacks. I also explained that many of the victims of such crimes were black as well.

After the meeting, I discovered that a reporter from the *Toronto Star* was in attendance, because he came up to me and started asking questions. Wally and I were shocked. This was highly sensitive and even volatile material. We immediately went to headquarters and met with Chief Marks and told him what happened. The chief knew there would be problems with this, but he stood by me. As it turned out, some others in the senior command of the Toronto police did not. They ran for the hills because they didn't want to be involved in the controversy and it began the very next day.

"Critics say police 'disgusting' to show race figures on crime," screamed the *Star*'s headline. The story said I had released police statistics showing that blacks made up 6 per cent of the population in the Jane-Finch area, but accounted for 82 per cent of robberies and muggings, 55 per cent of purse snatchings, and 51 per cent of drug offences in the previous year. The whole thing was just overwhelming with its misinformation, bantering, rhetoric, and accusations. Some of the attacks directed against me personally were nothing less than vicious. I was accused in various circles of using misleading statistics and of stereotyping the black community.

The next day the *Star* ran another story. "Police sweeps of Jane-Finch upset blacks." According to that story, some black leaders said I was the problem and one person said I had even declared war on black people. Then Ontario Solicitor General Joan Smith got into the act, along with Ontario premier David Petersen and Opposition Leader Bob Rae. They were all interviewed by the *Star* in yet another story, entitled "Stop collecting race statistics, police told." The tone of all these stories was that the police were racist and that I, as an individual, was racist as well.

I believe I was set up. I don't blame the reporter at that meeting because he was just doing his job and I don't blame the *Toronto Star* either. But I do blame the committee. The fact is, I never kept race-based stats, but was asked to prepare that information by the committee. So it was very galling to read in one of those stories that the chairman of the committee said the police had released this information on their own initiative. That was just a blatant lie.

At the time, my fourteen-year-old daughter was having serious health problems and in hospital. She was going through a lot of tests, we didn't know what was wrong with her, and it was a very difficult time for our family. One day, I was driving to the hospital to see her and on the way I was listening to a talk show on my car radio only to hear these vicious, vile attacks on me from people phoning in. I was depicted by some callers as a racist, bigoted cop, so I pulled over to the side of the road and called Wally from a pay phone. I told him that I'd had it, I wanted no part of this anymore, the whole thing was disgusting, and I was quitting. I was handing in my badge. I felt betrayed because the committee had left me to take all the flak when they were the ones who had requested the status in the first place. I told Wally I had made up my mind, but he talked me out of resigning.

In 2002, there was another controversy about alleged "racial profiling" by the Toronto Police Service and, once again, the *Toronto Star* was in the middle of it. This was when I was chief and, naturally, I was in the middle of it too. What is interesting is that right after I had become chief in Toronto in March 2000, the *Toronto Star* had made a request for information from the police database about arrest data concerning contacts we had with members of the community. One of the items on any arrest record is the race of the person being arrested. We didn't want to give them that information for fear of misuse or misinterpretation and appealed, but later we had to hand it over.

I was concerned that, without proper context this information could be improperly manipulated to create a great deal of harm to the hard-earned, police–community relationship and trust. And that's exactly what happened.

On October 18, 2002, I was interviewed by two *Toronto Star* reporters whom I knew, and they brought along a photographer. The general tone of that interview was that we were overpolicing the city's black community. They had their tape recorder running and we had ours running too. From my perspective, the tone of the questions was that the story was already written about the Toronto Police Service having been found guilty of racial profiling and of being a racist organization. The *Star* had never supported me for police chief from the get-go, so maybe they just wanted to show that I was the wrong guy for the job.

The next day, October 19, 2002, the story ran, alleging that the Toronto police was a racist organization and was targeting blacks. The headline was, "Singled out; *Star* analysis of police crime data shows justice is different for blacks and whites." The article referred to a "massive police database recording more than 480,000 incidents in which an individual was arrested, or ticketed for an offence dating back to 1996." The way I saw it, the paper was portraying itself as the saviour of society, while the police were depicted as the great Satan. Here's one paragraph from that story:

> Police are forbidden, by their governing board, from analyzing this data in terms of race, but the Star has no such restriction. The findings provide hard evidence of what blacks have long suspected—race matters in Canadian society, especially when dealing with police.

The story naturally included a reference to the 1989 fiasco: "Fantino, then a staff inspector, triggered a controversy by reporting to a race relations committee that blacks accounted for most crime in the Jane-Finch area." It also contained quotes from Scott Wortley, a University of Toronto criminologist, and Alan Borovoy, who was counsel to the Canadian Civil Liberties Association. Both of them came down hard on the police.

On the same day, October 19, the *Star* ran my response to all these allegations under the headline "There is no racism. We do not do racial profiling." In that article, I said the *Star* had been very selective in its use of data and didn't have all the facts. Over the next few days, the *Star* continued its series. "Treatment differs by division." "Police and race." "Police target black drivers."

The *Toronto Star* really feasted on this. Eventually, they interviewed Michael Friendly, a professor from York University who was said to be a statistics expert and who was the *Star*'s analyst for the data. His conclusion, according to the *Star*, was that based on his analysis of the statistics, we were targeting blacks. The paper also included my side of the story based on the edited interview with me. It included my denial that the police were racist and my statement that we arrested more than 50,000 people a year from many different races and backgrounds, and that the *Star* had taken a slice of the community and focused on that. In my view, the paper had an agenda. They started out with some preconceived notion and then set out to prove it, basically dropping a bombshell on the community and forcing all of us to live in the ashes.

I thought their behaviour was irresponsible.

We then hired our own consultant, Edward Harvey, a professor from the University of Toronto, a world-renowned expert on demographics. He got the same data the *Star* got. He said that the *Star*'s conclusions, based on the data, constituted "junk science" and had flawed methodology. He said the figures used by the *Star* had been obtained from the police database and were not designed for research.

The result of all this was that the Toronto police association filed a $2.7-billion lawsuit against the *Star*, alleging that its stories painted all of our police officers as racists. Another result was that the whole thing heightened tensions between the police and the city's black community, and definitely impacted policing in that community. Along with all the stories were columns, letters to the editor, talk shows, you name it. The whole thing just exploded.

I have never believed for a minute that the Toronto Police Service was engaged in racial profiling, which I regard as an abhorrent activity. If they were, I would have known about it. You can't hide something as systemic as what the *Star* was portraying. I think this was a perfect example of the media creating a story and running with it. But the *Toronto Star*, which is Canada's largest newspaper, has never been a friend to me. Many times I have regarded its coverage of issues involving the police, and me personally, as lacking.

On January 7, 2003, I held a town hall meeting in the Jane-Finch area. This was shortly after the *Star*'s much-ballyhooed series on race and crime. At the meeting, I mentioned that crime in Toronto had decreased by 7 per cent in the previous year. At one point a teenage girl spoke up. "How come you want us to respect the police when the police don't respect us black youth?" she said. I thought a comment like that was uncalled for and that it unfairly broadbrushed the city's entire police force. And I said as much. I said that youth have to be accountable, too, and that they shouldn't just make gratuitous and accusatory statements. But what appeared in the *Star* the next day? There was nothing positive at all. Nothing about crime decreasing. Nothing about people staying after the meeting to talk with me. Nothing about people cheering when I said what I did. But there was a lot about the girl's words and about me getting booed by a few. Their reporting was irresponsible, as was their entire series.

As for the girl's comment at the meeting, I felt it was a set-up. This young girl and some other teenagers were totally disrespectful in their behaviour throughout the proceedings. They were slouching and talking, and then out of the blue she came to the microphone and made the comment that she did, after which she ran out, followed by members of the media who smelled blood.

Unfortunately, when things like this get into print—even if they are dead wrong—they have a tendency of sticking to you. For example, if a young reporter wants to check me out on the Internet, one of the first things they might find is the Wikipedia listing. Wikipedia is a sort of online encyclopedia, but unlike the Encyclopedia Britannica or any other reputable publisher of information, material on this thing can be edited by anyone who has access to the website. It was launched in 2001, contains virtually millions of articles, and is considered one of the most widely visited websites in existence. But that doesn't mean the information is accurate. Still, I'm sure that more journalists than who would care to admit it, and who are doing stories and need some quick background, resort to it regularly.

Look me up on Wikipedia and what are the headlines? Well, there are three. The first is "Policing controversies" and under that you read that I had released race-based crime stats to the media, which is wrong; that I had "instituted child pornography investigation, Project Guardian" in London, which implies that I had fabricated the information; and that we "did not successfully find any evidence of child pornography." All this is totally incorrect. Then there is all the stuff about the *Toronto Star*'s statistical analysis of arrests, implying a racial bias on the part of the police department, which is complete bogus. The other two headlines are "Corruption scandals," which allegedly broke out under my tenure (as if I was responsible for them), and "Contract expiry," which got into all the shenanigans about why my contract was not renewed as Toronto's chief. And that's it. You spend almost forty years doing public service as a police officer and that's what they rack up on you.

Is there any mention about my being the Canadian police representative to a major conference on Law Enforcement in the Era of Global Terror, in Israel, in 2003? Nope. How about something about my role in developing an Intelligence Officer Exchange Program with the New York City Police Department in 2002? No. Anything about high-level briefings I attended with the FBI or Interpol? Uh-uh. Or maybe my getting appointed as a member of the Order of Ontario by the government of Ontario in 2004? Or appointed Commander of the Order of the Police Forces by the government of Canada in 2003? Or Commander of the Order of Merit to the Republic of Italy? The Order of St. John? Recipient of the Queen's Golden Jubilee Medal? Recipient of the International Association of Chiefs of Police Civil Rights Award in Law Enforcement, Education and Prevention? Or any number of things that have been bestowed on me by a large number of civic groups and community organizations?

No.

But my being an alleged racist and homophobe is front and centre. And so, the same things keep coming up over and over. Lies in. Lies out. You keep telling a lie often enough and some gullible people believe it. Today, even Wikipedia aside, much of what the media says about me is hand-me-down stuff that wasn't accurate to begin with. But like I say, it's all about the quick fix.

Many times I have been on television with a reporter who observed how well known I am and how I am best known for having compiled race statistics. This then is the mindset some reporters bring with them to an interview, reporters who don't do their homework, and there are a lot of those.

When I was being considered for the chief's job in London, Ontario, I had to explain at the interviews what, in fact, had happened back in 1989 in Toronto with all the brouhaha about the crime stats at Jane-

Finch. The people in London didn't want a racist bigot as their police chief, and who can blame them? And I had to explain what had happened yet again in 1994 when I competed for the top job in Toronto, and again in 1999, when I appeared before Toronto's Police Services Board to be considered for the job.

Then there are people who try to defame you to all and sundry. When I was chief in London, there was this guy named Battista who decided he was going to defame me wherever he could because of Project Guardian. So he started sending stuff about me by fax and email all over the place. I took him to court on a libel charge and he came to court in his pajamas and slippers. The court awarded me a $40,000 judgment, but of course, I never collected. What are you going to collect from such people? They've got nothing to lose and fear no consequences.

As far as black-on-black crime in Toronto is concerned, it is still very much an issue today. So let's look at the facts. A lot of black youth are preyed upon by the organized crime element with the enticement of high living, guns, and gangs, and along with that comes the violence. Crime itself has no particular denominator, but certain crime has certain elements to it. You take a community with a lack of infrastructure, no support systems, and lots of young people being left to their own devices, and you're going to have problems. Some of these high-density, subsidized-housing developments do nothing but warehouse people. They ghettoize people. This has been a big problem in Toronto and in many other cities as well, and the inevitable results are tragic for everyone. These things were built for disaster.

Dr. Peter Phillips, who was Jamaica's national security minister, once came to visit the Toronto police after I had met with the Jamaican consul-general and members of the city's Jamaican community. He asked me to visit Jamaica so our police could work with the Jamaican Constabulary Force, which is the only police force there, to engage in some problem-solving and to learn about their crime issues and what their police have to deal with. So three of us went to Kingston, Jamaica—Superintendent Wayne Cotgreave, Detective Doug Quan, and me. We met with their police and went out into the communities. Well, I was just shocked by the barbed wire strung across roadways to prevent drive-by shootings in some of those neighbourhoods. In Jamaica, the police often did their patrols wearing helmets and were backed up by Jamaican military personnel in armoured vehicles. The real problem was that young Jamaicans, including children, were exposed to all this violence.

Jamaica has a population of about 2.6 million and over 1,000 murders a year, so it was roughly a similar size to Toronto, but with *twenty times* the murder rate. A typical police station in Jamaica was very labour intensive with a lot of people on the ground, precious few computers, and not much in terms of electronic equipment. It was the same thing with schools. They were lacking in books, chalk, sports equipment, you name it. Toronto has a large Jamaican community that is decent, hard-working, and conscientious, and I figured we could make a difference. So we returned to Canada and reached out to our own police officers to gather needed supplies for those schools in Jamaica. We also went to local school boards and libraries and got companies involved as well. What began as a small endeavour became a huge collection of school supplies, sporting goods, and reading materials. We soon had *forty skids* to fill the cargo hold of a jumbo 767 airplane! Air Canada supplied the plane, the pilots, and the crew, and all the people were volunteers. So we went back to Jamaica a second time to deliver the goods, and with the help of the Jamaican Constabulary Force, identified the most deprived inner-city neighbourhoods of Kingston. Canada's High Commissioner to Jamaica, Claudio Valle, came with us.

In Jamaica, we were treated like royalty by the children wherever we went. And by the school staff, too. That whole exercise was about children and their quality of life. The company National Gym gave us soccer shoes, soccer balls, and soccer sweaters. Other companies like Grand & Toy and Hilroy gave us school supplies. You just had to see those children following us around. I was handing out Toronto police pins and it was like I was giving away gold. I'm sorry I didn't have thousands more with me. At the same time, our police developed joint initiatives and exchange programs with the Jamaican police. Later, I was walking in Toronto's annual Caribana Parade—Caribana is Toronto's Caribbean festival and one of North America's biggest cultural events, attracting over a million people—and I couldn't go two steps without citizens reaching out to shake my hand.

In Toronto's black community, the crime situation is a problem that has to be tackled by the leadership of that community as much as by anyone else. I have attended conferences in the U.S. hosted by the former governor of Florida about how to prevent crime in the black community. Those conferences focused on wide networks of people working together to understand key issues and to solve problems. Some U.S. cities like Boston have made tremendous turnarounds in their crime situation with community-based energy and local community leaders who aren't into fingerpointing and blaming. This has always been my approach as well.

We all have to live together. We can't play the blame game, which is easy for some people to do when they haven't read the small print and they haven't looked at anything beyond the headlines. That is sensationalism. It's a copout to blame me or the police in general for everything instead of dealing with the causes of these issues. And the causes of crime often start with the family breaking down, youth having nothing to do, and communities that are not engaged.

While I am tough on crime, I am also tough on the causes of crime. I have worked hard to help and address inadequacies in the system and I work hard to deal with discrimination and the violation of human rights, unfair practices, and unfair treatment. I know that a lot of people are oppressed and disadvantaged, and that a lot of people come from very humble beginnings. And I feel that we need to help them. I do this all the time and I think I'm respected for it. When you get respect, you show respect. And vice versa.

· 16 ·

Police and Politics

I N MY CAREER, I HAVE BEEN ACCUSED OF BEING RACIST, OF being homophobic, of conspiring against my fellow police officers, of accepting gratuities, and of being corrupt. When you occupy a high-profile public office like that of police chief, some people are bound to take a few shots at you. Unfortunately, what they say can end up in print, on the radio, and on TV, even when none of it is true. People are free to file a statement of claim that may contain the most vicious lies. They can accuse you and members of your family of anything they want, and all they have to do to qualify it is say the allegations are not proven. But the damage gets done. In reality, such allegations are often nothing more than a media release. One thing I have learned is that, while some people might make a lot of noise and sue for a million dollars, they will gladly settle for two bucks.

During an interview I gave not long ago, the host said that I seem to have attracted a lot of enemies. I replied by saying that I didn't feel badly about that because these enemies are all the right kind. In any case, I have also attracted a much larger number of supporters, so I must have been doing something right.

I am seen as a law-and-order guy, which is fine with me. If a police chief—if any police officer—doesn't stand up for law and order, they should get another job. But in Canada, a police chief must report to the local police services board, which in turn, reports to city council, and that's where politics can and often does come into the picture.

The people who hire you are invariably the people who will support you. I had the good fortune of spending most of my five years as police chief in Toronto working with a police services board that included Toronto mayor Mel Lastman. All the people on that board were very demanding, but I always felt they were fair-minded and reasonable.

Before the six municipalities of Metropolitan Toronto amalgamated in 1997, Lastman had served as mayor of one of those municipalities, North York, for some twenty-five years. One doesn't serve as mayor for a quarter of a century if people don't like what you do, and North York was no mere "suburb" of Toronto, but a large area with more than 600,000 residents in the north of the city. When those six municipalities amalgamated, Lastman ran for mayor of all Toronto and won, and was re-elected in 2000. I always found him to be decent, dedicated, hard-working, and fiercely loyal to Toronto. I don't think the city will ever have a better ambassador. He was also a mayor who felt very strongly about public safety, and law and order.

In 2002 and 2003, street gangs emerged as a growing problem in the city and I wanted to tackle it by forming a street-gang unit. The unit would involve police officers who were dedicated to dealing exclusively with this issue, which had come about from groups protecting their respective drug-dealing territories. I could see this problem developing and wanted to get ahead of the trend, but it meant adding resources at a time of severe fiscal constraints with the city budget which, of course, impacted the operating budget of the Toronto Police Service. The new street-gang unit would have seventeen officers and wouldn't come cheap. I went to Mayor Lastman with the idea, laid out the situation, and explained why I felt it was necessary, and he bought into it. It's true that, in 2005, Toronto saw a record number of gun-related homicides, many of them involving gangs. The media dubbed it the "summer of the gun." But I am sure the problem would have been much worse if we didn't have that street-gang unit in place.

After 9/11, Lastman was also very supportive of increasing funding to augment resources dedicated to the three major emergency services: police, fire, and Emergency Medical Services (EMS). And he was totally behind adding human resources dedicated to any counterterrorism intelligence work. Believe me, the man was no pushover. He had to be convinced that whatever was being sought was the right thing to do, and he always paid close attention to the bottom line. But once he was onside, he was committed and passionate and was never afraid to take on other city councillors who just didn't get it. There is no question that he was a good mayor for the police and a good mayor for law and order. He was also very trustworthy.

In November 2003, Lastman retired and new municipal elections were held. The run-off for mayor wound up between businessman John Tory, who was just entering politics, and David Miller, who was already a member of council. During the campaign, there was a lot of talk about issues involving public safety and policing.

Long before that election, the Toronto police did a study on staffing levels and determined that, to effectively do the job, we were short by more than 400 officers. How did we arrive at that? We examined the workload and came up with a formula for how a police officer's time is used. According to our formula, 60 per cent of the work was reactive, which referred to such things as answering calls, and 40 per cent was proactive, which referred to such things as problem solving and community policing. The 60/40 model gave us a target to reach so we could achieve optimum levels of policing, safety, and security for the city. It was based on all the factors that impact both the demands and availability of a police officer's time, and it took into account such things as officer safety and response times.

This then was our 60/40 formula. We applied it to current work levels and found that we needed at least another 400 officers. Because of this shortage, the actual availability of an officer's time was more like 80/20—80 per cent reactive and 20 per cent proactive. At the time, the Toronto Police Service had 5,250 officers in total. We needed more than

5,650. The Toronto Police Services Board approved the plan, but only if it were executed over a period of several years.

During the 2003 election campaign, John Tory picked up on this and said that the city would get 400 more police officers if he was elected mayor. Miller, on the other hand, said no to hiring more police officers. Shortly before the election, I was on CFRB radio, one of the city's most popular stations. The interviewer asked me, "Chief, can you use 400 more police officers?" and I said yes. This was interpreted by some in the media that I was supporting Tory for mayor, even though I had never said as much. Prior to the election, I didn't even know the man.

Meanwhile, I had been offered an extension of my contract as chief for another two years by the police services board. Then, after the election, which Miller won, the new police services board came in and the bantering began. The day before the first meeting of the new board, which was now without Mel Lastman, the then chairman of the board, Alan Heisey, told me there would be no problem extending my contract for another two years. But the very next day—December 11, 2003—he told me the current board would not be honouring the earlier decision about my contract, and further, that the new mayor, David Miller, did not want to move forward on the contract extension.

It was around this time that a few Toronto police officers, who had been under investigation, were formally charged for alleged corrupt practices under Ontario's Police Services Act. In some cases, criminal charges were laid. One day, the Lord Mayor of London, England, happened to be in the city and he and Miller were having a chat. Miller said to him, "Is your police force in jail? Mine is." This was caught on a TV clip. I didn't see this live, but later that day when I went to the studios of Citytv to do my monthly show called *The Chief*, I was shown a tape of what Miller had said. I was dumbfounded and had to watch it twice. They had me on camera and wanted a response. I certainly didn't want to attack the mayor, but at the same time, I was devastated by his comments, so I said I felt as if a stake had been driven through my heart. The police association representing the rank and file of the police service was very angry about Miller's comments. I spoke to the mayor the next day and recommended that he issue a letter of apology to the members of the Toronto Police Service, and he did.

Meanwhile, I had served notice to the new police services board that I wished to continue as chief, but there was a problem. At the time, the board, which previously had seven members on it, was down to six members. Miller chose not to be on it just yet and the province of Ontario was slow in appointing a seventh member which, by law, had to come from the provincial government. After being elected mayor, Miller had taken his seat on the Toronto Transit Commission (TTC) board, which was responsible for the city's public transit system, and planned to come onto the police services board later. The problem with the makeup of this police services board was that, of the six people who sat on it, three were pro-police and two were most definitely anti-police. These two, both from the left-leaning faction of city council, were appointed by Miller and attacked virtually everything we tried to do. Alan Heisey, the chair of the police services board, tended to be more of a fence-sitter. However, it seemed that just about every time a vote was held, it wound up in a tie. Needless to say, three members of the board were in favour of me continuing as chief and three were against. Eventually, Heisey, the chair, was forced to declare the board dysfunctional.

I think it's fair to say that I had a real problem working with this group. It was frustrating and really sapped my energy. But in spite of it all, the police force still retained its focus and remained very diligent about its duties and responsibilities towards the citizens. These board members challenged just about everything that came forward, including my retaining Judge Ferguson for his report on police corruption, and budget requests. Then, in the summer of 2004, the police services board decided not to renew my contract. No surprise there. But I still had my supporters on city council and they wanted to overturn that decision. This was rejected by a vote at city council, which I would describe as a body comprising two distinct groups with two distinct philosophies—the left-wingers and the right-wingers—and never the twain shall meet. Then my supporters created a protest movement with a "bring-back-the-chief" theme.

The whole thing got pretty ugly and became very much an "us-versus-them" kind of thing. The *Toronto Star*, as always, never had anything good to say about me and neither did two alternative newsweeklies. These were *NOW* magazine, which had once published my home address with a map showing how to get there, and EYE WEEKLY, which is owned by Torstar Corporation, the parent company of the *Toronto Star*. John Sewell, who was mayor of Toronto when Michael Sweet was killed—and who didn't think enough of attending Sweet's funeral—was a regular writer for EYE WEEKLY and never hesitated to take shots at me and the police in general. He came out praising the police-bashers on the police services board, calling them "progressive," and on May 27, 2004, wrote a piece criticizing how we had virtually destroyed a street gang called the Malvern Crew in Scarborough in the city's east end. The Malvern Crew was a violent gang that had been terrorizing the community. The takedown was the result of a fourteen-month investigation by our elite street-gang unit. More than 500 criminal charges were laid, with arrests not only in Scarborough, but also in three other municipalities—Ajax, Pickering, and Barrie—and it wasn't only the Toronto police who were involved, but also the York Regional Police Service, Peel Regional Police Service, RCMP, and OPP. This was a great success for the police and for the community. We arrested sixty-five members of the gang and effectively put them out of commission.

On the day of our press conference, we displayed the guns that had been seized and the only thing John Sewell could say about these guns in his article was that they hadn't all come from that gang. As if we were setting the whole thing up which, of course, was totally incorrect. Mind you, Sewell wasn't at the takedown, was he? He also got in a few shots about corruption in the police department and—wouldn't you know it—made sure to refer to my time as chief in London, Ontario, when we were breaking up a child porn–pedophilia ring; he said that charges in that case had stuck against only two people. In fact, Project Scoop, which later became Project Guardian, resulted in the conviction of sixty-one accused, with a conviction rate of 86 per cent and an average sentence of four years.

On July 23, 2004, the *Toronto Sun*, a newspaper that was generally supportive of the police, ran a cartoon depicting Miller as Adolf Hitler after Miller had ruled that a motion calling on the police services board to reconsider my contract was out of order. The editor of the *Sun* later said in a column that he regretted running the cartoon. So emotions were running high.

I had been appointed chief of the Toronto police on March 6, 2000, and my last day on the job was five years later, on February 28, 2005. I finished at seven o'clock in the evening by attending a recognition event at Queen's Park, which is the site of the Ontario legislature, to honour police volunteers who had worked with the Red Cross. By that time I had already been offered the job of commissioner of emergency management for the province of Ontario. So there I was on the last day of what was then my thirty-six-year career as a police officer.

It wasn't long after that—April 14, 2005—when Mayor Miller presented me with the Key to the City. Strangely enough, that ceremony took place after a *unanimous* vote by Toronto Council that supported the presentation. The vote included those councillors who sat on the police services board and who had voted against my contract extension. But that is city politics. Later that year, Miller announced that 150 new police officers would be hired for the Toronto Police Service, effectively going against what he had campaigned for in the earlier election campaign.

Still, David Miller and I got along professionally and were always cordial with each other. Some people like to think, and some media promoted the notion, that we were at odds, but that wasn't the case, at least as far as I was concerned. All the hype about the 400 new police officers and my allegedly supporting John Tory as mayor was sheer media-created sensationalism.

It wasn't the first time this had happened to me.

Today, I regard the whole episode about my contract as a twist of fate that wound up being the best thing that ever happened to me professionally. The very next day after stepping down as chief—March 1, 2005—I started my new job as Ontario's commissioner of emergency management. The job was at the level of a deputy minister and was connected to the Ontario Ministry of Public Safety and Correctional Services. I had responsibility for ensuring that all 444 municipalities in the province had business continuity plans—effectively, emergency plans—in place. We were still in the wake of 9/11 and it had become apparent that all Western governments should be prepared for worst-case scenarios and those scenarios could involve terrorism, as well as disasters and such emergencies as forest fires, flooding, storms, and chemical spills. I had to scan world events and advise the premier of Ontario and his cabinet on potential risks. I also had to deal with any emergencies that took place.

The job came with a lot of responsibility. The province of Ontario is the most populous in Canada with over twelve million people. What's more, in terms of sheer geography, it is twice the size of France! The skills I had learned in policing—organizational skills, problem solving, leadership, ability to negotiate outcomes and identify issues—all came in handy. In any emergency situation, the government still has to function and decisions have to be made. One thing we did when I was in emergency management was to put together a committee to advise the provincial government on any such emergency.

Probably the main thing that I learned on this job was just how vulnerable we were on a great many fronts such as security, climate change, natural disasters, health emergencies and pandemics, and even potential nuclear scenarios.

No sooner had I taken this new position than I was off to Israel with Monte Kwinter, Ontario minister of community safety and correctional services, and a delegation of Ontario police chiefs, to examine that country's counterterrorism procedures and policies, and it was on that trip when I heard about the four Mounties who had been killed in Alberta. Later I went to Pakistan with Michael Colle, Ontario minister of citizenship and immigration, right after a devastating earthquake had ripped into the country, taking 80,000 lives, injuring many more than that, and leaving countless people homeless. Ontario has a large southeast Asian population and a lot of families were deeply affected by this earthquake.

We went to see how we could help the people over there cope and to lend a hand any way we could. It's hard to imagine how a few minutes or even seconds of the earth shaking can cause such a terrible disaster, but seeing the destruction is something else. In Pakistan, we visited makeshift hospitals—they were nothing more than tents—and saw many children who were missing limbs because of the earthquake.

I was proud of Canada's response to that disaster. The Canadian Armed Forces and Canadian Red Cross were very active with relief efforts and, as far as the province of Ontario was concerned, Ontario premier Dalton McGuinty decided to not only send money but also a team of people who could investigate the situation and figure out how we could best help. Canadian military personnel were on the ground assisting with water purification, equipment, and repairs to water treatment plants damaged by the earthquake. The whole experience of seeing the devastation wrought by that earthquake was a flashback to the 1976 earthquake that hit northern Italy and destroyed the house where I was born. What happened in Pakistan, however, was much worse.

As emergency management commissioner, I was also involved in the relief effort for Hurricane Katrina in New Orleans. I organized the provincial response to that disaster. This involved partnering with the Canadian Red Cross to identify their most critical needs and then canvassing the provincial public service of Ontario and dispatching a team of sixty-eighty people who hailed from every sector of the government. They included crisis intervention specialists, experts in shelter management, and those who were skilled in leading groups and decision making.

Then there was Kashechewan. Kashechewan is a small, isolated native community in Northern Ontario that had been devastated by tainted water. It sits on the shore of James Bay near the Albany River. The flooding that takes place there is almost an annual event. When the spring thaw hits, ice makes its way down the river and gets caught in the mouth of the river. This leads to flooding and it happens because the community is below the river. A serious problem developed when a water plant became contaminated and people got sick, and then we had a health crisis on our hands. I was in charge of evacuating 1,300 people and coordinating the task with the Ontario Ministry of Natural Resources and the Canadian Armed Forces. It was a difficult assignment because the evacuation had to take place by air—there is no other way to get in and out of Kashechewan—and we had to find places for these people to go to. Some were sent to Ottawa, some to Sudbury, some to Timmins, as well as other cities and towns. The evacuation took a long time to do and when it was safe for people to return, some of them didn't want to go back home. I could understand why.

The conditions in Kashechewan are basically Third World. There is total disorder, with garbage strewn all over the place and graffiti on buildings, many of which are in a state of disrepair. The young have nothing to do and no opportunities. The people are helpless. I had never seen a place like that before and, as a Canadian, I felt ashamed that such communities existed in this country.

I was the commissioner of emergency management until October 29, 2006, and the next day I returned to policing in my current capacity as commissioner of the Ontario Provincial Police. I absolutely love this job and find it particularly refreshing after my last experience as chief. What I especially like is that there is no second-guessing of everything I do, as there was in Toronto. For example, when I was chief in Toronto and asked retired judge George Ferguson to prepare a report on police corruption, I thought I would have been thanked for getting something like this off the ground. After all, I was tackling police corruption. Instead, I was raked over the coals because I didn't do it through the police services board.

Some people you can never make happy.

On November 16, 2006, I was formally installed as the new OPP commissioner in an elaborate procession held at the Denison Armoury in Toronto. It featured the OPP's marching Pipe Band, many OPP officers, and such dignitaries as Ontario premier Dalton McGuinty, Ontario lieutenant-governor James Bartleman, Ontario Minister of Community Safety and Correctional Services minister Monte Kwinter, as well as representatives from the Canadian Armed Forces, and a number of police chiefs. Premier McGuinty welcomed me into the fold and I followed him with a speech. In that speech, I talked about something that has long been a burning issue with me. Impaired drivers. I promised that getting impaired drivers off the road would be a big priority for me in my role as OPP commissioner. In 2005, the OPP laid almost 11,000 charges for impaired driving throughout the province, but many of those people had gotten off because of court delays, case cancellations, plea bargains, and withdrawal of charges. The system didn't see the carnage, trauma, and tragedy that police officers see every day, and this was carnage, trauma, and tragedy that came directly from drunk drivers.

The sad thing about that day was having to mention the death that had taken place only three days earlier of Dave Mounsey, a constable from the Huron County OPP detachment. A month before, while responding to an emergency, he had been involved in a motor-vehicle collision. He died from his injuries, leaving his wife and three children. His funeral was held the day after my commissioning parade and I attended that as my very first duty as OPP commissioner.

There were, however, many things that excited me about becoming commissioner of the OPP and one of them was getting the chance to work closely with such people as Giuliano Zaccardelli, who at the time was commissioner of the RCMP.

He and I have been close friends for twenty years. We met in 1988 during security preparations for the G7 Summit in Toronto. At the time, he was an RCMP inspector assigned to handle security for the Italian delegation and I, of course, was working on security for the summit as well. Zaccardelli's background is very similar to mine. He came to Canada from Italy as a boy, but while my family went to Toronto, his wound up in Montreal. We both served on committees with the Canadian Association of Chiefs of Police, the International Association of Chiefs of Police, and the Criminal Intelligence Service Canada. I got to know him very well when I was chief in London and he was assistant commissioner of the RCMP for the Ontario Division. He and I also co-chaired an important meeting in Ottawa with fifty-four leaders from the Canadian police community; it was there where we first planned our National Strategy on Outlaw Motorcycle Gangs. Later, when I was chief in Toronto, we took that strategy a step further. As RCMP commissioner, Zaccardelli was a key player in putting that police strategy in place.

I have always thought of Zaccardelli as an honest, honourable man who was very proud of the RCMP and extremely proud to be one of them. He walked the talk and always went on about integrity and professionalism. He drove the RCMP agenda on a number of issues. For example, he strongly believed in the federal Mounties working with other police forces and law enforcement agencies, in terms of cooperating and sharing information and resources.

Zaccardelli was head of the largest police force in the country—the RCMP—and I was now head of the second largest—the OPP. We knew there would be many opportunities for us to work together on such things as joint-forces initiatives tackling organized crime and transnational crime, as well as intelligence sharing, counterterrorism, and training. But a few weeks after my commissioning parade, he resigned over the Maher Arar case. I feel that what happened to Zaccardelli is a classic case of how policing and politics get intertwined, especially at the top levels.

Maher Arar is a Canadian citizen, an engineer, who was born in Syria and who retained dual Canadian and Syrian citizenship. In 2002, he was held as a suspected terrorist during a stopover in New York City and was then sent to Syria where he said he was held in a cell and tortured for almost a year. He was later returned to Canada. It was alleged that the RCMP gave American authorities erroneous information about Arar, which is what led to his being apprehended. However, a Canadian government investigation concluded that Arar was innocent and he was awarded $10.5 million. Canadian prime minister Stephen Harper extended a formal apology to him and Justice Dennis O'Connor conducted an exhaustive inquiry into the Maher Arar case. The judge was fair and direct in his findings that although mistakes were made by the RCMP, he found no evidence of malice or intent to engage in wrongdoing by the force. However, as head of the RCMP, Giuliano Zaccardelli did the honourable thing by resigning as commissioner because he knew that this constant harangue over Arar would be very negative for the RCMP. In the short run and in the long run. And the RCMP is an organization Zaccardelli loved deeply. It is an organization he had served faithfully for thirty-six years.

During the whole Arar episode, Zaccardelli was under a lot of stress from all sides and I felt something should be done to honour this man and recognize the outstanding service he had given his country. So I formed a committee and we held a tribute dinner for him and his wife, Bette, in Woodbridge, Ontario. More than 550 people attended that dinner. It wasn't a high-profile kind of thing with politicians and celebrities, but an event with people from the local community. All the proceeds went to charity. We wound up raising $80,000 for Villa Leonardo Gambin and Villa Colombo Vaughan, which are both long-term-care facilities.

Why did we hold that dinner? Because those of us on the committee felt the media had effectively hijacked the message about Zaccardelli being a decent person. This is a man I know very well and any implications about him being less than honest are ridiculous. He and his family have sacrificed greatly for Canadian society and should not have been so viciously and personally attacked by some people in the media and by some political officials, most notably member of Parliament Mark Holland, who was co-chair of the public safety committee. Holland even accused Zaccardelli of having committed perjury when he had addressed that committee. Zaccardelli's character was publicly executed and in the politics of the world he became expendable. Incidentally, a second dinner was also held in his honour in Ottawa, and I went to that one, too. We had these dinners because somebody had to balance the public record.

I make no judgment about Maher Arar, but while he has been portrayed as a victim, I think to some degree Giuliano Zaccardelli was one as well.

·17·

The Post-9/11 World

O N SEPTEMBER 11, 2001, I WAS IN KENORA IN NORTHERN Ontario for a board meeting of the Ontario Association of Chiefs of Police. We had flown up the night before and that morning we were having breakfast. The plan was to have our meeting and then go fishing. It was supposed to be a relaxing day. We were summoned to our meeting and then someone said a plane had slammed into the World Trade Center in New York. Of course, we thought it was an accident. We all went to the TV and watched—by that time it was live coverage—and, lo and behold, the second plane went in before our very eyes. For a moment, I was totally and absolutely incredulous. I felt helpless and frustrated because now it was obvious something was going on and this was no accident. That chiefs' meeting included border chiefs from such cities as Windsor and Niagara Falls, so there was a great sense of urgency and immediacy on our part and everyone wanted to get back home as soon as possible. But who knew the extent of what was happening or if it involved Canada? As police chief of the biggest city in the country, I figured there was a chance this might impact Toronto, so I called my executive officer, Superintendent Wayne Cotgreave, who as it turned out had been trying to reach me.

Normally we would have driven west across the Manitoba border to Winnipeg and then flown back to Toronto from there, but that wasn't going to happen because of the no-fly order, so we found ourselves in a dilemma. A couple of chiefs had vans and planned to drive back home to their cities, but that wasn't feasible for those of us from the Toronto area. It would have taken ten hours to drive from Kenora to Thunder Bay, Ontario, and then the rest of the way would have taken days. The distance is enormous; Thunder Bay is on the north shore of Lake Superior and only an hour by car from the Minnesota border, but it's 1,400 kilometres to Toronto, so driving wasn't very practical, especially at a time like this. A small northern airline called Bearskin Airlines offered to take us back, but couldn't get a permit to fly.

We contacted the office of Canada's federal minister of transport and got permission from the minister himself, but were told we had to fly on either a military or police aircraft. RCMP Commissioner Giuliano Zaccardelli finally came to the rescue and sent a small RCMP aircraft to Kenora, which flew us to Buttonville, an airport just north of Toronto.

On the flight back, the pilots said it was eerie because no one was flying and there was no chatter in the air. Nothing. The only other aircraft were military planes and Medivac helicopters. There were no commercial planes anywhere. Our plane was a six-seater and, on the flight, I learned of the decision to evacuate all the tall buildings in downtown Toronto. But I knew that was no simple matter because when streets are flooded with people, you need a plan to evacuate the city and we didn't have such a thing. The experience of 9/11 demonstrated that we must have an evacuation plan focused on getting people out of a certain area very quickly. Later, I would commission the Toronto Police Service to develop a comprehensive evacuation plan for the city. We had never done that before.

It wasn't long after September 11 when I was standing at ground zero in New York City talking to two young Port Authority motorcycle officers. The site was still smouldering and it was obvious to me that these men were deeply traumatized. And no wonder. When the first plane hit, a call had gone out to Port Authority police to converge on the tower and help out. These two men had arrived just when one of the towers came down. One minute earlier and they would have been inside. They survived, but many of their colleagues didn't. Neither did my friend Fred Morrone.

Fred was the director of public safety for the Port Authority of New York and New Jersey Police Department. He had led that organization for five years, which put him in charge of a department with jurisdiction over three airports—JFK, LaGuardia, and Newark International—as well as the tunnels and bridges linking New York to New Jersey, the Port Authority bus terminal, the PATH interstate rail system, all the marine terminals in New York and New Jersey, and many other facilities. He was a member of the International Association of Chiefs of Police and, ironically, was on the IACP Subcommittee on Terrorism.

Fred was one of seventy-two officers from eight local, state, and federal agencies who died on 9/11. I had been on an FBI National Executive Institute training course with him. This was an executive training program offered by the FBI to chief executive officers of the largest law enforcement organizations in the United States, Canada, the United Kingdom, and Australia. Fred, John Thomas, who was deputy chief of the Chicago Police Department, and I were on this course together and the three of us got along very well. We were all about the same age and had similar thoughts and concerns about policing. We had met earlier that year and really hit it off. John, unfortunately, is also deceased now.

Fred Morrone was a good friend. He was a kind, gentle man and a real humanitarian. On that fateful morning, he was at a breakfast meeting when he got the call. He was last seen climbing up the stairs around the sixtieth floor and about to take charge. He was that kind of guy. About a month after 9/11, when feelings were still very raw, it was decided that the third leg of this FBI training course would be held in New York because of what had happened to him. When the group of us from that course were at ground zero we got a behind-the-scenes look at what was going on. And we got it up close. We saw the temporary morgue that was set up and the recovery of bodies that were being found every day. But what I remember most was that just behind the ruins, on a building still standing, was a plate-glass window that hadn't been shattered. Someone had written on the glass—in the dust and soot—the words: "You in big trouble now Bin." It was a message to Bin Laden.

I stood there thinking how vulnerable we were and that at any given time we could be violated by those intent on inflicting evil. I also remember thinking as a police officer what an awesome challenge it was to put all this together. This was a crime scene of mass murder like no one had ever seen before. It would mean organizing priorities, working across different agencies and, of course, dealing with your own personal feelings of trauma.

The first weekend in December after 9/11, Canadian senator Jerry Grafstein organized a Canada Loves New York Day in New York City, and my wife and I took part in that event. Canadian prime minister Jean Chrétien was there too. This was when I first met New York City mayor Rudolph Giuliani, a man who throughout the experience of 9/11 gave the whole world a lesson in what leadership is all about. Also in New York was the Toronto police video unit, which was producing a documentary. It would be called Emotional Rescue 9/11 and would later be used for training our police officers about how to handle emergencies like this. One big thing we learned in doing that documentary was the importance of managing post-traumatic stress.

Toronto police officers raised over $100,000 for the families of NYPD officers who died on 9/11, and when we held that Canada Loves New York Day, a group of us handed over the money to the New York City Police Patrolmen Benevolent Association. And the Toronto Fire Department also did its part by donating a fire truck to the New York Fire Department. On that day, I remember standing at the viewing site next to two young Toronto police officers, who didn't know a soul in New York, and they just broke down and cried. They had absorbed the enormity of the tragedy and knew that hundreds of bodies were still in the ruins and hadn't been recovered. It was so heartbreaking to see all the teddy bears, flowers, notes, photographs of missing loved ones, and memorials to police officers and firefighters.

The outpouring was unbelievable.

When I was in New York again on the third and final leg of that FBI training course, all the rubble from the World Trade Center was still being sent to Fresh Kills Landfill on the western shore of Staten Island, and a group of us—all chief executive officers from various police departments—were watching the meticulous and scientific search of rubble taking place. There were hundreds of police officers and forensic experts going through all of it. First, they sifted through it with rakes and gathered it up into a hopper. Then they put the rubble onto a vibrating screen, which sorted out a certain size of material. Then they put this material onto another vibrating screen, which sorted it in even finer detail. The police and forensic people were examining everything. At the time, those of us who had been Fred Morrone's classmates from that course saw this conveyor belt. Police officers were constantly picking off pieces of identification and items of jewellery from it. All of a sudden, a New York/New Jersey Port Authority shoulder flash appeared on the conveyor. This is the police insignia on the shoulder of the uniform. It was a profound moment and we all froze. We retrieved that shoulder flash and had it mounted on a plaque along with a cross made of recovered steel from the site. Today it stands as part of the memorial for Fred at the FBI Academy located on the United States Marine Corps Base in Quantico, Virginia.

As with many other victims of 9/11, Fred's remains were never recovered, but a very moving memorial service was held for him in the Newark Cathedral. The church was jam-packed with police and citizens. A pipe band played, and with the sound and the ambience, there wasn't a dry eye in the place. This man was very loved.

John Vigiano, a retired captain with the New York Fire Department, wasn't someone I knew personally, but I feel compelled to mention him because he lost two sons that day, one of them a firefighter and the other a police officer. His older son was John Junior, age thirty-six, a member of the NYFD and a father of two children. His younger son was Joseph, age thirty-four, a detective with the NYPD and a father of three, the youngest only three months old. Both brothers perished at the World Trade Center when they rushed in to help after the first tower was hit.

September 11 showed us that terrorism is all about making a statement and that statement can be made anywhere, but I don't think Canada realizes this. The country has a false sense of comfort and is naive. Many Canadians seem to think this is a U.S. issue and a U.S. problem. It isn't. The difference between Canadians and Americans is that Canadians are passive about terrorism and take much for granted, while Americans are absolutely certain it's not a question of if, but when. Personally, I don't think we have to worry about the likes of Bin Laden coming across our borders because the evil is now within. Today the whole philosophy of terrorism has been dispersed around the world by Bin Laden's rhetoric, which means people with his radicalized mindset are amongst us. The silent killer is here, and not only that, but we also have people in our midst who are sympathetic to terrorism and who hate Americans. At the same time, Canada is full of American institutions—banks, for example—along with individuals who raise funds for terrorism and who radicalize the young. This is the big danger. I don't know if they'll ever get Bin Laden and I don't think it even matters anymore, because his poison now permeates the world.

Canada is doing a lot to fight terrorism, but in the eyes of the international community it must do more. Bill C-36, the Anti-Terrorism Act, is good legislation that was enacted largely in response to 9/11. With this act authorities have new powers to deter, disable, identify, prosecute, convict, and punish terrorist groups. The act provides new investigative tools for law enforcement and security agencies, and strengthens laws against hate crimes and propaganda. At the same time, Bill C-36 comes with restrictions. For example, while it gave authorities extraordinary powers, it also imposed time limits. But there has been a debate on how long those powers can be in effect. From a police perspective, this can handcuff an investigation. There is a lot of rhetoric in Canada about this law and some people want it clawed back, but nothing in the bill has been abused and it does come with checks and balances.

Does Canada take terrorism seriously? As a country we don't take it as seriously as Americans or Europeans. In Italy, police officers do random checks on people right on the street. And we certainly don't take it as seriously as Israelis. In Israel, if you carry a bag and wear loose clothing, a police officer might pat you down and no one will scream about the abuse of human rights. But if this happened in Canada, we'd be in a human rights tribunal and the media would be jumping up and down. The difference is in attitude and in the perception and appreciation of the danger. And the danger is real.

In Israel, they're on the edge of this sort of thing. The safeguards Israel has in place deal with a high-threat environment. They have been acclimatized and for them terrorism is a reality, a fact of life, something they have to deal with every day. And they do. They are very strategic in their counterterrorism initiatives. Over there, police officers and military people are taught how to identify suicide bombers by their behaviour and dress. In most public places, military people will approach and if you have a parcel or bag, you are asked to open it up and nobody seems to mind. It's all seen to be for the greater good. Before you walk into a restaurant or any public place, for that matter, chances are there will be a security person. You can be questioned and patted down. Canada, by comparison, is very passive about terrorism. We are sitting back, but the day will come when we'll have to change our attitude. When the bombs go off, you just watch how things will go the other way with the knee-jerk reaction that takes place.

As mentioned earlier, in the fall of 2006, I was appointed commissioner of the Ontario Provincial Police. This job has brought me much closer to the issue of terrorism than I ever was before. It has exposed me to national and international intelligence about terrorist activities and threats. We are forever doing assessments, but the reality is that if terrorists want to attack you, they will.

In Canada, we overplay personal rights and entitlements to the detriment of the greater good. Here's an example. On December 26, 2005, a fifteen-year-old girl named Jane Creba was doing some Boxing Day shopping with her older sister when she was suddenly gunned down on Toronto's Yonge Street. Two gangs of youths were shooting at each other and six other people were wounded. The young girl died and there was a great public outcry. In the investigation that followed came an uproar about video cameras in the public domain and how they violated one's privacy. But what possible violation of privacy is there in the public domain when you're in the middle of the most travelled street in the country at high noon? Who would expect to have privacy in such a place? This kind of attitude is not conductive to preventing terrorism.

A few weeks after 9/11, Paul Martin, who was then Canada's finance minister and just two years away from being prime minister, was a guest at a fundraiser for the Tamil Eelam Society. Unbeknownst to Martin, this was an organization that raised money for the Tamil Tigers, a terrorist organization that has been waging a secessionist campaign against the Sri Lankan government. The Tamil Tigers want to create a separate state for Tamils in that country. Toronto has the biggest Sri Lankan community in the world outside of Sri Lanka, and the Tamil Tigers have indeed been terrorizing members of the local Sri Lankan community. I know for a fact that some businesses have had to pay a "head tax" to support this group's activities. So, here you have a senior member of the Canadian government endorsing a terrorist group with his presence while, at the same time, that same government is supposed to be fighting terrorism. Canada eventually did put the Tamil Tigers and other organizations like Hezbollah on their list of terrorist groups.

Maybe naiveté isn't the right word.

When I was chief in Toronto, I used to get all kinds of invitations to attend celebrations for various groups, but I always did my research to see what these groups were about and sometimes red flags went up. Some of these groups light candles and display photographs of people with machine guns all over the place. They make heroes out of terrorists.

I chose not to go to such events because, while I didn't know anything about the particular causes, my suspicions were aroused.

In Canada today, as in the United States and other Western countries, Muslims carry an added burden because of the rhetoric coming from some elements in their community. It's a big concern when community leaders speak out and seem to be apologists for terrorism even though they may not actively promote it. But I know a lot of people in the Muslim community and the great majority of them are decent, law-abiding citizens who just want to get by and who are deeply concerned about the rhetoric stemming from some circles in their community. At the same time, we know that many of the major Islamic charitable institutions in North America have been infiltrated by radical Islamists.

But there is a very significant difference between Muslims and terrorists. One of the negative residual aspects of all this rhetoric is that it causes anguish and concern to law-abiding citizens. It's just like it was with the Italians and the Mafia when I first joined the police back in the late '60s. It was assumed then that any Italian who was picked up by the police was Mafia, which was ridiculous. It's the same with Muslims today. I know how concerned they are with the smear on them as a people. There has been a backlash and they have sustained what is sometimes a racist, bigoted discriminatory response.

There are two images of Canada. One is how we see ourselves and the other is the bigger picture, which is how the world sees us. In many respects, that view is of a weak-kneed society that is not very discriminating about its borders and its jurisdictions and that too easily welcomes people who shouldn't be here. Canada is maturing, but we certainly aren't quick learners. We don't think we're on the hit parade of terrorists. One day, however, we are going to be shocked. Terrorists exploit vulnerabilities and weaknesses, which is why we can't afford to stop protecting ourselves. We must work diligently across borders and jurisdictions with the rest of the free democratic world. Neither Canada nor the U.S. can be a silo and a stand-alone society. Both countries are dependent on one another.

The biggest challenges facing Canada with regard to terrorism are its complacency and its approach to how terrorism should be fought. As for this latter issue, let me explain. The first line of defence against terrorism is vigilance on the ground in the community. This is where good relations with a diverse community are critical. The problem I have with Canada's approach to fighting terrorism is that the country regards the fight as a high-end, federal matter with terrorism being fought at the national level. This is how the fight is funded, but the sharing of information sometimes goes only one way. Down. It would be better if we reversed the pyramid because the massive numbers of ears and eyes are at the bottom end, not at the top. That doesn't mean we should all be spying on each other, but it does mean we should be maintaining safety and security and reporting any suspicious circumstances. I said as much when I testified in Ottawa at Senator Colin Kenny's Standing Senate Committee on National Security and Defence.

Senator Kenny is a man who has both his feet planted firmly on the ground. His committee invited me to appear when I was chief in Toronto, and I have appeared since that time as well. I think he and his committee are doing necessary work by putting such a strong focus on a very significant issue, which is the business of national security.

In June 2005, that committee released a report called Borderline Insecure to the Canadian Parliament. It made a lot of good points. It said an optimal target for terrorists in Canada is the Ambassador Bridge in Windsor, Ontario, because any problem there could lead to a continent-wide shutdown of the Canada–U.S. border. What would be the repercussions of that? Well, consider that 87 per cent of Canada's exports go to the U.S., most of it transported by truck, and that the Windsor-Detroit border gets more traffic than anywhere else. Also consider that one in four jobs in Ontario depends on exports to the U.S. and that two-way trade between Canada and the U.S. is worth more than U.S.$1 billion a day. The report of Senator Kenny's committee said *every four-hour delay* at the Windsor-Detroit crossing costs the economy of Ontario $7 million and the economy of Michigan $14.3 million. It also said that, without more attention paid to infrastructure issues dealing with the Canada–U.S. border, congestion and delay at the Windsor-Detroit crossing will cost an estimated *$20.8 billion a year* by 2030.

These concerns were also raised in the Smart Border Declaration signed by Canada and the United States in December 2001 and in the Security and Prosperity Partnership which came out of the March 2005 meeting in Waco, Texas, involving Canadian prime minister Paul Martin, U.S. president George W. Bush, and Mexican president Vicente Fox.

Senator Kenny's committee has addressed what it deems to be vulnerabilities at Canada's airports and seaports and along the coastlines. In fact, an editorial from the *Globe and Mail* of January 8, 2007, quoted Kenny as saying something that can only be construed as truly astonishing in this day and age: "There is virtually no security at Canada's airports." Even so, his committee has said that vulnerabilities at our land border crossings are the most serious of all.

Ed Flynn, who at the time of 9/11 was chief of the Arlington County, Virginia, police department, is a man I know from the International Association of Chiefs of Police. He made an excellent point about police leadership in a report called On-Scene Response and Security, Pentagon Terrorist Attack. This was in response to the 9/11 attack on the Pentagon. He said:

> While billions of dollars will and should be spent on federal-level preparedness and response to terrorism, one fact remains clear: the first responders to these acts will be beat cops—and they will need the leadership of their chiefs to do the right job.

I couldn't agree more. In March 2004, Senator Kenny's committee released a document called National Emergencies: Canada's Fragile Front Lines—An Upgrade Strategy. The committee sent a survey to first responders in 100 municipalities across Canada—police and fire detachments, ambulance services, doctors, nurses, emergency-response teams, and enlisted soldiers and reserves. The Executive Summary of that document says the following:

We discovered that first responders are not being listened to. They are not being communicated with. They are not being adequately funded. They often do not have the resources to do their jobs and often it is unclear as to where to go after those resources, partially because of tangled federal-provincial jurisdictions, and partially because of an apparent lack of urgency at various levels—including the federal government.

It went on to list specific examples where problems exist. Here are three of them:

- Health Canada has placed emergency supply caches across the country to be used in crises, but the vast majority of first responders don't know where those caches are located or even what they contain.
- Health experts identified several micro-organisms that could cause widespread illness and death if spread intentionally or accidentally, but there is no national plan to deal with such potential outbreaks.
- Most Canadians believe the Canadian Armed Forces will help out in times of national emergencies, but those forces are neither staffed nor equipped to do so.

In my own submission to Senator Kenny's committee, I said that first responders feel like marginal players on the preparedness stage even though they will be the lead actors in a crisis. I also said that improvements suggested by federal and provincial governments "fall seriously short in recognizing the need for local law enforcement to be made an integral part of the overall anti-terrorism problem." My only hope is that this committee is taken seriously and that one day Senator Kenny won't have to say "I told you so."

The fight against terrorism is on two levels. One level involves proactive, intelligence-driven, integrated, investigative work. The other level involves our ability to respond, if and when we are violated. We can't ignore the fact that there can be a fine line between radical, hate-motivated activity and extremists who actually engage in violence. This means that any hate-motivated activity directed against a specific group should be addressed head-on.

Ray Kelly, police commissioner of the city of New York, hit the nail on the head when he said "the lone wolf" represents the most significant threat. He said this at an IACP conference in Los Angeles in 2004, and his point was that one demented individual—a member of a terrorist cell or what have you—acting alone is the greatest danger.

I know Ray Kelly well and he is a man who doesn't look like the commissioner of America's largest municipal police department. He may be of small physical stature, but I can tell you that in the law enforcement community, he is a giant and widely respected. He is a strategic visionary thinker who isn't afraid to tell it like it is and he has shown tremendous leadership in the fight against terrorism with a clear focus on his prime responsibility—protecting his beloved New York City.

Paul Capellini, a detective with the NYPD, was the very first New York police officer seconded to Toronto in an exchange between the two police forces after 9/11. When he came to Toronto, he told us that big cities share a common bond—being targets of terrorists. He also said these cities must receive the necessary resources to fight terrorism. That means their respective federal governments must fund them so they can sustain investigations. This is very important because every terrorist act is a local event first. The local community gets threatened, and the local police cannot abdicate responsibility and just give way to federal authorities. Instead, they have to pair up with those federal authorities and work with them.

Today there is a cluster of U.S. law enforcement people in Toronto. That initial exchange between the New York and Toronto police forces proved to be a success, and it was our feeling that the threat against America was really a threat against democratic free countries and that terrorism could hit anywhere. Some time after 9/11, I went to Washington, D.C., to meet with American officials. I went with Bob

Runciman, who was Ontario minister of public safety and security, and Scott Newark, who used to be executive director of the Canadian Police Association and is now a security consultant. Paul Celucci, who was U.S. ambassador to Canada, was involved in this, too. The result is that today, FBI agents, Secret Service, and agents with the Bureau of Alcohol, Tobacco, Firearms and Explosives (ATF) work out of the U.S. consulate in Toronto. These law enforcement agencies within the U.S. Department of Justice are dedicated to preventing terrorism, fighting organized crime, and co-operating with Canadian law enforcement authorities. These people are in Toronto to work out cross-border and security issues and to help network with us so we can present a united front.

I first met Paul Celucci at that IACP conference in Toronto in October 2001. Right after 9/11. I was chief in Toronto and he was the U.S. ambassador to Canada. One of the events at that conference was called Host Chiefs Night and we turned it into a Tribute to America. Remember, this was just one month after 9/11 and feelings were still very raw. People everywhere were hurting and scared. Celucci came and made the most passionate and compelling speech. He brought spirit, encouragement, and patriotism, and I don't mean American patriotism, but free-world patriotism. He was just tremendous. This event was held at Toronto's Skydome, now called the Rogers Centre, and I don't think there was a dry eye in the house.

Sometimes in Canada decisions taken by the government make absolutely no sense and maybe the best example of that occurred in 1997. That was the year the Canadian government disbanded the Canada Ports Police. The Canada Ports Police was an on-site, around-the-clock, intelligence-driven agency dedicated to policing the country's ports. There are nineteen ports in all, the major ones being Vancouver, Montreal, Halifax, Quebec City, and in the Atlantic provinces, St. John's, Newfoundland, and Saint John, New Brunswick. The Canada Ports Police were specialized law enforcement officers who knew the ins and outs of the ports. They had contacts, experience, and an intimate knowledge of the business. When the government announced its intent to pull the plug on this agency, the Canadian Police Association, representing 40,000 front-line police officers in the country, was vehemently opposed, but the government went ahead and did it anyway. The apparent reasoning behind this decision was that the mere presence of the Canada Ports Police, which was employed by a regulatory body called the Canada Ports Corporation, was slowing down commercial trade, especially in the Atlantic provinces.

New York City is the biggest and most important port in the United States. It is one of the major ports of the world. The Canadian decision of 1997 would be like shutting down the Port Authority of New York and New Jersey Police Department—and replacing it with nothing. This is unthinkable. But that's what happened in Canada. And it happened right across the country.

The result of disbanding the Canada Ports Police was an explosion of organized crime activity at such ports as Vancouver where more heroin than we had ever seen before was being smuggled in. Getting rid of the Canada Ports Police turned out to be good news for criminal organizations like Hells Angels and, by the same token, also good for terrorists.

Scott Newark, who was part of that trip to Washington, D.C., and who was a Crown prosecutor in Alberta before becoming executive director of the Canadian Police Association, said abolishing the ports police was "the single most inexplicable and unjustified act" he had ever seen by the federal government in all the years he had been working in the criminal justice system.

The International Association of Airport and Seaport Police (IAASP) was formed in 1969 as an organization of police, law enforcement, and other agencies that protect airports and seaports around the world. The idea behind it is to foster communications and build professionalism in this important activity. Today Canada is the only member of the G8 and one of the few industrialized countries in the world without its own special police dedicated to the protection and security of its ports.

Mike Toddington was chief officer of the Vancouver detachment of the Canada Ports Police and later he became executive director of the

IAASP. He said that even when the Canada Ports Police was still around, drugs were a huge problem, especially at the port of Vancouver. According to a report he prepared, $1.2 billion was seized in illicit drugs from 1987 to 1994. Toddington said the interception rate was estimated to be less than 5 per cent of the actual total of drug traffic. This means that the illegal importation of drugs through the port of Vancouver would have been *$30 billion a year*, easily the most lucrative business conducted at the port.

We can only imagine what the numbers became once the Canada Ports Police was disbanded.

Consider that most American ports have their own police employed by the local port authority, as is the case with the Port Authority of New York and New Jersey Police Department. In Europe, special divisions of the police are specifically assigned to ports and transportation. In Asian cities like Singapore, auxiliary police are employed by the ports along with regular police permanently assigned to the ports. Hong Kong has a large division of port police exclusively responsible for the port area. States in Australia have their own dedicated harbour police or large marine divisions to patrol the waterways. The United Kingdom has its river police, which are absorbed into the London Metropolitan Police, and it also has the federal government Home Office with a special division of the National Police dedicated to the ports. In the Netherlands, the port police in Rotterdam constitute a special division of the National Police Service.

But Canada has nothing like this and the problem is that local police who respond to calls are limited to investigating, arresting, and prosecuting while, at the same time, they are not well versed in the whole business of dealing with the ports. They are also not well versed in the big picture involving international trade.

Just think of the organized crime activity that occurs at the ports—the contraband that constantly comes and goes and the potential corruption that always comes with it—and then all of a sudden the specialists who police it are pulled out. It is sheer lunacy. Since that 1997 decision, Canada's ports have been without a dedicated body of people who police the ports exclusively, on-site, around the clock. Instead, each port authority is responsible for its own security, which means you have local police forces who aren't dedicated to this activity, and the RCMP who, for the most part, aren't even on-site. In 2006, RCMP commissioner Zaccardelli told Senator Kenny's Senate national security committee that he had 124 RCMP officers stationed at the country's three largest airports and only thirty officers stationed at the nineteen ports. Thirty Mounties. That was it. He said: "In terms of vulnerability, our assessment is that the marine ports are the greatest single threat...in terms of organized crime and national security."

If any country is more lax with respect to its ports than Canada, I don't know what it is, but then Canada is pretty lax, period, when it comes to security. There is a big debate going on about whether we are going to arm border guards. On this side of the Canada–U.S. border, you've got very passive security; move a hundred yards the other way, and you've got very committed security. The contrast is very telling. The problem, I think, is that we're trying to insulate ourselves into believing it's not going to happen to us. This is Canada, we say.

Another big problem in Canada concerns the screening of people who want to come to this country. The screening should be done overseas, not when they get here, which, unfortunately, is how it works. Our first line of defence should be offshore. Another problem involves deportations. As a police officer, I knew of convicted bank robbers who had been deported ten different times—*ten times!*—and still they kept coming back.

Why does this happen? It's very simple. When you enter most countries around the world you fill out a form, and then you fill out another form when you leave the country. This is a system of inventory management and the inventory in question is people. With that second form, authorities know you have come and gone and, if you haven't completed that exit form in a prescribed amount of time, they start looking for you. But not in Canada. You come into this country and fill out a customs form, tell them how much liquor and tobacco you've got, and then you're home free. You don't have to sign anything when you leave and this is why we lose track of people here. We actually lose people. All kinds of people. Terrorists included. My point is that, until you do an inventory of who is coming into the country and who is going out, how do you know who's here? Well, you don't.

I think, above all, the most important thing in fighting terrorism is to create a united front with all the agencies involved. This means integrating everything we do. Sharing information. Avoiding duplication. Avoiding silos. Working strategically with joint forces. But there still has to be one umbrella entity that oversees and coordinates everything.

Fighting terrorism is largely a combination of proactive intelligence working with technology and, make no mistake, technology has come a long way. At many airports today, the technology is terrific, but we still must work harder at knowing who is flying on those airplanes. At the same time, people must have freedom of movement, but let's not lose perspective on this. When you consider how much air travel goes on, the chances of being mugged on the street are far greater than they are of being victimized on an aircraft. But that doesn't mean we let up on security.

We can't.

The day after 9/11, I was involved in something quite remarkable. Once we realized we were facing a significant terrorism threat—though we still didn't know for sure the origin—we knew we needed information. A lot of information. At the time, all kinds of databanks and sources of information were housed with many different agencies. Jack Hooper was the national security expert at the Canadian Security and Intelligence Service (CSIS) in Ontario. CSIS is the federal agency with a mandate to protect the national security interests of Canada. Jack and Staff Superintendent Rocky Cleveland of the Toronto Police Service brought all the different agencies together. The purpose was to take advantage of our collective wisdom, intelligence, and information and sort everything out. This was a great example of joint forces co-operating with each other. Every law enforcement agency and every national security agency that was operating in the city was brought together in one room. The Toronto Police Service. The RCMP. The OPP. The CSIS. The federal department of Immigration and Customs. They all had their best technical people there and this had never happened before. Ever. What's more, it happened quickly and there was no reluctance on anyone's part. We integrated all the different databanks and analyzed the information everyone had to see if we could connect the dots.

In that exercise, we shared and analyzed information, and were very open with each other. That was the most significant, visionary example of how fighting terrorism should work. Everybody—all the databanks and all the agencies—in one room. Working together. Fully integrated. Strategically focused. Seeking out that vital piece of information someone may have to enable us to connect the dots, to identify suspects, to target the right individuals, and to be tactical in surveillance and other investigative techniques.

This is precisely the kind of response we need to fight terrorism, and I'm not talking about one city or even one country. I'm talking about working across agencies, across cultures, and across borders and jurisdictions. Everybody working together. That meeting we had was all about survival and out of it came threat assessments and a sense of what we should be doing. Unfortunately, it took 9/11 to make it happen.

· 18 ·

Innovations in Crime Fighting

W HEN I WAS CHIEF IN LONDON, WE DEVELOPED A USER-focused, records management system and it was done with a vision. The vision was to support and sustain the individual police officer on the street, and to make that officer safe and more efficient. We felt information was the key. The idea was that, if the officer was suspicious about a certain vehicle, he or she would key in the license number on the in-car computer and the system would reach out to all the available databanks. The officer would then get the name of the registered owner of the vehicle, along with the person's history and photograph, and all this information would be displayed on the computer screen right in the cruiser. We also wanted to make the system voice-activated so officers didn't have to take their eyes off the road. They would just say the license number and the information would appear before they had even stopped the vehicle.

London was at the forefront of developing such a records management system, which was no surprise because this sort of thing can be created more cost-effectively in a smaller police department than in a bigger one. After we developed it, we took the system a step further. Because the criminal element is very transient, we wanted to be able to interface with other police departments, and we did. Today, all major police forces in Canada have this technology. Now an officer in Ottawa can access information held by the police in London or Vancouver and get whatever they want. Before, you couldn't do that directly because all the systems were stand-alone.

Another interesting thing we did in London involved the use of traffic enforcement vehicles equipped with "subdued markings." These cars looked like ordinary vehicles—unmarked cars—but they weren't because the decals identifying them as police showed up only when a headlight was shone on them, and then the vehicles lit up like Christmas trees. The advantage was that a speeding driver might think nothing of passing such a car, only to learn a moment later that he had blown right by the police. These vehicles had all the necessary technology to pursue dangerous drivers: forward-looking radar, rear-looking radar, and radar-detecting radar, which tells if a motorist has an anti-radar device.

I can't take credit for this idea. In fact, a traffic sergeant in London thought it up. But the job of a police chief is to throw out snowballs that other people make for you. If they're good snowballs, they will stick. I thought this was a great idea, a major innovation, and other police departments have adopted it as well. When I left London and went to the York Regional Police, I made sure that York Region got these vehicles, and when I returned to Toronto as chief, I made sure they got them as well.

In York Region, we also designed a state-of-the-art, mobile Breathalyzer unit in a specially equipped vehicle that was used to apprehend suspected impaired drivers. This was a big van and you could call it "one-stop shopping." Here's how it worked. After being pulled over, the suspected impaired driver got out of his car and came through the back door of the van to a receiving area. He was booked and read his rights and everything was filmed. Then he was taken to a private booth, where he could call a lawyer. Then he went to the Breathalyzer station and did the test. If he failed, he was handcuffed and taken away. The whole thing was done in the vehicle and was a great time saver. We used it on our Reduced Impaired Driving Everywhere (RIDE) program. It was fast, efficient, and convenient, and it effectively brought the police station right to the roadside. Again, this was another practical idea.

But by far the greatest innovation I have ever been involved in has been CETS (Child Exploitation Tracking System), which was developed by the Toronto Police Service. I have long had a keen interest in the issue of victimization of children because I see children as the most vulnerable segment in society, and I also see pedophiles as brutal, manipulative monsters. Through Project Guardian in London, I learned a lot about this problem, and through Interpol, I learned a lot about sex tourism and how pedophiles use the Internet to their own advantage. I attended many conferences and spoke at many of them about such things.

When I became chief in Toronto, I got Paul Gillespie, who was then a staff sergeant, to head up a special unit—the Child Exploitation Section of the Sex Crimes Unit. Paul had the same kind of passion I had for this issue. He was very computer savvy and always saw the big picture. He was also a family man with children of his own. Not long after we put the unit in place, he became increasingly aware of the limitations of the police in these types of investigations. He also became increasingly aware of the extraordinary ability of the bad guys to hide, imbed, or encrypt pornography online. He was always telling me about the technological challenges the police faced and about the heart-rending child pornography and victimization he was finding on his computer screen every day. Believe me, this job was not for the timid or faint of heart.

One day in early 2003, Paul decided to send an email to Bill Gates of Microsoft, asking him for help in dealing with the computer-facilitated, sexual exploitation of children. I only found out about this after the fact. Protocol would have required something like that to go through the chief or some other high-ranking officer, but in a moment of exasperation Paul decided to email Bill Gates. Paul knew that Microsoft technology was being widely used for both lawful and unlawful purposes, so he figured who better to help than Bill Gates. He also knew that Gates and his wife had a reputation, even back then, for getting involved in causes. This was a cause. Here is the email Paul sent to Bill Gates:

My name is Detective Sergeant Paul Gillespie of the Toronto Police Service. I am in charge of the Child Exploitation Section of the Sex Crimes Unit. I have 10 investigators assigned to me who are responsible for online child pornography investigations. My office seized over 2 million movies and images of child abuse last year and we are absolutely inundated with case files. Although the Internet is a wonderful thing, it has changed our lives forever. As the former director of the F.B.I. so accurately observed, combining an age old problem with modern technology is proving to be an almost insurmountable task for investigators.

By virtue of their age, intelligence and limited life experience, children are totally vulnerable as victims of sexual exploitation and abuse. Children are the "perfect" victims, and we are not very good at identifying them. I am frustrated and I need help. The Internet has dramatically increased the access of sex offenders to the population they seek to victimize. While child pornography crimes are not new, the methods in which the crimes are carried out are new and are changing as technology changes.

There are an alarming number of adults producing and distributing child pornography on the Internet. Investigating child exploitation on the Internet poses a number of challenges to investigators. Offenders use various techniques to frustrate investigators: disguising not only their personal identity but their Internet identity, utilizing computer software designed to defeat the forensic retrieval of evidence, and encryption.

The Toronto Police Service is committed to saving children. We are hosting an International Seminar in Toronto from September 22nd to 26th, 2003. Would you or anyone in your company be available to come to our seminar and present your

thoughts or possible solutions to these very important concerns
to the 500 investigators and child care workers in attendance? We
need your help. It's all about the kids.

Yours truly,

Detective Sergeant Paul Gillespie

Toronto Police Service, Sex Crimes Unit, Child Exploitation
Section

Well, lo and behold, if Paul didn't get a response. It came a couple of
weeks later in the form of a phone call from the corporate communications department at Microsoft Canada. Frank Clegg, who at the time was
president of Microsoft Canada, had been instructed by Bill Gates himself
to contact the officer who had sent the email to see if Microsoft could
help in any way. This then was the foundation for what has become a
wonderful example of how law enforcement can partner with private
enterprise for the greater good. Since then, I have never missed an
opportunity to praise Microsoft, Bill Gates, Frank Clegg, and their whole
team for what they have done.

In October 2003, Paul Gillespie was interviewed on CNN about child
pornography and he pulled no punches in explaining the problem. In his
interview, he talked about the horrific images of child abuse that he had
seen. Most people wouldn't believe this material even existed. He talked
about children—even babies—being brutalized, raped, tortured, tied
up, and hung upside down. He explained how like-minded individuals
traded this material online as if it were baseball cards. What's more, these
people were operating in an environment with no borders and no international laws regulating the flow of these images.

In his interview on CNN, this is what Paul said:

It's not unusual to recover 100,000 . . . 200,000 . . . 500,000
images of abuse and we're not very good at identifying the poor
children. So I decided one day in January, staring at my wall . . . I
have a saying on the wall. It's by Einstein. It says, "The significant

problems we face cannot be solved at the same level of thinking we were at when we created them." And all of a sudden it occurred to me. I'm not sure who created this problem, the police aren't dealing with it very well, and the only person I can think of is Mr. Gates who might have an idea as to how we might handle things or make it a little better.

So off went the email and the rest, as they say, is history. Well, thank goodness for Einstein.

Soon, I joined Paul and a few others and we all went to Microsoft's corporate headquarters in Redmond, Washington, just outside Seattle, to meet with the company's senior management. The Canadian president of Microsoft, Frank Clegg, led our presentation. We wanted to ensure that Bill Gates and his senior staff were onside. Microsoft, in turn, wanted to be assured that Paul would continue to work closely with the company's technical people, so that this technology could be used worldwide by any law enforcement agency that wanted it.

On our visit to Redmond, Microsoft treated us as if we were their best customers. Their boardroom was the most impressive boardroom I have ever seen and, they showed us great respect. After that, we had many meetings at Microsoft's Canadian headquarters in Mississauga, Ontario, and I got to know Frank Clegg very well. You won't find a finer gentleman and a more caring person in the corporate world than this man. He might have been the president of Microsoft Canada, but he was very welcoming and always had a lot of time for us. He didn't delegate. He handled this project himself. What really impressed me about Microsoft was that the company wasn't only being a good corporate citizen, it was also assuming responsibility for the fact that it had facilitated, unintentionally of course, the abuse of children that was taking place every day on the Internet. So it wanted to help correct that.

The Toronto police and Microsoft worked together to develop technology that would help investigators deal with child pornography on the

Internet. And this wouldn't be local. It would be international. As of
2007, Microsoft had invested U.S.$10 million into CETS.

Once we had the buy-in from Microsoft, things happened very
quickly. In January 2004, we held a two-day conference with representatives from twenty Canadian police agencies and representatives from the
FBI, the United States Department of Homeland Security, the National
Center for Missing and Exploited Children, which was a civilian agency
in the U.S., the National Child Exploitation Coordination Centre, which
was run by the RCMP in Canada, Interpol, and Europol. There were also
representatives from the United Kingdom—from the National Crime
Squad and Scotland Yard. The National Crime Squad, which in 2006
became the Serious Organized Crime Agency, reports to the Home
Office in London and deals mainly with organized crime, drug trafficking, illegal arms dealing, computer crime, and high-tech crime. As for
Scotland Yard, many people don't realize this, but it's not a national
police or law enforcement agency in the U.K. It refers to the headquarters of the Metropolitan Police Service in London, England. This then
was a truly international gathering and the purpose was to let everyone
kick the tires, as it were, so we could all get an idea of what requirements
were necessary to build the kind of system we had in mind. I should add
that Microsoft picked up the tab for getting all those people to and from
the meeting, as they did with every other meeting we had.

Shortly after that, our own Toronto police began using the first version of CETS. We called it the Alpha version. By the spring of 2004, we
were doing hands-on workshops for U.S. law enforcement agencies. In
December 2004, a later version of CETS was housed at RCMP headquarters in Ottawa, and police forces from across Canada began connecting
to the system. In May 2005, Microsoft Canada established the CETS
Center of Excellence in Toronto and started rolling out the system
internationally.

How does CETS work? It uses custom software that helps police combat the online exploitation of children, which includes child
pornography and "luring." Luring occurs when a sexual predator pre-

tends he is someone else by establishing an online identity and then entices children into a meeting. CETS uses what is called MapPoint technology, which permits radius searches of every address in the database. For example, let's say a local police department learns of an attempted child abduction at a certain address. That address is then put into the system and up comes every suspect who lives within one kilometre of that address or three kilometres or five kilometres—whatever you want. The CETS database is an intelligence database that includes not only convicted offenders, but also suspects. When online identities are queried, the system automatically searches all public newsgroups on the Internet.

The big advantage of CETS is that it allows for collaboration and information sharing among different police services. It enhances the effectiveness of individual police investigators and also teams of investigators by giving them the tools to store, search, share, and analyze large volumes of information.

Before CETS came along, every police force in Canada doing an investigation involving child pornography did so on its own. It was an independent investigation. There was no mechanism for sharing information with other police forces. So, if a suspect engaged in a certain modus operandi in one jurisdiction and then did the same thing in another jurisdiction, the two police forces involved wouldn't know about each other's suspects. In short, they wouldn't be able to connect the dots. Many enterprising criminals took advantage of this by spreading their victims across different jurisdictions so that they would never get caught.

A good example of what happens when information can't be shared is what we in the police community call "blue on blue." A police officer from one agency will go online seeking out pedophiles by pretending that he or she is a young person. Sooner or later they get hit on and a meeting is arranged. What happens sometimes is that two cops show up, one of them pretending to be a kid and the other pretending to be a pedophile. Blue on blue. This is how police often try to find out who these people are, but the problem is that neither force knows what the other is doing.

CETS bridges this gap. It allows for different police forces—not only within Canada but around the world—to share information. The electronic distribution of child pornography doesn't stop at borders or jurisdictions, so why should a police investigation? With CETS, it doesn't have to. CETS allows police and law enforcement agencies to work together, seamlessly and effectively, to investigate suspects and apprehend criminals. CETS makes child exploitation investigations more effective by reducing the duplication of efforts by police and by allowing agencies to combine all available information about investigations and suspects. With CETS, police and law enforcement agencies, no matter where they are located, can access a centralized database so that child exploitation investigators can match data with other investigators who might be referencing the same people or the same online identities.

The system's first success involved an investigation that originated in the U.S. What it did was link up non-obvious relationships. In 2004, the FBI was monitoring an Internet chat room involving child pornography in Washington, D.C. The FBI discovered that one of the administrators of this chat room lived in London, England, so London's Metropolitan Police Service got involved. This then led to a Toronto connection and the Toronto police got involved as well. But the Canadian suspect couldn't be identified. At least, not yet. Three months later, another U.S. investigation, this time by the Department of Homeland Security—it was called Project Falcon and once again it concerned child pornography—turned up sixty-two people in the Toronto area who were involved in this thing. All their identities went into the system and up came a "hit" with the previous information from the London investigation and that earlier Toronto connection. The offender was identified, a search warrant was issued, and when the police arrived they found him on his computer with a camera right beside him. This man had been sexually abusing a four-year-old girl and had distributed her image on the Internet. He was charged with eleven counts, including sexual assault, and possession and distribution of child pornography, and later was convicted. He got four and a half years.

Shortly after that, CETS showed its worth again. Toronto investigators had information about a suspected distributor of child pornography—a high-school teacher—and his name was run on the system. Many hits were returned, each with different versions of his first and last names. All the complaints for these different names contained the same basic information. The suspect picked up young boys off the street, paid them with money or alcohol or drugs, engaged in sex, and then took pictures of the boys. He was arrested, charged with several counts of child pornography, and convicted.

But let's not kid ourselves. While CETS has found and saved children around the world, the numbers saved are only a drop in the ocean. There are reasons for this, the main one being that there still is no significant deterrent for people who engage in this type of criminal activity. To a large degree, society and most definitely the courts, treat such material as film or photographs too lightly and always raise the issue of freedom of speech or freedom of expression. Until we accept the fact that this material is irrefutable evidence of the most brutal crime short of murder that can be committed against a child, and we hand out sentences that are appropriate, these people will not be deterred.

In 2006, Paul Gillespie, who was by then a detective sergeant, retired from the Toronto Police Service after a twenty-seven-year career to become a private consultant. He had become the face and voice of child pornography investigations and was widely known as Canada's, and maybe even the world's, top Internet cop. He and his team in Toronto, which by the fall of 2006 had twenty experts in its unit, deserve a lot of credit for what they achieved. Paul's retirement was a great loss to the police, but he has continued the fight against those who exploit children on the Internet by lending his expertise to police all over the world. With the help of Microsoft, he set up an international training facility in Toronto to teach others how to use CETS. Of course, Microsoft's involvement has also continued. In fact, the company assigned five full-time software architects to developing CETS 2.0, which was released in the summer of 2007 and which featured significant improvements over the previous version. Paul also began working with an Internet safety group called the Kids Internet Safety Alliance (KINSA). KINSA is involved with training, education, and advocacy concerning the issue of child pornography in developing countries. Former Microsoft Canada president Frank Clegg and I are the two Founding Patrons of KINSA.

In the summer of 2007, CETS was rolled out to police forces in the United Kingdom, Brazil, Indonesia, and Italy. I am extremely proud of CETS and consider it one of the major accomplishments I have been associated with in my career. When CETS was launched, Microsoft took out full-page ads in newspapers and magazines. With the ad was a large photograph of law enforcement people from across Canada who were involved in developing the system. We all got together at the Fairmont Royal York Hotel in Toronto for the shot. In the front row were myself; RCMP commissioner Giuliano Zaccardelli; David Hemler, who by then had succeeded Frank Clegg as president of Microsoft Canada; and Nancy Anderson, who was vice president and deputy general counsel for Microsoft in Redmond, Washington. Behind us was a large group of people from police services and law enforcement agencies across Canada. Standing in the middle of the pack was Paul Gillespie, and you couldn't miss him because he's six-five.

The ad also ran an article called "Protecting the Innocent" by David Butt, a former prosecutor who had conducted many cases involving child pornography and who is a top expert in the field. David is a Canadian who graduated with a master's degree from Harvard Law School. He has a brilliant legal mind and a wonderful way with words. This is his article that ran with the ad:

Thousands of new child abuse images appear on the Internet every month. They are not happy snapshots of cute tweenies on the beach, all coy smiles and bare bottoms. They are explicit images of the sexual abuse of prepubescent children, toddlers and infants that can only be described as sexual torture.

One can enter chat rooms posing as a ten-year-old and within minutes be set upon by sexual predators like vultures. In other chat rooms, child abusers crow about the sexual conquest of their own young children. If bank robbers felt safe enough to brag openly on street corners about each heist, we would be socially incensed.

No one can deny the Internet's immeasurable benefits. Technology and the Internet are essential classroom tools. In school and on the job, technologically literate kids go farther, faster than those who are not.

But this only heightens the need to confront Internet child abuse. How is that to be done? In three ways. First, we need to get up to speed—and fast—on the dangers facing our children online. We must also educate our children about Internet dangers without scaring them from exploring its wonders. This is important work for families, communities, technology companies, schools and governments everywhere.

Second, we must apprehend and punish Internet child predators. To do this, police need tools and resources they do not yet have. Courts must emerge from the glacial fog that impedes their moral vision. They must denounce Internet child abusers with real punishments that properly reflect the horror that is child abuse. Criminal law responses are not enough either—they address harm already inflicted. Our children deserve a society where danger is removed before harm is done.

Third, we must prevent harm to children by making cyberspace socially and technologically hostile to child abusers. This is a daunting challenge. It requires creativity, insight, persistence, adaptation and co-operation. It requires concrete support across the Internet technology industry. It requires action by governments locally, provincially, nationally and internationally. It requires a deep understanding of pedophilia. And it requires social mechanisms, like the U.K. Internet Watch Foundation, to foster an Internet social climate overtly unwelcoming to child abuse.

Internet child abuse is a tragedy that transcends political boundaries through commercial Internet technology. It will be prevented only on the same terms: through partnerships among governments and commercial actors across political boundaries. Some have already shown, by deeds, they care about eliminating Internet child abuse. And while real work has just begun, Canada is a world leader thanks to brave individuals willing to take some unusual leaps forward.

Toronto Police Detective Sergeant Paul Gillespie, Microsoft Canada Co. and the RCMP deserve our praise for their passionate response to this problem. Overcome with the flood of Internet child abuse, Gillespie e-mailed a plea for help to Bill Gates, who read it, and tasked Microsoft Canada to work closely with Toronto Police in developing a solution.

Today, police have free access to the Child Exploitation Tracking System or CETS, powerful Internet investigative software without equal in the world. Twenty-five police forces across Canada have adopted the tool, including Calgary, Charlottetown, Durham Regional, Edmonton, Halifax, Halton Regional, Hamilton, London, Manitoba, Niagara Regional, Ottawa, Peel Regional, Toronto, Saskatoon, Saint John, Sudbury, Vancouver, Victoria, Regina, Rothesay in N.B., Waterloo Regional, York Regional as well as the Ontario Provincial Police, Surete du Quebec and the Royal Newfoundland Constabulary.

The federal government has also funded the RCMP to create a nationwide cyber-linked CETS Investigative Network—another world's first. And Microsoft continues to think outside the corporate box by working to bring CETS to police services worldwide.

Governments and commercial actors must show they care enough about child abuse to step outside their traditional spheres to respond. With CETS, Canada is leading the way, setting a powerful example that is already making a difference.

I applaud Microsoft for its work in developing CETS and for attaching its good name to such an ad. I also applaud David Butt for telling it like it is.

CETS aside, the Toronto Police Service has also done some other important things to help fight crime. Notable among these is the DASH-BOARD Project. In any big city, the police can only make good decisions based on information at their disposal. In Toronto, we had a tremendous amount of information, but it was in different places and unless someone went to all the databanks and printed out everything, they couldn't get the "big picture." It's like going to the local hardware store for a home project. You might have to make fifteen stops at the store, and maybe some other stores too, to get all the things you need. DASHBOARD brings all that information together so you don't have to travel around. It's all about retrieving information. This was a huge problem for us and involved both the accuracy of data and the availability of data. The trouble with having information all over the map—and having it hard to retrieve when you want it—is that it makes a police force *reactive* instead of *proactive*. We wanted to be more proactive. We also wanted to know corporately and locally how well we were performing.

We called our system DASHBOARD because in a car you see everything on the dashboard—speed, gas gauge, oil gauge, alarm indicators—and we wanted to see everything, too. We developed two versions of the system, one with information pertinent to the local unit commander, and another with information pertinent to the corporate level. That one had a view of everything. The big picture. DASHBOARD was a statistics-based, management system that allowed us to be proactive, to deploy resources, and to keep one's finger on the pulse of the community. We targeted things like gun calls, theft of vehicles, crime occurrences, calls for service, 911 calls, officer performance, you name it, and we did it over several years. Then we crunched the numbers and came up with trends and patterns.

We also looked at occurrences of hate crimes, the number of firearms processed, the total number of hours spent on calls for service and administrative calls, and our response times for such emergencies as assaults in progress, indecent exposure, or a person with a knife. We looked at collision statistics, arrests, how many parking tags were issued, complaints made against the police. In short, we looked at everything.

By the time I left the Toronto Police Service in 2005, I could look back at the five years I had served as chief and see what trends had taken place. I could see that over those five years, the overall level of reported crime had actually dropped. There was a perception in the community that crime in the city had, in fact, gone up, but our numbers looked at reported crime and the numbers didn't show that.

The interpretation of all this data was critical because it allowed us to develop strategies to counter any apparent trends. For example, one of the issues we addressed was traffic collisions involving police officers. We felt many of these collisions were preventable, so once we had the stats we developed a video for police officers called "Arrive Alive" and it became part of every police officer's training. The end result was a dramatic decrease in collisions involving officers.

The issue of gun crimes was another big concern. Gun-related crimes were increasing in number, so getting together all this data was instrumental in the Toronto police installing its specialized unit targeting gangs and gun crime, and that unit proved very successful as we took countless numbers of guns and gunmen off the street.

We didn't invent the idea of a statistics-based management system for the police. The New York City Police Department deserves credit for that. They developed a system called Compstat—for Computer Statistics—and we adapted it for Toronto. The NYPD built a system where the decision makers on the ground had access to all this valuable information instantaneously. Their system was the model and it has since been customized and tailored by many different police forces.

A police chief is always looking at best practices and I thought the New York system would work well in Toronto. After I became commissioner of the OPP, I made sure we got it there, too.

Another thing the NYPD has is helicopter patrols. So does the LAPD and pretty well every other big-city police department in the United States. There is no question that a helicopter is a big-ticket item, but it can maximize police resources on the ground and enhance safety in the community. The helicopter comes with an array of sophisticated technology. For example, it can identify heat sources on the ground that represent a person running from the police in the dark. Or an elderly person who is missing. Or a car that was ditched but the engine is still hot. Or even the origin of a marijuana grow operation. It can do all these things. It also has the ability to shine a spotlight on an area that is under police investigation. A helicopter allows for better deployment of police tactical units on the ground, and it allows you to better observe people and vehicles that are escaping from the police.

Helicopters make the police more effective. A helicopter maximizes police resources on the ground. When I was chief in London, a large city in terms of area but not population, we ran a three-month test with a helicopter and it proved very effective. After I went to York Region, we had an offer from the Weston family who wanted to donate a helicopter, a used one, with no strings attached. We took it and later traded it in for a better machine, which the York Regional Police still have to this day. In fact, Toronto borrows it all the time because they don't have one of their own.

When I was chief in Toronto, we once used a helicopter on trial and it helped us find a criminal. A man who had just committed an armed robbery was thought to be in a park in the north end of the city. Police officers and police dogs were scouring the park for him but couldn't find him anywhere. We brought in the helicopter with its infrared imaging technology, which can detect body heat, and spotted him right away on the roof of a small building.

Across the world today, more than 500 police departments have helicopters. York Region, which is immediately north of Toronto, has the one I just mentioned. So does the Durham Regional Police, located east of Toronto. So does the police department in Calgary, a city one-quarter the size of Toronto. But the biggest city in Canada doesn't have one. Go figure.

In 2004, I was clamoring for a helicopter for the Toronto Police Service, and during the presentation of the police budget to city council, an exchange took place that got all over the media. I was asked if I needed a helicopter for the police force. While I was responding, one city councillor, Howard Moscoe, who had never been a friend of the police, began a diatribe. It was nothing less than a rant. He called the helicopter proposal "pure testosterone" and sarcastically suggested that the helicopters be equipped with Sidewinder missiles to chase criminals. "Do we need a helicopter to track down drug dealers in Parkdale?" he said. "It's tough to land a helicopter on a donut shop." People like that, and I've met many of them in my time, have no idea what they are talking about. Not a clue. If anti-police politicians like this guy had their way, the police would still be using carbon paper.

Without question, the single-most expensive item on the budget in any police force is people. Any chief wants to maximize the use of those human resources with technology and with the effective use of tools. A helicopter is such a tool. Now that I'm with the OPP, we have two helicopters and also a fixed-wing aircraft. Mind you, the jurisdiction of the OPP is the entire province of Ontario. But I will gladly loan either of our OPP helicopters to Toronto any time.

When Rudy Giuliani was mayor of New York City, he didn't just say he was going to clean up the city, he also put in place tools that would allow various entities, including the police, to do their job better. He saw New York the way it was and didn't like it, so he wanted to change things. Under his watch, it became a much cleaner city with less crime and virtually no people living on the street, and that's how it is today. His administration developed a computerized data system for homeless shelters, which led to better management of those shelters and which helped countless people get off the street. It led to better utilization of the available bed space with a strategy that more accurately reconciled needed bed space with the actual need. There was also more compliance and enforcement with regard to bylaws. Quality-of-life issues were a big topic with his administration, too. For example, you could no longer park yourself in the middle of the street and do whatever you wanted because it just wasn't going to be tolerated anymore. Giuliani also bolstered the number of officers on the police department, and such a commitment didn't come without a price. It was a huge price. But that investment has paid off handsomely because New York's reputation as a crime-ridden, filthy city has become a thing of the past.

The formula is easy. You look at the situation and if you don't like it, you find a way to go from what you don't like to what you aspire to. Toronto is the biggest city in Canada and the fifth biggest city in North America, after New York, Los Angeles, Chicago, and Houston. But the city has some serious problems. There is a proliferation of homeless people, especially in the downtown core. Traffic—gridlock—is terrible and getting worse by the day. Gun-related crime is increasing. And the feeling persists that the city is getting dirtier and more rundown. There are also far too many areas with high concentrations of public housing developments, which do nothing but warehouse people. Still, we have to keep things in perspective. For a city of its size, Toronto is still safe. Its homicide rate and rate of crime in general is only a fraction of what it is in most big American cities.

But let's go back to New York again. I remember visiting New York when you feared where you were going. You were told not to go here and not to go there. You couldn't walk a block without being accosted by someone. However, today it is a clean, well-managed city. In 2006, it was even named the most courteous big city in the whole world in a survey by *Reader's Digest*. So much for the old stereotype of rude New Yorkers. Today, I go there often and never have to step over a homeless person and am never accosted for money. Which is definitely not the case in Toronto.

In New York, the transit police and the housing police were absorbed into one big police department, which eliminated duplication, created greater depth of resources, and created more integrated services to the public. The city has four times the population of Toronto, but nine times as many police officers. There is no question that under Giuliani the visibility of the police increased significantly and they are still very visible today.

Police being visible on the street and in the community deters crime. It's a fact. Pure and simple. The city I know best is Toronto, and here's what I think it should do: it should significantly increase its number of police officers. The cost would be great, some people at city hall would scream bloody murder, and we can only speculate about the outcry in the media. But in the long run, the city would be better off. It would offer better protection and services to its citizens and it would attract more tourism and more business investment.

If you want to attract tourism to a city, hype up safety in a big way and make it value-added in terms of how people feel about where they live, where they work, and how they raise their families. I have no doubt that the importance of safety in a big city—any big city—is vastly under-rated and, in most cases, under-resourced. New York City has proven that when you spend the time, devote the attention, and deploy the resources to deal with quality-of-life issues, the model works. It's a mat-ter of not only having the city appear safe but actually *making* it safe and ensuring that its residents *feel* safe. Today New York is a showpiece for what visionary leadership can do and this has continued under Mayor Michael Bloomberg and Police Commissioner Ray Kelly.

Sure, there are all kinds of wonderful technologies available to assist the police, not only in information technology, but also in the sciences. Advances in DNA and the forensic sciences help police gather evidence to convict those who are guilty and, at the same time, clear suspects who are innocent. We have laser technology that helps you find fingerprints that otherwise wouldn't be obvious. We have technology that identifies and links the casings and bullets from firearms, so you can analyze and interpret what happened in a situation with multiple shootings. Informationwise, we have central repositories that deal with specific things like organized crime. Canada has a system called the Financial Transactions and Reports Analysis Centre of Canada (FINTRAC), which tracks the movement of any amounts of money over $10,000, and it has been used to track laundered money that has a terrorist link. In the fall of 2006, Canada's minister of finance, Jim Flaherty, reported transac-tions of over $5 billion in the year previous, which was double the amount of a year earlier, and of this total some $256 million was said to involve financing for terrorist activity.

I mentioned gridlock. In the downtown core of any big city, it's a huge problem when motorists enter a busy intersection and can't make the light, so they push ahead and get stuck and tie everything up. This creates a real mess. New York City has an innovative traffic management system. They put police officers at major, four-way intersections and passed new bylaws that hammer motorists hard with a heavy fine if they get caught blocking traffic in an intersection. But a city like Toronto can't do that because it doesn't have nearly enough police officers in traffic enforcement, on the ground, to keep the traffic moving. Another thing New York did was not allow deliveries in certain areas during the middle of the day. A good idea.

In the future, science and technology will continue to make new improvements to assist the police. But policing will always remain a people business. Police still have to talk to people and do one-on-one interviews. Just look at the two biggest cities in the United States: New York and Los Angeles. In terms of sheer numbers, the ratio of the police force to the population in New York is far greater than what it is in Los Angeles. So the approach to policing in those two cities is obviously very different. Like I say, having police on the street deters crime and gives people a greater sense of comfort and safety. New York understands this. But many cities don't.

· 19 ·

When All Is Said
and Done

A FEW YEARS AGO WHEN THE ANNUAL ST. PATRICK'S DAY
Parade was being held, some dignitaries from Ireland were in
Toronto as our special guests. I was chief of police and was
escorting them to the reviewing stand, and on the way we had to walk
over derelicts who were sprawled across the sidewalk on blankets. It was
downtown and we were in a public place in the middle of a public event.
One of our guests, a very senior officer from an Irish police service,
turned to me and, as we stepped over these people, said in amazement,
"You allow this?" I was embarrassed. All I could tell him was this is the
way it is.

When I joined the police, we used to have a law called the Vagrancy
Act. If people were wandering around aimlessly without any means of
support or were bothering pedestrians, we could pick them up. Later,
the powers that be felt this law was a violation of the rights of the
homeless, so it was repealed. But nothing replaced it and now there is
a proliferation of homeless people on the streets. Many of them are
addicts or mentally ill, yet society seems willing to let them be and
even die because we think that by doing something about their
predicament we are somehow encroaching upon their rights. This is
way out of whack. For one thing, they need help. For another, don't

ordinary citizens also have a right not to be bothered, not to have to step over these people, and not to be accosted on street corners with demands for money?

There was nothing wrong with the Vagrancy Act. It was neither oppressive nor tyrannical. It was about getting homeless people off the street, getting them into the kind of shelter they needed, and then getting them some help. Today the hypocrisy, at least in a city like Toronto, is such that you can't sleep on City Hall property—a by-law prohibits it—but it's okay across the street and pretty well everywhere else. This is shameful.

You didn't see this sort of thing, at least to the same degree, back in the late '60s when I joined the police. Of course, there is a huge difference in attitudes between then and now. In those days, people had more respect for law and order, more respect for each other, and more respect for another person's property. Attitudes have changed and so have values.

I recall a conference in the United States where the speaker was talking about how things used to be. He mentioned the proverbial Mrs. Brown, a little old lady who was home all day and who kept her eye on the street only to see Little Johnny misbehaving. She went to his home and told his parents what he was doing and the parents thanked her. Fast-forward to today. If Mrs. Brown intercepted Little Johnny, he might call her an old bag and tell her to mind her own business, and if she went to his parents they'd threaten her with a lawsuit. This is what has changed. That same speaker also looked at the things kids consider important. Family, church, school, and community were all high on the list in the old days, but now it's video games. This is what kids consider important now.

And laws have changed along with those attitudes. Laws today encourage people to claim entitlement to all kinds of rights but, at the same time, we don't seem to place a very high priority on accountability.

Crime has no single cause and there is no single answer as to how to stop it. It is a dynamic issue with many variables, but let's focus on the criminal justice system. As one who has spent his career in it, I can tell you that the system—at least, in Canada—leaves a great deal to be desired. For starters, people who break the law should know that there will be certain and severe penalties, especially for crimes of violence. But there aren't. We should have truth in sentencing with no bargain-basement sentences handed out. But we don't. In fact, because the jails are so overcrowded today there is a situation in Toronto's Don Jail where "three-for-one sentences" are offered to accused who are waiting to go to court; upon conviction they get a *discount*, so for every day spent in jail they get three days off their sentence.

What's more, recidivists—career criminals—should be held accountable for the choices they make. But they're not. As well, victims of crime should be accorded all the services, respect, and consideration they are entitled to, but they don't get these things because our justice system isn't geared to look after victims. Not by a long shot. Instead, the system is geared to the rights of the criminals and to making sure everything works for them.

At the end of the day, how many people in the justice system really feel that they receive justice? Not many, I can tell you. But then, our system of justice isn't really justice at all. It's more of a production line or a *process*. And not a very efficient one at that. Process is everything.

When I was in homicide, a murder trial might take two weeks. I went to court with a couple boxes of documents and that was it. But now I'd need a truck to cart everything over. The fact is, in spite of all the advancements and innovations that have been made, we are not administering better justice today and, as far as the police are concerned, far too many resources go to facilitating what is still a very labour-intensive system. The result? Police officers are not on the street as much as they should be, doing what they are mandated to do: keeping the peace, preventing crime, and dealing with offenders.

Police today are burdened with extraordinary demands involving bureaucratic, labour-intensive work. Everything is process-driven, so while we may have more police than before, the *visibility* and *availability* of those officers to do that core-function police work are drastically reduced because of all the time spent on paperwork. When I was a young officer, we always had enough spare people around to walk the beat. There was never a shortage. But today policing is all about dealing with shortages, so even though we may have more police, the local station can't possibly provide the same degree of coverage it once did.

Consider that citizens today must go to a police station to make a complaint or go to a collision-reporting centre to report a car crash. Before, when people went on vacation, they'd drop in at the local police station, inform us they were going to be away for a couple weeks, and ask us to check on their home. And we did. If a family went to the local police station with such a request now and met a young officer, that officer would be flabbergasted and would tell them the police don't do such things. We even used to do calls for bicycle thefts. Not now.

Today the police are overworked and underutilized.

When I worked the night shift in a patrol car, I would check properties constantly. When I was a beat cop, I would physically check doors to make sure they were locked. I would survey fire escapes and rooftops of businesses with a flashlight and sometimes catch people breaking and entering. I could do those things because we operated at the street level on the ground and in the laneways where criminals operated. Another thing about those days is that individual officers were held accountable for what happened in their areas of patrol. If there was a break-in during the night on your beat and you were at home sleeping, you could expect a call from the sergeant first thing in the morning. He'd ask, "Where were you? Why didn't you discover the break-in?"

We don't do this anymore and the public is very much aware of the visible absence of the police. Older people especially are aware of it because they remember how it used to be. And criminals are aware of it, too. Would you leave money on the veranda for the delivery man today? Would you leave your front door or your car unlocked? Of course not. But this is what people used to do. Not anymore, and for good reason.

Police used to be more proactive than they are now. Today they are more reactive, but it's not their fault. It's not their fault because they are run off their feet going from call to call. So, in spite of all the new equipment and all the new technology, our communities are not being policed as well as they were years ago.

I have long advocated a complete review of the entire criminal justice system because it is badly broken. It would mean taking a good hard look at the laws and the processes that have been put in place and which are largely a millstone around the neck of police officers. It would also mean looking at the core mandate of the police and asking ourselves some hard questions: What is it we want the police to do? How can we best help them achieve that mandate? How much crime are we, as a society, willing to tolerate?

Do you know why trials take so long? Because police have to meet the microscope test on everything they do. Police are expected to operate in a no-fault environment where their every action must be perfect. Letter perfect. If a murder has just been committed and the murder weapon is right there—in plain view—the police still need a search warrant before they can seize it. They are under extraordinary scrutiny and let's not forget that laws are always changing and evolving and that sometimes rulings are inconsistent, so exactly *what* you are supposed to do in a given situation isn't always crystal clear.

The bottom line is this. Today it's harder to be a cop and easier to be a crook.

It no longer seems to even matter if a person is guilty. When I joined the police force, 10 per cent of my time was spent on paperwork and matters of process, but ask a young police officer about this today and it's up to 50 per cent. What's the result? With the exception of some cities like Boston and New York, police no longer walk the beat because of the cost. Policing is a big chunk of any city's budget and the cost for a single police officer now—in terms of salary, benefits, equipment, and training—can be $100,000 a year.

What we have to do is streamline the process, so police officers can get back to those core function-mandated responsibilities—crime fighting, crime prevention, working at the community level, and being visible. That's what police are supposed to do, but they aren't doing these things as much as before and society suffers because of it, as does the reputation of policing.

As far as police oversight is concerned, I believe police must be held accountable to a higher degree than ordinary citizens. Of course they should. However, police oversight and governance have become an industry unto themselves. How many bodies of police oversight exist now? The Special Investigations Unit (SIU). The public complaints system. Mandatory inquests. Inquiries. We have oversight upon oversight dealing with police activity.

No wonder many fine police officers retire early and take jobs in the private security industry. Private security, especially since 9/11, has grown exponentially to the point where the number of people working in it is actually higher than the number of those in law enforcement. It's also far more lucrative and without the headaches. I've had many offers myself, but law enforcement happens to be my passion.

After I left the Toronto Police Service in 2005, I was asked by the mayor of Vaughan, which is the community where I live, to chair a task force. It would make recommendations about safety and security with a focus on education, prevention, and community participation. This task force would report to the local council. I got twenty community-spirited citizens together and we did a lot of research. We looked at cities in Canada, the United States, and overseas. We examined all the best practices we could find and threw in some ideas of our own. On September 18, 2006, we reported to council. I think our eleven recommendations can apply to any city.

1. Institute a Community Safety Committee to develop expertise in crime prevention and community safety.
2. Hire a full-time safety and security coordinator to be the point of contact and liaison for the mayor's task force and also for the newly created Community Safety Committee, the local police force, school boards, and community groups.

3. Enhance and support community-based programs such as Neighbourhood Watch that have proven to be effective in achieving enhanced safety and security as long as they are maintained.

4. Enhance the capacity of by-law enforcement officials, especially with regard to deterring vandalism and other disturbances which often involve youths.

5. Establish a grow-op registry to create a public record listing all buildings in the community that have been raided and identified by police as "grow ops"—households illegally growing marijuana plants.

6. Enhance community safety and crime prevention through environmental or urban design (i.e., making sprinkler systems in residential homes mandatory).

7. Establish a community safety website to encourage citizen participation.

8. Encourage stronger relationships between neighbours (i.e, waive permit fees for events involving local ratepayer associations).

9. Undertake a comprehensive traffic safety study to look at the effectiveness of such things as stop signs, speed bumps, and inadequate parking facilities.

10. Designate as "drug-free zones" any area within a 300-metre radius of local schools, parks, and other city-owned facilities to give public prosecutors and judges extra ammunition in sentencing those convicted of possession or distribution of illicit drugs.

11. Encourage and support city council to increase the presence of not-for-profit groups serving youth, seniors, and women.

Public safety cannot be left solely to the police. The primary function of the police is preserving the peace and maintaining order in the community, but nowadays police have been relegated to being the *janitors* of society because much of what they do involves things that slip through the cracks. By that I mean things that haven't been dealt with by society at large. For example, look at the notoriously bad planning of high-density, public housing complexes designed with front doors that open out to courtyards with the result that everyone is always in everyone else's face. Drug dealers are just like water because they find the course of least resistance, so this is where they congregate. You end up with crack dealing and shootings and young people who have nothing to do, so they turn to gangs. It's a vicious cycle. We must break that cycle and better-planned public housing is one way to do it, but a lot of other things must be done as well.

A few years ago when I was a member of the International Association of Chiefs of Police Crime Prevention Committee, I helped define what I felt was a realistic philosophy of crime prevention. In a nutshell it's this: *community safety is everyone's responsibility and crime prevention is everyone's business.* The City of Vaughan has tried to address this head-on and I think every city, no matter where it is, should do the same. Abraham Lincoln once said, "What truly motivates people is values" and he was right. It's all about values.

I consider myself lucky that I learned these values when I was young. My family came to North America with nothing. We were from a humble background and didn't speak the language and it was a struggle. But the embedded teachings of my parents were such that I was expected to be a good person and not cause any embarrassment to my family or to the Italian community. I was taught that we were guests in the country and should be appreciative of that fact. That's how it was and my parents' words have stayed with me to this day.

There are three tracks to my life—my family, my job with its oath of office, and my community. Throughout my life, I have been guided by my moral compass and my moral compass is about being ethical, honourable, and trustworthy. It's about being straight with people. I always say in life that it's important to know who you are, what you are here to do, and whom you are here to serve. And this is especially true of a police officer.

• • •

Sometimes when I'm downtown near Toronto police headquarters, I drive by the memorial plaque to Michael Sweet and all the events of that horrible night from 1980 come back to me. The plaque says:

> *This street is dedicated to the memory of*
> *Police Constable Michael Sweet,*
> *52 Division, Toronto Police Service.*
> *He was shot and killed while responding*
> *to an armed robbery on March 14, 1980.*
> *He paid the supreme sacrifice while serving*
> *the community.*
> *May 7th, 2000*
> *A fitting tribute to a very fine officer*

I am glad there is some recognition of this young man who lost his life in the line of duty. His family was present the day we unveiled that plaque—his widow, Karen, who had since remarried and moved to England, and his three daughters who, of course, were all grown up. I met them that day for the very first time and it was a proud moment that provided a bit of closure for me. They were grateful and appreciative that the memory of a husband and father had not waned over all these years. The street dedicated in his name is in 52 Division where he once worked and the street sign says "Michael Sweet Avenue." Right below that is the motto of the Toronto Police Service—"To serve and protect." That's what it's all about.

No doubt, there will be more parole hearings for Michael Sweet's killer, Craig Munro, and I intend to appear at every one of them. And no doubt Jamie Munro will continue to lobby to come back to Canada from Italy. I plan to be involved in that process too, either preventing him from returning to this country or ensuring that he go directly to jail the moment he steps foot on Canadian soil.

Michael Sweet was a police officer who shouldn't have died and he didn't have to die. In one country alone, the United States, some 17,000 police officers have lost their lives, going all the way back to 1792. It's a staggering number. Today the National Law Enforcement Memorial in Washington honours them. In Canada, the more than 800 police officers who have been killed in the line of duty are honoured at the Canadian Police and Peace Officer's Memorial on Parliament Hill in Ottawa.

Not long ago I was in Boston attending an IACP conference and a young police officer was being honoured in a special ceremony. He had responded to a radio call concerning a home-invasion robbery. The door to where this robbery was taking place was locked, but police managed to get through it and this particular officer was the first one in. Two men were inside—one of them was attempting to stab a man and the other was attempting to stab a woman. The officer was faced with this situation: one of the men was coming at him in very close quarters with a gun and the other was coming at him with a knife. So he shot and killed them both and, in the process, saved the lives of two innocent victims. Of course, the local authorities investigated what happened, but what many people don't understand is "the fear factor."

That police officer had fired something like ten shots, but when he sat down later to recount what had happened, he didn't recall taking any shots at all. Not one. Police are traumatized in a situation like that and then when everything goes under the microscope the officer is expected to act like a robot and explain exactly what happened in a blow-by-blow fashion. But police are not robots. Or *robocops*. They are human beings and being able to recall every intimate detail isn't always possible. One thing is for sure, though; that young police officer was a true hero.

Today, we as a society are working overtime to hold the police accountable to the nth degree, which is fine, but we're not doing as much with the criminal element. I don't stand for what is perfect. Perfection is not of this world. But I do stand for what is right. I have always been on the side of law and order, and I try to treat people with dignity and respect. However, I feel that victims of crime are getting a raw deal while, at the same time, the system turns itself upside down to facilitate and accommodate those who break the law.

The system isn't balanced.

My son was once hit by an impaired driver and the case was thrown out because of court delays. I once had my car broken into and would have liked to catch the culprit in the act and turn him over to the police. But all this is small potatoes compared to people who are violently hurt or to families who lose a loved one through a criminal act. And let's not forget that a lot of offenders who do these crimes are undeterred repeat offenders. They haven't been rehabilitated. In fact, I would argue that rehabilitation is a total myth. The jails do not rehabilitate people. They warehouse people. And they are full of the same badass offenders who keep going in and out over and over again. What's the solution? There is no easy solution. But one thing I do know is that a lot more work must be done with young people, especially children.

Another myth is that police budgets are a burden on society and a burden on the taxpayer. Far from it. In fact, police budgets are one of the best investments a city can make. They make communities safe and secure, they improve the quality of life, and they enhance the economic viability of the community.

We, the police, are the last resort on the production line of societal breakdown and disenfranchised people. But you need us and you need us badly. Just try to think for a moment what it would be like if we weren't there. My entire career as a cop has been based on this simple principle: that breaking the law and victimizing people should result in certain and severe consequences. Based on my almost forty years of police service, I think we still have a long way to go.

Acknowledgement

Many people were very helpful in providing information and assistance in the preparation of *Duty: The Life of a Cop*. Special thanks must go to a number of police officers and former officers with the Toronto Police Service, including former chief David Boothby, as well as Randy Bested, Dan Hayes, John Latto, Doug Ramsey, and Michael Sale. A very special thanks must go to Paul Gillespie, who was most helpful in interviews and also in answering a never-ending list of questions about the Child Exploitation Tracking System, and pretty well anything else to do with the issue of child pornography and the abuse of children. Attorney David Butt was also of invaluable assistance in this area. Consultant Antonio Nicaso always made available his extensive knowledge of organized crime, and was a tremendous source of information. In addition, there are several members of the legal community who are deserving of thanks. They include former Ontario Justice George Ferguson, as well as Michael Demczur, Earl Levy, Robert McGee, Scott Newark, and Steve Sherriff. A 'thank you' as well to the Hon. Senator Consiglio DiNino, Adrian Humphreys of the *National Post*, Allan McInnis of the Ontario Court of Appeal, Sergeant Scott McKee at CBF Edmonton military prison, Michael Toddington of the International Association of Airport and Seaport Police, former MP Randy White, and Peter Collins, who is manager of the Forensic Psychiatry Unit with the Ontario Provincial Police. And also to the following individuals from Correctional Service Canada: Annette Allen, Holly Knowles, Charlie Stickell, and Peter White. Sincere apologies to anyone who may have been left out. From Key Porter, it was a pleasure to work with Jonathan Schmidt, editor par excellence, and we must also recognize that this book would not have been possible without the keen support of Jordan Fenn, and agent Bill Hanna. Finally, a most heartfelt thanks to Liviana Fantino, who was always so gracious in opening up her home, and of course to Julian Fantino, a consummate gentleman and first-class guy, who just happens to wear blue.

—J. A.

Index